Language and Computers

Language and Computers

Markus Dickinson, Chris Brew
and Detmar Meurers

A John Wiley & Sons, Ltd., Publication

Blackwell Publishing was acquired by John Wiley & Sons, in February 2007. Blackwell's publishing program has been merged with Wiley's global Scientific, Technical, and Medical business to form Wiley-Blackwell.

Registered Office
John Wiley & Sons, Ltd, The Atrium, Southern Gate, Chichester, West Sussex, PO19 8SQ, UK

Editorial Offices
350 Main Street, Malden, MA 02148-5020, USA
9600 Garsington Road, Oxford, OX4 2DQ, UK
The Atrium, Southern Gate, Chichester, West Sussex, PO19 8SQ, UK

For details of our global editorial offices, for customer services, and for information about how to apply for permission to reuse the copyright material in this book please see our website at www.wiley.com/wiley-blackwell.

The right of Markus Dickinson, Chris Brew, Detmar Meurers to be identified as the authors of this work has been asserted in accordance with the UK Copyright, Designs and Patents Act 1988.

Library of Congress Cataloging-in-Publication Data

Dickinson, Markus.
Language and computers / Markus Dickinson, Chris Brew, Detmar Meurers.
    p. cm.
  Includes index.
    ISBN 978-1-4051-8306-2 (cloth) – ISBN 978-1-4051-8305-5 (pbk.) 1. Computational linguistics.
2. Natural language processing (Computer science) I. Brew, Chris. II. Meurers, Detmar.
III. Language and computers
  P98.D495 2013
  410.285–dc23

                                    2012010324

A catalogue record for this book is available from the British Library.

Cover design by www.cyandesign.co.uk

Set in 10.5/13pt Minion by SPi Publisher Services, Pondicherry, India

1 2013

Brief Contents

Contents

Contents

What This Book Is About

The computer has become the medium of choice through which much of our language use is channeled. Modern computer systems therefore spend a good part of their time working on human language. This is a positive development: not only does it give everyone on the internet access to a world of information well beyond the scope of even the best research libraries of the 1960s and 1970s, it also creates new capabilities for creation, exploitation, and management of information. These include tools that support nonfiction, creative writing, blogs and diaries, citizen journalism and social interactions, web search and online booking systems, smart library catalogs, knowledge discovery, spoken language dialogs, and foreign language learning.

This book takes you on a tour of different real-world tasks and applications where computers deal with language. During this tour, you will encounter essential concepts relating to language, representation, and processing, so that by the end of the book you will have a good grasp of key concepts in the field of computational linguistics. The only background you need to read this book is some curiosity about language and some everyday experience with computers.

This is indeed why the book is organized around real-world tasks and applications. We assume that most of you will be familiar with many of the applications and may wonder how they work or why they don't work. What you may not realize is how similar the underlying processing is. For example, there is a great deal in common between how grammar checkers and automatic speech-recognition systems work. We hope that demonstrating how these concepts recur – in this case, in something called *n*-grams – will reinforce the importance of applying general techniques to new applications.

The book is designed to make you aware of how technology works and how language works. We focus on a few applications of language technology (LT), computational linguistics (CL), and natural language processing (NLP). LT, CL, and NLP are essentially names for the same thing, seen from the perspectives of industry, linguistics, and computer science, respectively. The tasks and applications were chosen because: (i) they are representative of techniques used throughout the field; (ii) they represent a significant body of work in and of themselves; (iii) they connect directly to linguistic modeling; and (iv) they are the ones the authors know best. We hope that you will be able to use these examples as an introduction to general concepts that you can apply to learning about other applications and areas of inquiry.

How to use the book

There are a number of features in this textbook that allow you to structure what you learn, explore more about the topics, and reinforce what you are learning. As a start, the *relevant concepts* being covered are typeset in bold and shown in the margins of each page. You can also look those up in the *Concept Index* at the end of the book.

The Under the Hood sections included in many of the chapters are intended to give you more detail on selected advanced topics. For those interested in learning more about language and computers, we hope that you find these sections enjoyable and enlightening, though the gist of each chapter can be understood without reading them.

At the end of each chapter there is a *Checklist* indicating what you should have learned. The *Exercises* also found at the end of each chapter review the material and give you opportunities to go beyond it. Our hope is that the checklist and exercises help you to get a good grasp of each of the topics and concepts involved. We recognize, however, that students from different backgrounds have different skills, so we have marked each question with an indication of who the question is for. There are four designations: most questions are appropriate for all students and thus are marked with ALL; LING questions assume some background and interest in linguistics; CS questions are appropriate for those with a background in computer science; and MATH is appropriate for those wanting to tackle more mathematical challenges. Of course, you should not feel limited by these markers, as a strong enough desire will generally allow you to tackle most questions.

If you enjoy the topic of a particular chapter, we encourage you to make use of the *Further reading* recommendations. You can also follow the page numbers under each entry in the *References* at the end of the book to the place where it is discussed in the book.

Finally, on the book's *companion website* http://purl.org/lang-and-comp we have collected resources and links to other materials that could be of interest to you when exploring topics around language and computers.

Overview for Instructors

Everyday natural language processing tools, such as those mentioned in the previous section, provide new educational opportunities. The goal of our courses is to show students the capabilities of these tools, and especially to encourage them to take a reflective and analytic approach to their use.

The aim of this book is to provide insight into how computers support language-related tasks, and to provide a framework for thinking about these tasks. There are two major running themes. The first is an emphasis on the relation between the aspects of language that need to be made explicit to obtain working language technology and how they can be represented. We introduce and motivate the need for explicit *representations*, which arises from the fact that computers cannot directly work with language but require a committment to linguistic modeling and data structures that can be expressed in bits and bytes. We emphasize the representational choices that are involved in modeling linguistic abstractions in a concrete form computers can use.

The second running theme is the means needed in order to obtain the knowledge about language that the computer requires. There are two main options here: either we arrange for the computer to *learn from examples*, or we arrange for experts to *create rules* that encode what we know about language. This is an important distinction, both for students whose primary training is in formal linguistics, to whom the idea that such knowledge can be learned may be unfamiliar, and for the increasing number of students who are exposed to the "new AI" tradition of machine learning, to whom the idea of creating and using hand-coded knowledge representations may be surprising. Our view is that the typical real-world system uses a synthesis of both approaches, so we want students to understand and respect the strengths and weaknesses of both data-driven and theory-driven traditions.

Chapter-by-chapter overview

Chapter 1. Prologue: Encoding Language   This chapter lays the groundwork for understanding how natural language is used on a computer, by outlining how language can be represented. There are two halves to this chapter, focusing on the two ways in which language is transmitted: text and speech. The text portion outlines the range of writing systems in use and then turns to how information is encoded on the computer, specifically how all writing systems can be encoded effectively. The speech portion offers an overview of both the articulatory and the acoustic properties of speech. This provides a platform for talking about automatic speech recognition and text-to-speech synthesis. The chapter closes with a discussion of language modeling in the context of speech recognition.

Chapter 2. Writers' Aids   This chapter sets out to (i) explain what is currently known about the causes of and reasons for spelling errors; (ii) introduce the main techniques for the separate but related tasks of nonword error detection, isolated-word spelling correction, and real-word spelling correction; and (iii) introduce the linguistic representations that are currently used to perform grammar correction – including a lengthy discussion of syntax – and explain the techniques employed. The chapter describes classical computational techniques, such as dynamic programming for calculating edit distance between words. It concludes with a discussion of advances in technology for applying spelling correction to newer contexts, such as web queries.

Chapter 3. Language Tutoring Systems   In this chapter, we seek to (i) introduce some fundamentals of first and second language acquisition and the relevance of language awareness for the latter; (ii) explain how computer-assisted language learning (CALL) tools can offer feedback for exercises without encoding anything about language in general; (iii) motivate and exemplify that the space of well-formed and ill-formed variation arising in language use often is well beyond what can be captured in a CALL tool; (iv) introduce the idea that the need for linguistic abstraction and generalization is addressed in tokenization and part-of-speech tagging as two fundamental NLP processing steps, that even such basic steps can be surprisingly difficult, and how part-of-speech classes are informed by different types of empirical evidence; (v) motivate the need for analysis beyond the word level and syntactic generalizations; and (vi) showcase what a real-life intelligent language tutoring system looks like and how it makes use of linguistic analysis for both analysis and feedback. The chapter ends with a section discussing how in addition to the context of language use and linguistic analysis, learner modeling can play an important role in tutoring systems.

Chapter 4. Searching   To cover the task of searching, the goals of this chapter are (i) to outline the contexts and types of data in which people search for information (structured, unstructured, and semi-structured data), emphasizing the concept of one's information need; (ii) to provide ways to think about the evaluation and improvement of one's search results; (iii) to cover the important concept of regular expressions and the corresponding machinery of finite-state automata; and (iv) to delve into linguistic corpora, illustrating a search for linguistic forms instead of for content. The middle of the chapter provides more in-depth discussion of web searching, including how webpages are indexed and how the PageRank algorithm is used to determine relevance for a query.

Chapter 5. Classifying Documents　This chapter aims to (i) explain the idea of classifiers and machine learning; (ii) introduce the Naive Bayes and Perceptron classifiers; (iii) give basic information about how to evaluate the success of a machine learning system; and (iv) explain the applications of machine learning to junk-mail filtering and to sentiment analysis. The chapter concludes with advice on how to select a machine learning algorithm and a discussion of how this plays out for a consulting company employing sentiment analysis as part of an opinion-tracking application designed to be used by corporate customers.

Chapter 6. Dialog Systems　The goals of this chapter are (i) to introduce the idea of dialog systems; (ii) to describe some of the ways in which researchers have conceptualized dialog, including dialog moves, speech acts, and conversational maxims; (iii) to show some of the ways of classifiying dialog systems according to their purpose and design; and (iv) to illustrate how to measure the performance of dialog systems. We spend some time discussing the difficulties in automating dialogue and illustrate this with the example of the early dialog system Eliza.

Chapter 7. Machine Translation Systems　Starting from the general idea of what it means to translate, in this chapter we (i) introduce the idea of machine translation (MT) and explain its capabilities and limits; (ii) indicate the differences between direct MT systems, transfer systems, and modern statistical methods; and (iii) set machine translation in its business context, emphasizing the idea of a translation need. The chapter includes extended discussion of IBM's Model 1 translation model and of the Noisy Channel Model as applied to translation. It also discusses the translation needs of the European Union and those of the Canadian Meteorological Service, and contrasts them with the very difficult requirements for a satisfactory translation of a Shakespeare sonnet. The chapter concludes with a discussion of the likely consequences of automated translation for the career prospects and training choices of human translators.

Chapter 8. Epilogue: Impact of Language Technology　The final chapter takes a look at the impact of language technology on society and human self-perception, as well as some of the ethical issues involved. We raise questions about how computers and language technology change the way information can be accessed and what this means for a democratic society in terms of control of information and privacy, how this changes learning and teaching as well as our jobs through upskilling and deskilling, and the impact on human self-perception when faced with machines capable of communicating using language. The goal of the chapter is to raise awareness of such issues arising through the use of computers and language technology in the context of real life.

How to use the book

A typical way to use the material in this book is in a quarter-length course assuming no mathematical or linguistic background beyond normal high-school experience. For this kind of course, instructors may choose to cover only a subset of the chapters. Each chapter is a stand-alone package, with no strict dependencies between the topics. We have found this material to be accessible to the general student population at the Ohio State University (OSU), where we originally developed the course.

To support the use of the book for longer or more advanced courses, the book also includes Under the Hood sections providing more detail on selected advanced topics, along with development of related analytical and practical skills. This kind of use is more appropriate as part of a Linguistics, Computer Science, or Communications major, or as an overview course at the nonspecialist graduate level. The Under the Hood topics have been useful in semester-length courses at Georgetown University and Indiana University, as well as honors versions at OSU.

Accompanying the book there is a website containing course materials, such as presentation slides, at http://purl.org/lang-and-comp/teaching.

Acknowledgments

This book grew out of a course that was offered for the first time in the winter quarter of 2004 at the Ohio State University (OSU): Linguistics 384, *Language and Computers*. A special thanks to the chair of the Department of Linguistics at the time, Peter Culicover, as well as the Director of Undergraduate Studies in Linguistics, Beth Hume, for having the foresight to recognize the potential for such a course and supporting its development and approval as a general education requirement course at OSU.

There would not be a book were it not for Danielle Descoteaux, who heard about the course and our ideas to turn it into a book and encouraged us to realize this with Wiley-Blackwell. Her sustained enthusiasm for the project made sure we stayed on the ball. We are also very grateful to our project editor Julia Kirk, who continued to be supportive and friendly despite our slow progress.

Drafts of this book benefited significantly from feedback on the course at OSU, as well as similar courses taught at Georgetown University (GU) and Indiana University (IU). The instructors shared many good ideas and pointers to relevant materials, for which we would like to thank particularly Stacey Bailey, Xiaofei Lu (who also provided the Chinese characters for this book), Anna Feldman, DJ Hovermale, Jon Dehdari, Rajakrishnan Rajkumar, Michael White, Sandra Kübler, Ross Israel, and the computational linguistics community at our universities for encouragement and neat ideas for the course and book. Thanks also to Lwin Moe for providing figures of the Burmese writing system; to Tony Meyer and Ayelet Weiss for help on the Hebrew examples; and to Wes Collins for providing Mam examples in chapter 7.

We wish to specially acknowledge Jason Baldridge at the University of Texas, who has continually tested book chapters, provided insightful suggestions for the book and associated courses, and diligently encouraged us to get the book completed.

While it would take too long to name them individually, the students at OSU, GU, and IU who took these courses have been a joy to teach, and their feedback on particular exercises and requests for clarifications on material have definitely made the book better.

A number of people read drafts or partial drafts and provided useful comments. Thanks to Amber Smith for her comments and discussion on integrating the book material into a real course, to Johannes Widmann for his comments on the Language Tutoring Systems chapter, and Keelan Evanini and Michael Heilman at Educational Testing Service (ETS) for extensive and extremely helpful comments on every aspect of the book, from the structure of the chapters through the best way to talk about neural networks to correcting typographical mistakes (including the especially awkward ones in the sentences advocating the use of spell checkers). Sheena Phillips, Jason Quinley, and Christl Glauder also helped us improve the book by carefully proofreading the final version - thanks!

Speaking individually, Markus Dickinson would like to thank Stephanie Dickinson for her encouragement and support during the last few years of this project, and also for her willingness to discuss specificity, sensitivity, and other classification metrics at the dinner table. Lynn Weddle deserves credit for responding to a Facebook post and suggesting Bart and Lisa Simpson for an example in the Searching chapter – although she had no idea it had to do with a book or would lead to an acknowledgment.

Chris Brew thanks Sheena Phillips for everything, and specifically for being exactly the right person to answer the question: "Is this too British?" Matthew and Jamie Brew gave helpful advice on the design of the cover, pointing out things that the older generation just did not see.

Detmar Meurers would like to thank Markus and Chris for the excellent collaboration and being such reliable colleagues and friends, Walter Meurers for emphasizing the importance of connecting research issues with the real world, and Kordula De Kuthy, Marius, Dario, and Cora for being around to remind him that life has a meaning beyond deadlines.

1

Prologue

Encoding Language on Computers

1.1 Where do we start?

One of the aims of this book is to introduce you to different ways that computers are able to process natural language. To appreciate this task, consider how difficult it is to describe what happens when we use language. As but one example, think about what happens when a friend points at a book and says: "He's no Shakespeare!". First of all, there is the difficulty of determining who is meant by "he". Your friend is pointing at a book, not at a person, and although we can figure out that "he" most likely refers to the author of the book, this is not obvious to a computer (and sometimes not obvious to the person you are talking with). Secondly, there is the difficulty of knowing who "Shakespeare" is. Shakespeare is the most famous writer in the English language, but how does a computer know that? Or, what if your friend had said "He's no Lessing!"? English majors with an interest in science-fiction or progressive politics might take this as a reference to Doris Lessing; students of German literature might suspect a comparison to G.E. Lessing, the elegant Enlightenment stylist of German theater; but in the absence of background knowledge, it is hard to know what to make of this remark.

Finally, even if we unpack everything else, consider what your friend's statement literally means: the author of this book is not William Shakespeare. Unless there is a serious possibility that the book *was* written by Shakespeare, this literal meaning is such a crushingly obvious truth that it is difficult to see why anyone would bother to express it. In context, however, we can tell that your friend is not intending to express the literal meaning, but rather to provide a negative evaluation of the author relative to Shakespeare, who is the standard benchmark for good writing in English. You could do the same thing for a slim book of mystical poetry by saying "She's no Dickinson!", provided the hearer was going to understand that the reference was to American poet Emily Dickinson.

Language and Computers, First Edition. Markus Dickinson, Chris Brew and Detmar Meurers.
© 2013 Markus Dickinson, Chris Brew and Detmar Meurers. Published 2013 by Blackwell Publishing Ltd.

Or consider a different kind of statement: "I'm going to the bank with a fishing pole." Most likely, this means that the speaker is going to a river bank and is carrying a fishing pole. But it could also mean that the speaker is going to a financial institution, carrying a fishing pole, or it could mean that the speaker is going to a financial institution known for its fishing pole – or even that the river bank the speaker is going to has some sort of notable fishing pole on it. We reason out a preferred meaning based on what we know about the world, but a computer does not know much about the world. How, then, can it process natural language?

From the other side of things, let us think for a moment about what you may have observed a computer doing with natural language. When you get a spam message, your email client often is intelligent enough to mark it as spam. Search for a page in a foreign language on the internet, and you can get an automatic translation, which usually does a decent job informing you as to what the site is about. Your grammar checker, although not unproblematic, is correct a surprising amount of the time. Look at a book's listing on a site that sells books, like Amazon, and you may find automatically generated lists of keywords; amazingly, many of these words and phrases seem to give a good indication of what the book is about.

If language is so difficult, how is it that a computer can "understand" what spam is, or how could it possibly translate between two languages, for example from Chinese to English? A computer does not have understanding, at least in the sense that humans do, so we have to wonder what technology underlies these applications. It is these very issues that we delve into in this book.

1.1.1   Encoding language

There is a fundamental issue that must be addressed here before we can move on to talking about various applications. When a computer looks at language, what is it looking at? Is it simply a variety of strokes on a piece of paper, or something else? If we want to do anything with language, we need a way to represent it.

This chapter outlines the ways in which language is represented on a computer; that is, how language is encoded. It thus provides a starting point for understanding the material in the rest of the chapters.

If we think about language, there are two main ways in which we communicate – and this is true of our interactions with a computer, too. We can inter- **text** act with the computer by writing or reading **text** or by speaking or listening to **speech** **speech**. In this chapter, we focus on the representations for text and speech, while throughout the rest of the book we focus mainly on processing text.

1.2   Writing systems used for human languages

If we only wanted to represent the 26 letters of the English alphabet, our task would be fairly straightforward. But we want to be able to represent any language in any **writing system** writing system, where a **writing system** is "a system of more or less permanent marks used to represent an utterance in such a way that it can be recovered more or less exactly without the intervention of the utterer" (Daniels and Bright, 1996).

And those permanent marks can vary quite a bit in what they represent. We will look at a basic classification of writing systems into three types: alphabetic, syllabic, and logographic systems. There are other ways to categorize the world's writing systems, but this classification is useful in that it will allow us to look at how writing systems represent different types of properties of a language by means of a set of characters. Seeing these differences should illustrate how distinct a language is from its written representation and how the written representation is then distinct from the computer's internal representation (see Section 1.3).

For writing English, the idea is that each letter should correspond to an individual sound, more or less, but this need not be so (and it is not entirely true in English). Each character could correspond to a series of sounds (e.g., a single character for *str*), but we could also go in a different direction and have characters refer to meanings. Thus, we could have a character that stands for the meaning of "dog". Types of writing systems vary in how many sounds a character represents or to what extent a meaning is captured by a character. Furthermore, writing systems differ in whether they even indicate what a word is, as English mostly does by including spaces; we will return to this issue of distinguishing words in Section 3.4.

One important point to remember is that these are systems for writing down a language; they are not the language itself. The same writing system can be used for different languages, and the same language in principle could be written down in different writing systems (as is the case with Japanese, for example).

1.2.1   Alphabetic systems

We start our tour of writing systems with what should be familiar to any reader of English: alphabets. In **alphabetic systems**, a single character refers to a single sound. As any English reader knows, this is not entirely true, but it gives a good working definition. **alphabetic system**

We will look at two types of alphabetic systems. First, there are the **alphabets**, or phonemic alphabets, which represent all sounds with their characters; that is, both **alphabet** consonants and vowels are represented. Many common writing systems are alphabets: Etruscan, Latin, Cyrillic, Runic, and so forth. Note that English is standardly written in the Latin, or Roman, alphabet, although we do not use the entire repertoire of available characters, such as those with accents (e.g., *è*) or **ligatures**, combinations of **ligature** two or more characters, such as the German ß, which was formed from two previous versions of *s*.

As an example of an alphabet other than Latin, we can look at Cyrillic, shown in Figure 1.1. This version of the alphabet is used to write Russian, and slight variants are used for other languages (e.g., Serbo-Croatian). Although some characters correspond well to English letters, others do not (e.g., the letter for [n]). The characters within brackets specify how each letter is said – that is, pronounced; we will return to these in the discussion of phonetic alphabets later on.

а	б	в	г	д	е	ё	ж	з	и	й
[a]	[b]	[v]	[g]	[d]	[je]	[jo]	[ʒ]	[z]	[i]	[j]

к	л	м	н	о	п	р	с	т	у	ф
[k]	[l]	[m]	[n]	[o]	[p]	[r]	[s]	[t]	[u]	[f]

х	ц	ч	ш	щ	ъ	ы	ь	э	ю	я
[x]	[ts]	[tɕ]	[ʂ]	[ɕɕ]	[-]	[ɨ]	[ʲ]	[e]	[ju]	[ja]

Figure 1.1   The Cyrillic alphabet used for Russian

     Some alphabets, such as the Fraser alphabet used for the Lisu language spoken in
diacritic Myanmar, China, and India, also include **diacritics** to indicate properties such as a
word's tone (how high or low pitched a sound is). A diacritic is added to a regular
character, for example a vowel, indicating in more detail how that sound is supposed
to be realized. In the case of Fraser, for example, *M:* refers to an [m] sound (written
as *M*), which has a low tone (written as :).

abjad   Our second type of alphabetic system also often employs diacritics. **Abjads**, or consonant alphabets, represent consonants only; some prime examples are Arabic, Aramaic,
and Hebrew. In abjads, vowels generally need to be deduced from context, as is illustrated by the Hebrew word for "computer", shown on the left-hand side of Figure 1.2.

מחשב	מחשב	מחשב
b š x m	*b š x m*	*b š x m*
[maxʃev]	[mexuʃav]	[mexaʃav]
'computer'	'is digitized'	'with + he thought'

Figure 1.2   Example of Hebrew (abjad) text

     The Hebrew word in its character-by-character transliteration *bšxm* contains no
vowels, but context may indicate the [a] and [e] sounds shown in the pronunciation
of the word [maxʃev]. (Note that Hebrew is written right to left, so the *m* as the
rightmost character of the written word is the first letter pronounced.) As shown in
the middle and right-hand side of Figure 1.2, the context could also indicate different pronunciations with different meanings.

     The situation with abjads often is a little more complicated than the one we just
described, in that characters sometimes represent selected vowels, and often vowel
diacritics are available.

A note on letter–sound correspondence   As we have discussed, alphabets use letters
to encode sounds. However, there is not always a simple correspondence between a
word's spelling and its pronunciation. To see this, we need look no further than
English.

English has a variety of non-letter–sound correspondences, which you probably labored through in first grade. First of all, there are words with the same spellings representing different sounds. The string *ough*, for instance, can be pronounced at least five different ways: "cough", "tough", "through", "though", and "hiccough". Letters are not consistently pronounced, and, in fact, sometimes they are not pronounced at all; this is the phenomenon of silent letters. We can readily see these in "knee", "debt", "psychology", and "mortgage", among others. There are historical reasons for these silent letters, which were by and large pronounced at one time, but the effect is that we now have letters we do not speak.

Aside from inconsistencies of pronunciation, another barrier to the letter–sound correspondence is that English has certain conventions where one letter and one sound do not cleanly map to one another. In this case, the mapping is consistent across words; it just uses more or less letters to represent sounds. Single letters can represent multiple sounds, such as the *x* in "tax", which corresponds to a *k* sound followed by an *s* sound. And multiple letters can consistently be used to represent one sound, as in the *th* in "the" or the *ti* in "revolution".

Finally, we can alternate spellings for the same word, such as "doughnut" and "donut", and **homophones** show us different words that are spelled differently but spoken the same, such as "colonel" and "kernel". **homophone**

Of course, English is not the only language with quirks in the letter–sound correspondences in its writing system. Looking at the examples in Figure 1.3 for Irish, we can easily see that each letter does not have an exact correspondent in the pronunciation.

Spelling	Pronunciation	Meaning
samhradh	[sauruh]	'summer'
scri'obhaim	[shgri:m]	'I write'

Figure 1.3 Some Irish expressions

The issue we are dealing with here is that of **ambiguity** in natural language, in this case a letter potentially representing multiple possible sounds. Ambiguity is a recurring issue in dealing with human language that you will see throughout this book. For example, words can have multiple meanings (see Chapter 2); search queries can have different, often unintended meanings (see Chapter 4); and questions take on different interpretations in different contexts (see Chapter 6). In this case, writing systems can be designed that are unambiguous; phonetic alphabets, described next, have precisely this property. **ambiguity**

Phonetic alphabets You have hopefully noticed the notation used within the brackets ([]). The characters used there are a part of the International Phonetic Alphabet (IPA). Several special alphabets for representing sounds have been developed, and probably the best known among linguists is the IPA. We have been discussing problems with letter–sound correspondences, and phonetic alphabets help us discuss these problems, as they allow for a way to represent all languages unambiguously using the same alphabet.

Each phonetic symbol in a phonetic alphabet is unambiguous: the alphabet is designed so that each speech sound (from any language) has its own symbol. This eliminates the need for multiple symbols being used to represent simple sounds and one symbol being used for multiple sounds. The problem for English is that the Latin alphabet, as we use it, only has 26 letters, but English has more sounds than that. So, it is no surprise that we find multiple letters like *th* or *sh* being used for individual sounds.

The IPA, like most phonetic alphabets, is organized according to the articulatory properties of each sound, an issue to which we return in Section 1.4.2. As an example of the IPA in use, we list some words in Figure 1.4 that illustrate the different vowels in English.

bead: [bid]		boot: [but]
bid: [bɪd]		book: [bʊk]
bade: [be(i)d]	bud: [bʌd]	bode: [bo(ʊ)d]
bed: [bɛd]		bought: [bɔt]
bad: [bæd]		body: [bɑdi]

Figure 1.4 Example words for English vowels (varies by dialect)

At http://purl.org/lang-and-comp/ipa you can view an interactive IPA chart, provided by the University of Victoria's Department of Linguistics. Most of the English consonants are easy to figure out, e.g., [b] in "boy", but some are not obvious. For example, [θ] stands for the *th* in "thigh"; [ð] for the *th* in "thy"; and [ʃ] for the *sh* in "shy".

1.2.2 Syllabic systems

syllabic system **Syllabic systems** are like alphabetic systems in that they involve a mapping between characters and sounds, but the units of sound are larger. The unit in question is syllable called the **syllable**. All human languages have syllables as basic building blocks of speech, but the rules for forming syllables differ from language to language. For example, in Japanese a syllable consists of a single vowel, optionally preceded by at most one consonant, and optionally followed by [m], [n], or [ŋ]. Most of the world's languages, like Japanese, have relatively simple syllables. This means that the total number of possible syllables in the language is quite small, and that syllabic writing systems work well. But in English, the vowel can also be preceded by a sequence of consonant several consonants (a so-called **consonant cluster**), and there can also be a conso-cluster nant cluster after the vowel. This greatly expands the number of possible syllables. You could design a syllabic writing system for English, but it would be unwieldy and difficult to learn, because there are so many different possible syllables.

abugida   There are two main variants of syllabic systems, the first being **abugidas** (or alphasyllabary **alphasyllabaries**). In these writing systems, the symbols are organized into families.

All the members of a family represent the same consonant, but they correspond to different vowels. The members of a family also look similar, but have extra components that are added in order to represent the different vowels. What is distinctive about an abugida is that this process is systematic, with more or less the same vowel components being used in each family.

To write a syllable consisting of a consonant and a vowel, you go to the family for the relevant consonant, then select the family member corresponding to the vowel that you want. This works best for languages in which almost all syllables consist of exactly one consonant and exactly one vowel. Of course, since writing is a powerful technology, this has not stopped abugidas from being used, with modifications, to represent languages that do not fall into this pattern. One of the earliest abugidas was the Brahmi script, which was in wide use in the third century BCE and which forms the basis of many writing systems used on the Indian subcontinent and its vicinity.

As an example, let us look at the writing system for Burmese (or Myanmar), a Sino-Tibetan language spoken in Burma (or Myanmar). In Figure 1.5, we see a table displaying the base syllables.

က	ခ	ဂ	ဃ	င
[ka̩]	[kʰa̩]	[ga̩]	[ga̩]	[ŋa̩]
စ	ဆ	ဇ	ဈ	ည
[sa̩]	[sʰa̩]	[za̩]	[za̩]	[ɲa̩]
ဋ	ဌ	ဍ	ဎ	ဏ
[ta̩]	[tʰa̩]	[da̩]	[da̩]	[na̩]
တ	ထ	ဒ	ဓ	န
[ta̩]	[tʰa̩]	[da̩]	[da̩]	[na̩]
ပ	ဖ	ဗ	ဘ	မ
[pa̩]	[pʰa̩]	[ba̩]	[ba̩]	[ma̩]
ယ	ရ	လ	ဝ	သ
[ya̩]	[ya̩] ([ra̩])	[la̩]	[wa̩]	[θa̩]
	ဟ	ဠ	အ	
	[ha̩]	[la̩]	[a̩]	

Figure 1.5   Base syllables of the Burmese abugida

As you can see in the table, every syllable has a default vowel of [a̩]. This default vowel can be changed by adding diacritics, as shown in Figure 1.6, for a syllables that start with [k]. We can see that the base character remains the same in all cases, while diacritics indicate the vowel change. Even though there is some regularity, the combination of the base character plus a diacritic results in a single character, which distinguishes abugidas from the alphabets in Section 1.2.1. Characters are written from left to right in Burmese, but the diacritics appear on any side of the base character.

က [ka̱]	ကု [ku̠]	ကေး [kéi]	ကို [kò]
ကာ [kà]	ကူ [kù]	ကယ့် [ke̠]	ကီး [kó]
ကား [ká]	ကူး [kú]	ကယ် [kè]	ကော [kɔ̠]
ကိ [ki̠]	ကော့ [ke̠i]	ကဲ [ké]	ကော် [kɔ̀]
ကီ [kì]	ကေ [kèi]	ကို့ [ko̠]	ကော [kɔ́]
ကိး [kḭ]			

Figure 1.6 Vowel diacritics of the Burmese abugida

syllabary   The second kind of syllabic system is the **syllabary**. These systems use distinct symbols for each syllable of a language. An example syllabary for Vai, a Niger-Congo language spoken in Liberia, is given in Figure 1.7 (http://commons.wikimedia.org/wiki/Category:Vai_script).

An abugida is a kind of syllabary, but what is distinctive about a general syllabary is that the syllables need not be organized in any systematic way. For example, in Vai, it is hard to see a connection between the symbols for [pi] and [pa], or any connection between the symbols for [pi] and [di].

1.2.3   Logographic writing systems

logograph   The final kind of writing system to examine involves **logographs**, or logograms. A logograph is a symbol that represents a unit of meaning, as opposed to a unit of sound. It is hard to speak of a true logographic writing system because, as we will see, a language like Chinese that uses logographs often also includes phonetic information in the writing system.

To start, we can consider some non-linguistic symbols that you may have encountered before. Figure 1.8, for example, shows symbols found on US National Park Service signs (http://commons.wikimedia.org/wiki/File:National_Park_Service_

pictograph   sample_pictographs.svg). These are referred to as **pictographs**, or pictograms, because they essentially are pictures of the items to which they refer. In some sense, this is the simplest way of encoding semantic meaning in a symbol. The upper left symbol, for instance, refers to camping by means of displaying a tent.

Some modern systems evolved from a more pictographic representation into a more abstract symbol. To see an example of such character change, we can look at the development of the Chinese character for "horse", as in Figure 1.9 (http://commons.wikimedia.org/wiki/Category:Ancient_Chinese_characters).

Figure 1.7 The Vai syllabary

Originally, the character very much resembled a horse, but after evolving over the centuries, the character we see now only bears a faint resemblance to anything horse-like.

There are characters in Chinese that prevent us from calling the writing system a fully meaning-based system. **Semantic-phonetic compounds** are symbols with a meaning element and a phonetic element. An example is given in Figure 1.10, where we can see that, although both words are pronounced the **semantic-phonetic compound**

Figure 1.8 US National Park Service symbols (pictographs)

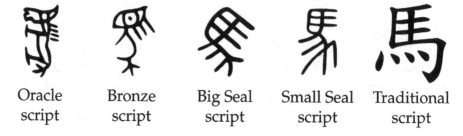

| Oracle script | Bronze script | Big Seal script | Small Seal script | Traditional script |

Figure 1.9 The Chinese character for "horse"

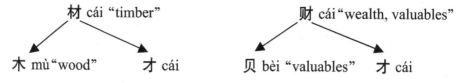

Figure 1.10 Semantic-Phonetic Compounds used in writing Chinese

same, they have different meanings depending on the semantic component. Of course, it is not a simple matter of adding the phonetic and semantic components together: knowing that the meaning component of a semantic-phonetic compound is "wood" by itself does not tell you that the meaning of the compound is "timber".

1.2.4 Systems with unusual realization

In addition to writing systems making use of characters differentiated by the shape and size of different marks, there are other writing systems in existence that exploit different sensory characteristics.

Perhaps best known is the tactile system of Braille. Braille is a writing system that makes it possible to read and write through touch, and as such it is primarily used by the blind or partially blind. We can see the basic alphabet in Figure 1.11 (http://commons.wikimedia.org/wiki/File:Braille_alfabet.jpg). The Braille system works by using patterns of raised dots arranged in cells of up to six dots, in a 3 x 2 configuration. Each pattern represents a character, but some frequent words and letter combinations have their own pattern. For instance, the pattern for *f* also indicates the number 6 and the word "from". So, even though it is at core an alphabet, it has some logographic properties.

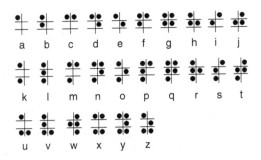

Figure 1.11 The Braille alphabet

An interesting case is the **chromatographic** writing system supposedly used by the Benin and Edo people in southern Nigeria (http://purl.org/lang-and-comp/chroma). This system is based on different color combinations and symbols. We have some reservations in mentioning this system, as details are difficult to obtain, but in principle both color and shape can encode pronunciation. **chromatographic**

1.2.5 Relation to language

As we mentioned before, there is no simple correspondence between a writing system and a language. We will look at two examples, Korean and Azeri, which will highlight different aspects of the unique ways languages are written.

Korean The writing system for Korean is a hybrid system, employing both alphabetic and syllabic concepts. The writing system is actually referred to as *Hangul* (or *Hangeul*) and was developed in 1444 during the reign of King Sejong. The Hangul system contains 24 letter characters, 14 consonants and 10 vowels. But when the language is written down, the letters are grouped together into syllables to form new characters. The letters in a syllable are not written separately as in the English system, but together form a single character. We can see an example in Figure 1.12 (http://commons.wikimedia.org/wiki/File:Hangeul.png), which shows how individual alphabetic characters together form the syllabic characters for "han" and "geul". The letters are not in a strictly left-to-right or top-to-bottom pattern, but together form a unique syllabic character. Additionally, in South Korea, *hanja* (logographic Chinese characters) are also used.

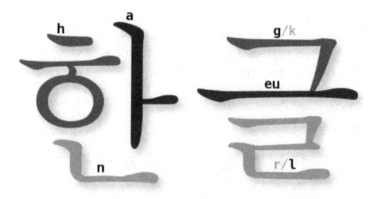

Figure 1.12 Composition of the characters for "Hangeul"

Azeri Azeri is a language whose history illustrates the distinction between a language and its written encoding. Azeri is spoken in Azerbaijan, northwest Iran, and Georgia, and up until the 1920s it was written in different Arabic scripts. In 1929, however, speakers were forced to switch to the Latin alphabet for political reasons. In 1939, it was decided to change to the Cyrillic alphabet, to bring Azeri more in line with the rest of the Soviet Union. After the fall of the USSR in 1991, speakers went back to the Latin alphabet, although with some minor differences from when they had used it before. Azeri is thus a single language that has been written in many ways.

1.3   Encoding written language

1.3.1   Storing information on a computer

Given the range of writing systems, we now turn to the question of how to encode them on a computer. But to address that, we have a more fundamental question: How do we encode anything on a computer?

To answer that, we need to know that information on a computer is stored in **bits**. **bit**
We can think of the memory of a computer as, at its core, a large number of on–off
switches. A bit has two possible values, 1 (yes) or 0 (no), allowing us to flip the
switches on or off. A single bit on its own does not convey much information, but
multiple bits can come together to make meaningful patterns. It is thus often more
convenient to speak of a **byte**, or a sequence of 8 bits, e.g., 01001010. **byte**

These sequences of bits tell the computer which switches are on and which are off,
and – in the context of writing systems – a particular character will have a unique
pattern of on–off switches. Before we fully spell that out, though, let us consider a
better way to think of sequences of bits, other than just a sequence of mindless 0s
and 1s.

Bit sequences are useful because they can represent numbers, in so-called **binary** **binary**
notation. They are called binary because there are only two digits to work with.
The base ten numbers we normally use have columns for ones, tens, hundreds, and
so on; likewise, binary numbers have their own columns, for ones, twos, fours,
eights, and so on. In addition to base two and base ten, there are encodings such as **hexadecimal**
hexadecimal, where there are 16 digits (0–9 and then the letters A–F).

In **Big Endian** notation, the most significant bit is the leftmost one; this is the **Big Endian**
standard way of encoding and is parallel to decimal (base ten) numbers. The positions
in a byte thus encode the top row of Figure 1.13. As we can see in the second row of
the figure, the positions for 64, 8, and 2 are "on", and $64 + 8 + 2$ equals 74. The binary
(base two) number 01001010 therefore corresponds to the decimal number 74.

128	64	32	16	8	4	2	1
0	1	0	0	1	0	1	0

Figure 1.13   Example of Big Endian notation for binary numbers

Little Endian notation is just the opposite, where the most significant bit is the **Little Endian**
rightmost one, but it is less common. In both cases, the columns are all powers
of two. This is just like with decimal numbers, where the columns are all powers of
ten. As each digit is here limited to either 0 or 1 (two choices), we have to use
powers of two.

Converting decimal numbers to binary
Although many of you are likely already familiar with binary numbers, it is instructive
to see how to convert from decimal to binary notation. We will consider the division
method of conversion and walk through an example, converting the decimal number 9
into a 4-bit binary number.

The division method is easy to calculate and moves from the least significant to
the most significant bit. Because every column has a value that is a multiple of 2, we
divide by 2 with every step. In Figure 1.14, for example, we divide 9 by 2 and find
that we have a remainder. A remainder after dividing by 2 means that we started
with an odd number. Since 9 is odd, the rightmost bit should be 1.

Decimal	Remainder?	Binary
9/2 = 4	yes	1
4/2 = 2	no	01
2/2 = 1	no	001
1/2 = 0	yes	1001

Figure 1.14   The division method

The trick now is to take the resulting value, in this case 4, and divide it by 2. The same principle is at work here: if there is no remainder, it means that the starting number (4) was even, and this bit needs to be switched off for that to happen.

1.3.2   Using bytes to store characters

With 8 bits (a single byte) and each byte storing a separate character, we can represent 256 different characters (= 2^8). This is sufficient for many applications and more than enough for anyone wishing simply to type in Latin characters for English. With 256 possible characters, we can store every single letter used in English, plus all the auxiliary characters such as the comma, the space, the percent sign, and so on.

ASCII

ASCII   One of the first encodings for storing English text used only 7 bits, thus allowing for 128 possible characters. This is the **ASCII** encoding, the American Standard Code for Information Interchange. We can see most of the ASCII chart in Figure 1.15.

32		48	0	65	A	82	R	97	a	114	r
33	!	49	1	66	B	83	S	98	b	115	s
34	"	50	2	67	C	84	T	99	c	116	t
35	#	51	3	68	D	85	U	100	d	117	u
36	$	52	4	69	E	86	V	101	e	118	v
37	%	53	5	70	F	87	W	102	f	119	w
38	&	54	6	71	G	88	X	103	g	120	x
39	'	55	7	72	H	89	Y	104	h	121	y
40	(	56	8	73	I	90	Z	105	i	122	z
41	)	57	9	74	J	91	[	106	j	123	{
42	*	58	:	75	K	92	\	107	k	124	—
43	+	59	;	76	L	93	]	108	l	125	}
44	,	60	<	77	M	94	^	109	m	126	~
45	-	61	=	78	N	95	_	110	n	127	DEL
46	.	62	>	79	O	96	'	111	o		
47	/	63	?	80	P			112	p		
		64	@	81	Q			113	q		

Figure 1.15   The ASCII chart

Omitted from the chart are codes 1–31, since these are used for control characters, such as a backspace, line feed, or tab. A nice property is that the numeric order reflects alphabetic ordering (e.g., 65 through 90 for uppercase letters). Thus, we can easily alphabetize the letters by comparing numbers. Although we have written the base ten number, for ease of reading, the binary number is what is used internally by the computer.

You might already be familiar with ASCII or other character-encoding systems, as many communications over email and the internet inform you of different encodings. Emails come with lots of information about themselves. Specifically, Multipurpose Internet Mail Extensions (MIME) provide **meta-information** on the text, or information that is part of the regular message, but also tell us something about that message. MIME information tells us, among other things, what the character set is; an example can be seen in Figure 1.16.

meta-information

```
Mime-Version: 1.0
Content-Type: text/plain; charset=US-ASCII
Content-Transfer-Encoding: 7bit
```

Figure 1.16   MIME example

Unicode

We have just mentioned ASCII and that there are other encoding systems, and, as you may recall, one of our goals is to be able to encode *any* language. With only 128 possible characters, ASCII clearly is insufficient for encoding the world's writing systems. How, then, do we go about encoding writing systems other than the Latin alphabet?

One approach is simply to extend the ASCII system with various other systems. For example, ISO-8859-1 is an 8-bit encoding that in addition to ASCII includes extra letters needed for French, German, Spanish, and related languages; ISO-8859-7 is for the Greek alphabet; ISO-8859-8 for the Hebrew alphabet; and JIS-X-0208 encodes Japanese characters. While multiple encoding systems make it possible to specify only the writing systems one wants to use, there are potential problems. First, there is always the possibility of misidentification. Two different encodings can use the same number for two different characters or, conversely, different numbers for the same character. If an encoding is not clearly identified and needs to be guessed, for example by a web browser displaying a web page that does not specify the encoding explicitly, the wrong characters will be displayed. Secondly, it is a hassle to install and maintain many different systems in order to deal with various languages.

Unicode (http://www.unicode.org) is a system that addresses these problems by having a single representation for every character in any existing writing system. While based on the earlier discussion we have some idea about the variety of writing systems, we may not have a good feel for how many characters there are to encode in the world. Unicode, version 6.0, has codes for over 109,000 characters from alphabets, syllabaries, and logographic systems. While this sounds like a lot, it should be noted that Unicode uses 32 bits to encode characters. The number of distinct characters a system can encode is equal to 2^n, where n is the number of bits: with 7 bits, we had 2^7 ($=128$) possibilities. With 32 bits, we can store $2^{32} = 4,294,967,296$ unique characters.

At this point, we should consider the situation: Unicode allows for over four billion characters, yet only needs about 100,000. If we use 32 bits to encode every character, that will take up a lot of space. It seems as if ASCII is better, at least for English, as it only takes 7 bits to encode a character. Is there any way we can allow for many characters, while at the same time only encoding what we really need to encode?

The solution Unicode uses is to have three different versions, which allow for more compact encodings: UTF-32, UTF-16, and UTF-8. UTF-32 uses 32 bits to directly represent each character, so here we will face more of a space problem. UTF-16, on the other hand, uses 16 bits ($2^{16} = 65,536$), and UTF-8 uses 8 bits ($2^8 = 256$).

This raises the question: How is it possible to encode 2^{32} possibilities in 8 bits, as UTF-8 does? The answer is that UTF-8 can use several bytes to represent a single character if it has to, but it encodes characters with as few bytes as possible by using the highest (leftmost) bit as a flag. If the highest bit is 0, then this is a single character or the final character of a multi-byte character. For example, 01000001 is the single-character code for A (i.e., 65). If the highest bit is 1, then it is part of a multi-byte character. In this way, sequences of bytes can unambiguously denote sequences of Unicode characters. One nice consequence of this set-up is that ASCII text is already valid UTF-8.

More details on the encoding mechanism for UTF-8 are given in Figure 1.17. An important property here is that the first byte unambiguously tells you how many bytes to expect after it. If the first byte starts with 11110xxx, for example, we know that with four 1s, it has a total of four bytes; that is, there are three more bytes to expect. Note also that all nonstarting bytes begin with 10, indicating that they are *not* the initial byte.

Byte 1	Byte 2	Byte 3	Byte 4	Byte 5	Byte 6
0xxxxxxx					
110xxxxx	10xxxxxx				
1110xxxx	10xxxxxx	10xxxxxx			
11110xxx	10xxxxxx	10xxxxxx	10xxxxxx		
111110xx	10xxxxxx	10xxxxxx	10xxxxxx	10xxxxxx	
1111110x	10xxxxxx	10xxxxxx	10xxxxxx	10xxxxxx	10xxxxxx

Figure 1.17   UTF-8 encoding scheme

To take one example, the Greek character α ("alpha") has a Unicode code value of 945, which in binary representation is 11 10110001. With 32 bits, then, it would be represented as 00000000 00000000 00000011 10110001. The conversion to UTF-8 works as follows: if we look at the second row of Figure 1.17, we see that there are 11 slots (x's), and we have 10 binary digits. The 10-digit number 11 10110001 is the same as the 11-digit 011 10110001, and we can rearrange this as 01110 110001, so what we can do is insert these numbers into x's in the second row: 11001110 10110001. This is thus the UTF-8 representation.

1.4 Encoding spoken language

We now know that we can encode every language, as long as it has been written down. But many languages have no written form: of the 6,912 known spoken languages listed in the *Ethnologue* (http://www.ethnologue.com), approximately half have never been written down. These unwritten languages appear all over the world: Salar (China); Gugu Badhun (Australia); Southeastern Pomo (California); and so on.

If we want to work with an unwritten language, we need to think about dealing with spoken language. Or, more practically, even if a language has a written form, there are many situations in which we want to deal with speech. Picture yourself talking to an airline reservation system on the phone, for example; this system must have some way of encoding the spoken language that you give to it. The rest of this chapter thus gives a glimpse into how computers can work with speech. Even though the book mainly focuses on written text, it is instructive to see how spoken and written data are connected.

1.4.1 The nature of speech

In order to deal with speech, we have to figure out what it looks like. It is very easy to visualize spoken language if we think of it as phonetically transcribed into individual characters, but to **transcribe**, or write down, the speech into a **phonetic alphabet** (such as the IPA we saw before) is extremely expensive and time-consuming. To better visualize speech and thus encode it on a computer, we need to know more about how speech works and how to measure the various properties of speech. Then, we can start to talk about how these measurements correspond to the sounds we hear.

transcribe

phonetic alphabet

Representing speech, however, is difficult. As discussed more fully below, speech is a continuous stream of sound, but we hear it as individual sounds. Sounds run together, and it is hard for a computer to tell where one ends and another begins. Additionally, people have different dialects and different sizes of vocal tracts and thus say things differently. Two people can say the same word and it will come out differently because their vocal tracts are unique.

Furthermore, the way a particular sound is realized is not consistent across utterances, even for one person. What we think of as one sound is not always said the same. For example, there is the phenomenon known as **coarticulation**, in which neighboring sounds affect the way a sound is uttered. The sound for k is said differently in "key" and the first sound in "kookaburra". (If you do not believe this, stick one finger in your mouth when you say "key" and when you say "koo"; for "key" the tongue touches the finger, but not for "koo".) On the flipside, what we

coarticulation

think of as two sounds are not always very different. For instance, the *s* in "see" is acoustically very similar to the *sh* in "shoe", yet we hear them as different sounds. This becomes clear when learning another language that makes a distinction you find difficult to discern. So both articulatory and acoustic properties of speech are relevant here; let's now take a closer look at both of these.

1.4.2 Articulatory properties

articulatory phonetics

Before we get into what sounds look like on a computer, we need to know how sounds are produced in the vocal tract. This is studied in a branch of linguistics known as **articulatory phonetics**. Generally, there are three components to a sound, at least for consonants: the place of articulation, the manner of articulation, and the voicing.

place of articulation

The **place of articulation** refers to where in the mouth the sound is uttered. Consider where your tongue makes contact with your mouth when you say [t] (*t* in *tip*) as opposed to when you say [k] (*k* in *key*, *c* in *cool*). For [t], the tip of your tongue touches the area of your mouth behind your upper teeth (what is called the alevolar ridge), whereas for [k], the back of your tongue rises to the back of the roof of your mouth (i.e., the velum).

manner of articulation

While place makes some distinctions, there are sounds said at nearly the same point in the mouth that come out differently, due to the **manner of articulation**. For example, [s] (*s* in *sip*, *c* in *nice*), like [t], is an alveolar consonant, uttered with the tongue behind one's upper teeth. However, [t] involves a complete stoppage of air (and thus is commonly called a stop consonant), whereas [s] allows a narrow stream of air to continually pass through the constriction (and is referred to as a fricative).

voicing

The final distinction involves **voicing**, or whether or not one's vocal cords vibrate during the utterance. Your vocal cords are in your throat, so you can easily compare sounds by putting a hand on your throat and feeling whether there are vibrations. For example, [s] and [z] (*z* as in *zoo*) are both alveolar fricatives, but [s] is unvoiced and [z] is voiced.

1.4.3 Acoustic properties

acoustic phonetics

While studying articulation provides important distinctions, to which we will continue to refer in the following, to represent spoken language on a computer we need speech properties that we can quantify, which brings us to **acoustic phonetics**. Acoustic properties of speech refer to the physical characteristics of sound. **Sound waves** that we speak are simply "small variations in air pressure that occur very rapidly one after another" (Ladefoged, 2005). When these waves hit a recording device, we can measure how often they hit, how loud they are, and so on.

sound wave

continuous

discrete

As mentioned before, sound is **continuous**, but computers store data in **discrete** points, as illustrated in Figure 1.18, and thus can only capture the general pattern of

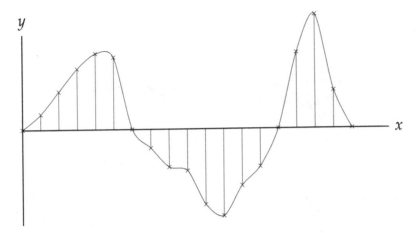

Figure 1.18   A continuous line with evenly spaced discrete points

the sound. The quality of a recording depends on the **sampling rate**, or how   **sampling rate**
many times in a given second we extract a moment of sound. The sampling rate is
measured in samples per second, commonly referred to as **Hertz** (Hz).   **Hertz**

The higher the sampling rate, the better the recording quality, though it takes
more space to store. For capturing the frequencies of language sounds when using
the telephone, 8,000 samples per second turn out to be adequate, and 16,000 or
22,050 Hz is often used when recording speech.

Some of the properties of speech we are interested in include the **speech flow**,   **speech flow**
the rate of speaking and the number and length of pauses. This is easy enough to
measure in units of time (i.e., seconds). The **loudness**, or **amplitude**, is the amount   **loudness**
of energy a sound has. Again, we have an intuitive sense of what it means to measure
amplitude; loudness of sounds is typically measured in decibels.   **amplitude**

Most important for classifying sound waves into individual speech sounds are the
frequencies associated with each sound. As we will see below, the frequency – or   **frequency**
how fast the sound waves repeat – is the basis on which we are able to tell sounds
apart. Frequency can be measured in terms of cycles per second, again referred to as
Hertz.

To get a feel for how sounds are represented on a computer, we start with a
waveform, shown in an **oscillogram**. Figure 1.19 represents the word "Thursday": as   **oscillogram**
time passes on the x-axis, we can observe the changes in amplitude, or loudness, on
the y-axis. All phonetic figures in this chapter were produced using Praat (http://
www.fon.hum.uva.nl/praat/). The first vowel in the figure has the loudest sound and
there is essentially silence in the middle of the word, due to the stop consonant [d].

The **pitch** of a sound – how high or low it is – provides additional information,   **pitch**
especially for vowels. Speech is composed of different frequencies all at once (due to   **fundamental**
the way sound reverberates in the vocal tract): there is a **fundamental frequency**,   **frequency**
or pitch, along with higher-frequency **overtones**. These overtones give unique character to each vowel. We also have **intonation**; that is, the rise and fall in pitch. For   **overtone**
example, the intonation at the end of questions in English typically rises.   **intonation**

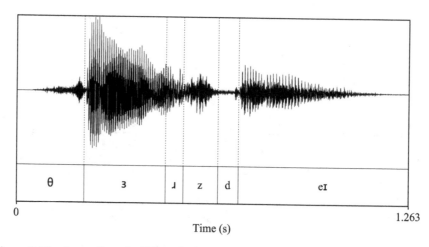

Figure 1.19   A waveform for "Thursday"

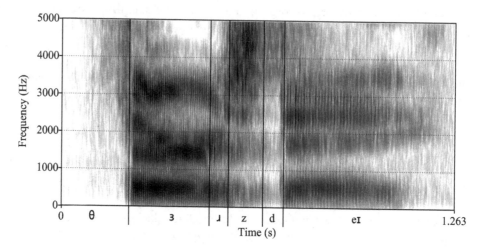

Figure 1.20   A spectrogram for "Thursday"

spectrogram   Finally, we can analyze spoken language using a **spectrogram**, which is a graph to represent the frequencies of speech (y-axis) over time (x-axis). As we can see in Figure 1.20, each sound is a complex unit made of different frequencies. In fact, what we observe in a spectrogram will help us the most in automatically determining what sound was uttered, to which we turn next.

1.4.4   Measuring speech

A spectrogram has various measurable properties that tell us what the sounds are. Under the Hood 1 on *Reading a spectrogram* provides more details, but we will sketch a few general properties here. These are questions you can ask when looking at a spectrogram:

1. How dark is the picture?

   This tells us how loud each sound is and is measured in decibels. Different sounds differ in their loudness, including some sounds – such as [d] – that involve a moment of complete silence. Compare [θ] and [z] in Figure 1.20, which show that [θ] is not as loud.

2. Where are the lines the darkest?

   The darkest lines tell us which frequencies (measured in Hertz) are the loudest and the most important for determining the sound. Each vowel has roughly three prominent frequency bands, and the vowels are distinguished by these bands. For voiced sounds, we typically also see a low dark band.

3. How do these dark lines change?

   One last point involves how the frequencies change over time. When we have stop consonants like [t] or [k], there appears to be nothing in the spectrogram by which we can distinguish the sounds, and yet we make the distinction quite easily. It turns out that the transitions of the vowel bands before and after the consonant are unique.

It is these measurements that represent speech on the computer. In other words, to a computer, speech is nothing but a sequence of various numeric measurements. After we discuss reading a spectrogram, we will delve into turning these measurements of speech into text.

Under the Hood 1
Reading a spectrogram

The first thing to note about reading a spectrogram is that the word boundaries are not at all clear-cut. As mentioned before, there are no pauses between words. To know what a word is, what is needed is information about the structure of the language we are looking at. Consider, for example, hearing a string in a foreign language such as "skarandashom". Can you tell where the word boundary is? If you speak Russian (and understand the transliteration from Cyrillic), you might recognize the break between "s" ('with') and "karandashom" ('(a) pencil'). Otherwise, you probably did not know the boundaries.

But what about the individual sounds? Let us start with the different kinds of consonants. When discussing the articulatory properties of speech, we distinguished the manner of articulation – how air is passed through the channel – and it turns out that sounds with similar manners have commonalities in their

(Continued)

Under the Hood 1
Reading a spectrogram
(Cont'd.)

acoustic properties. We will examine three kinds of consonants: fricatives, nasals, and stops. For each type of consonant, we will give a brief articulatory description and then the acoustic distinctions that make it prominent.

We start our analysis with fricatives – in English, these include [f] (*f* in *fist*, *ph* in *photo*), [v] (*v* in *vote*), [s], [z], [θ] (*th* in *thigh*), [ð] (*th* in *thy*), [ʃ] (*sh* in *she*), and [ʒ] (the final sound of *rouge*). All of these involve air passing turbulently through the mouth: the tongue raises close to a point of constriction in the mouth, but it does not completely touch. With this turbulent air, we will see a lot of "noise" in the spectrogram. It is not completely noise, however; you can look at where the shading is darkest in order to tell the fricatives apart. For example, although it varies by speaker, [s] has its energy concentrated in the higher frequencies (e.g., close to 5000 Hz), as illustrated in Figure 1.21.

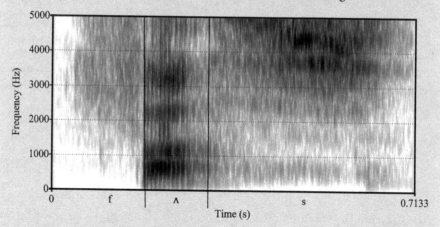

Figure 1.21   A spectrogram for "fuss"

On the other hand, [ʃ] peaks lower (e.g., around 3500 Hz), and [f] does not really have a prominent peak, as also shown in the figure. The voiced sounds [z], [ʒ], and [v] pattern mostly like [s], [ʃ], and [f], respectively. The main difference is that these sounds are voiced. Voicing, which is the movement of vocal cords, causes there to be low-frequency energy, though it is a bit hard to see precisely in the spectrogram for the word "fuzz" in Figure 1.22. (Note, however, that the voicing difference co-occurs with a distinct difference in the length of the vowel.)

The next consonant type to look at is the set of stop consonants, also called *plosives*: [p] (*p* in *pad*), [b] (*b* in *boy*), [t], [d], [k], and [g] (*g* in *go*). As with fricatives, there are more stops in other languages than English. What all of these sounds have in common is that, to make them, the tongue makes a complete closure with part of the mouth.

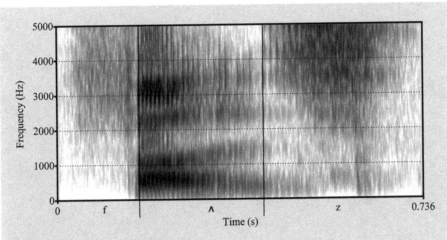

Figure 1.22 A spectrogram for "fuzz"

But if there is a stoppage of air, then stops actually involve a lack of sound. So how is it that we hear differences? First of all, we should note that stops are often accompanied by a burst of air – what is called aspiration – that translates into noise (similar to a fricative) in a spectrogram right after the stoppage. We can see this in Figure 1.23, at the end of the [t] sound. Secondly, and more importantly, the way we hear a distinct stop sound – e.g., [t] vs. [k] – is in the surrounding vowels. The vowels surrounding a consonant transition into the stop and then out of it again; that is, their formants (see below) move up or down, depending on the consonant. We will not go into the exact ways to read the transitions, as it is rather complex; the interested reader can refer to sources in the *Further reading* section.

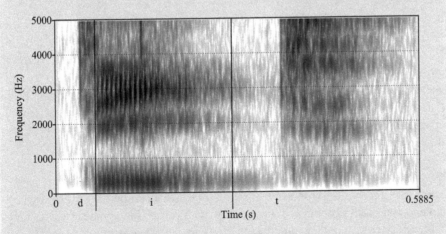

Figure 1.23 A spectrogram for "deet"

We can now turn to vowels, which can be difficult to tell apart. Articulatorily speaking, a key aspect of vowels is where in the mouth the tongue is raised:

(*Continued*)

Under the Hood 1
Reading a spectrogram
(Cont'd.)

front, middle, or back. We can also talk about vowel height: whether the tongue is raised high, low, or somewhere in between. Some of the vowels in English are given in Figure 1.24: [i] (*beet*), [e] (*bait*), [æ] (*bat*), [ə] (the *a* in *sofa*), [u] (*boot*), [o] (*boat*), and [ɑ] (the *a* in *father*). See also Figure 1.4.

	Front	Middle	Back
High	i		u
Mid	e	ə	o
Low	æ		ɑ

Figure 1.24 Some of the major vowels in English

Vowels are generally distinguished by their three bands of frequencies: these are the vowel formants. We refer to these as F1, F2, and F3. Conveniently, there is a nearly direct correspondence between the formant values and the location of the tongue in the mouth. The higher the F1 value, the lower the tongue is – for example, [ɑ] has one of the highest F1 values. While F1 is associated with vowel height, F2 is associated with vowel frontness: the higher the F2 value, the further forward in the mouth the tongue is. Thus, [i] has one of the biggest F2 values. (The F3 value, by the way, can often be hard to see.) In Figure 1.23, for example, the [i] in "deet" has a low F1 band and a high F2, with the F3 value slightly higher.

1.4.5 Relating written and spoken language

automatic speech recognition (ASR)

text-to-speech synthesis (TTS)

Written and spoken forms of language are clearly relatable. If we can automatically relate the two, then we can perform two very practical tasks: **automatic speech recognition (ASR)**, which maps sound to text, and **text-to-speech synthesis (TTS)**, which maps text to sound.

Automatic speech recognition (ASR)
Automatic speech recognition is the process by which a computer converts a speech signal to text. Such systems, are enormously practical, as they can be integrated into dialogue systems, can allow doctors to dictate patient diagnoses in one quick pass, and so on.

    In general, ASR systems go through three steps. First, speech is digitally sampled, as was discussed above. As this converts continuous speech into a discrete **information loss** representation, this will naturally involve **information loss**. Secondly, the speech samples are converted into measurable units, as was also discussed above; this is referred to as **acoustic signal processing**. Here, the digital samples are converted into, among other things, recognizable frequencies, giving the computer a repre- sentation of speech to work with. These frequencies are used for the third step, the recognition of sounds, groups of sounds, and words. The frequencies can be used to identify speech sounds, but, as we discussed before, the interpretation of a given frequency is often ambiguous, since different people speak differently. For example, a [t] might sound like a [d]. Thus, more sophisticated analysis will likely be added to this step; the Under the Hood section on language modeling provides more information below. *(acoustic signal processing)*

Given these basics, there are different kinds of ASR systems. The main distinction we can make is between speaker-dependent and speaker-independent ASR systems. **Speaker-dependent** systems work for a single speaker, whereas **speaker-independent** systems work for any speaker of a given variety of a language, for example American English. Given the range of pronunciations across different people, speaker-dependent systems are clearly more accurate. This is why there are also **speaker-adaptive** systems, which start out as independent systems but begin to adapt to a single speaker in order to improve accuracy. *(speaker-dependent, speaker-independent, speaker-adaptive)*

We can also distinguish ASR systems based on their domain. ASR systems that are built for a particular domain, for instance flight reservations, are optimized for dealing with flight vocabulary, and their vocabulary size may be much smaller than general-purpose ASR systems.

Text-to-speech synthesis (TTS)

The reverse of automatic speech recognition is text-to-speech (TTS) synthesis, which converts words into speech. This might seem like a trivial task: couldn't we simply record a voice saying phrases or words and then play back those words in the appropriate order?

While this might work for talking toy dolls, when we deal with technology such as dialog systems (see Chapter 6), the computer system generates written sentences that need to be synthesized on the fly. Thus, we have to be able to break the text down into smaller units that can be converted into speech. This is challenging, given that writing system representations are often phonetically ambiguous.

The main idea behind speech generation is to adjust the values of the frequencies, the loudness, and so forth, to produce the correct sounds. Since we know what frequencies correspond to which vowels, for example, we can play those frequencies to make the speech sound like the right vowel. Of course, as we mentioned before, sounds are always different, across time and across speakers. One way to help in the process of generating speech is to have a database of speech and to use **diphones** – that is, two-sound segments – to generate new utterances. The contextual information found in diphones helps with two different issues: (i) the fact that every sound is spoken differently depending on the neighboring sounds; and (ii) the fact that phonetically ambiguous characters are less ambiguous in context. *(diphone)*

Under the Hood 2
Language modeling for automatic speech recognition

Although we have talked a great deal about the acoustic information that goes into speech recognition, acoustics is not the only source of information. For example, if the system already recognized the previous words correctly, then knowing these correct words could help us get the next word correct.

Consider what happens when a system thinks that it has recognized a syllable sounding like [ki]. Without knowing anything about the context, the most likely word is "key" but, given all the fluctuations in how speakers say a word, this could also be "Guy", "keep", "keyed", "keen", or even the latter part of "ski".

The problem is that all of these are plausible words or parts of words for that sound: sounds like [g] and [k] are easily confused; final consonants can be dropped; and the preceding sound may or may not be a part of this word (e.g., "his skis" and "his keys" sound nearly identical). While certain facts about pronunciation are useful – for example, the likelihood of dropping a [p] at the end of a word – what we really need is some notion of the wider context.

Specifically, knowing something about the previous word can help. Consider if the previous word was recognized as "is": all of a sudden, "keep" and "key" are less likely. If the previous word was "the", we have a different set of best candidates: in this case (assuming no previous s sound), "key" is probably the best choice. The intuition is that facts about the (previous) context should give us better word guesses. Now, the question is: How can we capture this intuition in a computationally practical way?

One concept that will help here and in the chapters to come is that of an *n*-gram, a stretch of text *n* units long (here, words). We can use *n*-grams to approximate language, as they say something about language, without capturing the entire structure, and they constitute a very efficient technique for language processing. Finding, for example, every two-word sequence in a text is quick and easy.

N-grams help in a variety of natural language processing (NLP) applications, including the task in which we are interested, namely word prediction. We can look at the previous words (i.e., the previous $n-1$ words) to predict the next word. If we use 3-grams, or trigrams, we will use the previous two words to predict the current word.

Let us start with a phrase like "I dreamed I saw the knights in", the first seven words of the Neil Young song "After the Gold Rush". Before we get into technical points, what do you think the next word is? Even if they have never heard the song, many people will answer with "shining" or "armor" (the correct word, in this case). In fact, if you had seen the phrase "knights in" and were asked to predict the next word, your choices would likely be the same. That is, we often only need two words to be able to say something useful about the next word. (Of course, homophones, such as *nights in*, as in The Moody Blues' "Nights in White Satin", could cause a problem here.)

We will return to this point in a moment, but first, let us lay out the more mathematical properties of this situation. In order to make sense of *n*-gram information, we want to know how likely an *n*-gram is. Thus, we will use probabilities. A probability captures the likelihood of something happening. For example, maybe the probability of seeing someone carrying an open umbrella on a given college campus is 10%.

What we will actually need to do is look at the probability of one event if we know something about another related event. Let us walk through an example to see what this means. Consider the probability of seeing a professor walking across the Ohio State campus carrying an open umbrella. The weather in Ohio is usually quite good, so this probability is low, say 10%. But if we know that it has been raining for the last three hours, then our estimate of the probability increases markedly. In the language of probability, we call the fact that it has been raining for the last three hours the conditioning event, and the fact that we actually observe the professor with the umbrella the conditioned event. The idea of using conditional probabilities here is to take account of the fact that rain influences the behavior of professors. Of course, this tendency cannot be totally relied on, because professors are notoriously erratic and insensitive to their environment. But, on average, it remains true that rain will increase the rate at which umbrellas are present and open.

Similarly, the idea of language modeling is to form conditional probabilities that reflect our judgment about the influence that the previous words will have on their successors. In the case of "I dreamed I saw the knights in", the conditional probability we are interested in is the probability of the next word given that we have already seen "I dreamed I saw the knights in".

Mathematically, we denote conditional probabilities by using a | symbol. We can read something like $P(A|B)$ as "the probability of A given B". In this case, if we want to know the likelihood of "armor" being the next word, we are interested in $P(armor|I\ dreamed\ I\ saw\ the\ knights\ in)$.

But this seems like a strange probability. Do we really need seven words to predict the eighth one? Most of these words are unimportant for predicting the next word. Furthermore, if we have to do word prediction with a computational system, it will take us an enormous amount of memory to store all these 8-grams, or 10-grams, or 25-grams, or however long.

The solution for this situation is simple: we use our intuition from before – that we only need a few words accurately to predict the next word – and approximate this probability. A trigram approximation for this string is in (1), where ≈ means "is approximately equal to". This says that we should only look at the previous two words to predict the next word.

(*Continued*)

Under the Hood 2
Language modeling for automatic speech recognition
(Cont'd.)

1. $P(armor|I\ dreamed \ldots knights\ in) \approx P(armor|knights\ in)$

Common approximations are to use bigrams ($n=2$) or trigrams ($n=3$). The choice of how long an n-gram should be is a tradeoff between robustness and accuracy. The shorter the n-gram, the more examples we can find – after all, for a string of four words there is a single 4-gram, but two 3-grams, three 2-grams, and four 1-grams (or unigrams). So the chance of finding the same bigram twice in a text is greater than that of finding the same trigram twice. The lower the value of n, the more instances of such n-grams we find, meaning that a system will be able to account for more situations and thus be more robust.

One remaining question is: What do we do when we encounter a trigram we have never seen before? For example, someone might utter "eat loaves" and we have never seen this phrase before, so we are not sure what the next word should be. While we will not delve into this topic too deeply, systems employ techniques for dealing with unknown data, often called smoothing. One such technique is to back off to a shorter n-gram when the current one cannot be found. For example, in this scenario we would check all bigrams starting with "loaves" in order to predict the next word (e.g., *of*).

Continuing our "knights in armor" example, if the system is deciding between "armor", "harmful", and the two-word sequence "arm or", an n-gram model as we have outlined should be able to tell us that "armor" is the preferred word.

Recall also the similar example at the beginning of this section, namely trying to decide between "keen", "key", and "keyed", among other choices. When we put all this information together in a given context, one probability should outweigh another, as in (2). Using these probabilities, the system's best guesses at speech sounds can be turned into sequences of real words.

(2) $P(key|the) > P(keen|the) > P(keyed|the)$

The concepts of using n-grams and probabilities will recur throughout this book, such as in the writers' aids section on using n-grams to assist with spelling correction, Section 2.3.1, and in Under the Hood 11 in the machine translation chapter, where some of the theoretical underpinnings of using probabilities to recover information are given.

Checklist

After reading the chapter, you should be able to:

- Describe different types of writing systems and how they vary in their use of phonetic and semantic properties. Explain why it is possible for a language (such as Azeri) to be written in several different writing systems, and what this shows about the relationship between the written and spoken forms of language.
- Recognize that numbers can be represented in different ways, and understand how to convert between representations, especially converting numbers between base two and base ten representations.
- Explain what Unicode is useful for and how the UTF-8 encoding scheme works.
- Have an understanding of how the physics and biology of the articulatory system allow speech sounds to be produced.
- Be able to sketch how modern technology allows the acoustic properties of speech sounds to be measured, and know how to recognize some speech features by looking at spectrograms.
- Explain the tasks of automatic speech recognition and text-to-speech synthesis, and distinguish between speaker-dependent and speaker-independent approaches.
- Understand the value of statistical models in building language technology, and be able to explain how *n*-grams are used for language modeling for ASR (if you read Under the Hood 2).

Exercises

1. **ALL:** Go to http://www.omniglot.com and pick a syllabary. Take a paragraph from a novel written in English and transliterate it into this syllabary.
   (a) What difficulties do you encounter?
   (b) Is there any *information loss* in your transliteration? If it were transliterated back into the Latin alphabet, what ambiguities would you find?

2. **LING:** Assume you've been given power to alter the Latin alphabet for the purpose of better writing down English words.
   (a) Keeping it as an alphabet, what would you change, add, or remove? Why?
   (b) Could you just use the IPA to write down English? What problems would you encounter (on a global scale)?
   (c) Could you convert the alphabet into a system similar to Hangeul for Korean? How would it work?
   (d) Assume you have to propose 100 words to take on some logographic properties in their writing. What would be a reason for converting the alphabet into a (more) logographic system of writing? What types of words would you select for the first 100? Why?

3. **MATH**: As mentioned briefly, *hexadecimal* numbers have 16 digits: 0–9 and the letters A–F. They are commonly used in computing because they more compactly represent the numbers that are often used for bytes than binary numbers do.
    (a) Describe how hexadecimal numbers work, working through the base ten number 46 as an example.
    (b) Describe a procedure for converting numbers from a binary (base two) to a hexadecimal (base sixteen) representation.

4. **ALL**: Discuss the optimal way to design UTF-8, in terms of the average number of bytes per character and the number of users of a given writing system.

5. **ALL**: The speech waveforms and spectrograms shown in this chapter were produced using Praat (http://purl.org/lang-and-comp/praat), but there are other useful speech analysis software kits, such as Wavesurfer (http://purl.org/lang-and-comp/wavesurfer).
    (a) Download one of these software packages and make yourself comfortable with using it.
    (b) Pick your favorite book and record yourself reading the first sentence (or 20 words, whichever comes first).
    (c) Record a friend saying the same thing.
    (d) Compare and contrast spectrograms of your different spoken language examples, describing how what you see corresponds to what you both said and what the differences are.

6. **ALL**: Explain why automatic speech recognition (ASR) is an irreversible process. Make reference to the concept of *information loss* in your answer.

7. **ALL**: Come up with a list of 10 bigrams that vary in how predictable the next (third) word should be and write them down. For example, "to the" can be followed by a large number of items, "edge of" seems to have a more limited set, and "the United" is even further restricted.
    (a) Interview at least 10 friends, asking them to fill in the blanks. Record their answers.
    (b) Do you find that the strings are as predictable as you thought they were? Why or why not?

8. **CS**: To get a firmer grasp on how *n*-grams work and how they can be used to predict a word – as is done for ASR – write a program that takes a text file as input and stores all unigrams and bigrams.
    (a) Read in a new text file and, for each word (i.e., unigram), predict the most probable next word.
    (b) How accurate is your simple word-guessing program? Is it better or worse on different kinds of texts?

Further reading

More information on writing systems, including various graphics, can be gleaned from websites such as http://www.omniglot.com. Additionally, there are books on writing systems, such as Daniels and Bright (1996). Sproat (2000) offers a unique treatment, which focuses on computational properties of writing systems, and Sproat (2011) extends the writing system discussion to language technology and its impact on society. Both are highly recommended. Turning from writing systems to language, a thorough set of information on the world's languages can be found in the *Ethnologue* (Gordon, 2005). For an accessible overview of topics related to language and how language can be studied, check out *Language Files* (Mihaliček and Wilson, 2011). As a reference book, you can find comprehensive information in David Crystal's *Cambridge Encyclopedia of Language* (Crystal, 2011).

For an introductory look at automatic speech recognition and language modeling, the Jurafsky and Martin (2009) textbook is a valuable resource. There are also papers such as Madnani (2009) that provide good overviews of language modeling, and you can check out practical toolkits, such as SRILM (Stolcke, 2002), at http://purl.org/lang-and-comp/srilm. For thorough introductions to the field of phonetics, Ladefoged (2005) and Johnson (2003) are recommended. The latter is especially good for examining the acoustic properties of speech.

2

Writers' Aids

2.1 Introduction

A few years ago, the following email was heavily circulated around the internet:

Aoccdrnig to a rscheearch at Cmabrigde Uinervtisy, it deosn't mttaer in waht oredr the ltteers in a wrod are, the olny iprmoetnt tihng is taht the frist and lsat ltteer be at the rghit pclae. The rset can be a toatl mses and you can sitll raed it wouthit porbelm. Tihs is bcuseae the huamn mnid deos not raed ervey lteter by istlef, but the wrod as a wlohe.

The text is surprisingly readable, even though the claims made in the message are not entirely true. Various people pointed out, for example, that in general it is not enough to get the first and last letters right (see, e.g., http://purl.org/lang-and-comp/ cmabridge), so the example text is well chosen. Nonetheless, the message does make you wonder whether correct spelling is just an unnecessary torture invented by middle school teachers. If people can understand badly spelled text just as well as correctly spelled text, why should anyone bother to get the spelling right?

There are a number of reasons why standard spelling is useful and important. Consider, for instance, the spelling of family names: for this, spelling is not standardized, so you will encounter variation. You are asked to call someone called "Vladimir Zygmunt", so you look him up in the telephone book. But alas, no such entry appears under Z. So you turn to look for alternative spellings and under S you discover "Siegmund." Among the many entries, you cannot find a "Vladimir", though. Browsing through the different first names you come across the alternative spelling "Wladimir" and finally find the entry you were looking for under "Wladimir Siegmund". Without an agreed standard spelling for English words, similar detective work would be necessary

Language and Computers, First Edition. Markus Dickinson, Chris Brew and Detmar Meurers.

every time we want to look up a word in a dictionary or thesaurus. A word such as "itinerary" might, for example, be found under *I*, but without standard spelling it might also be listed as "etinerary" under *E*, or as "aitinerary" under *A*. Standard spelling makes it possible to find a word in a single, predictable place.

Standard spelling also makes it easier to provide a single text that is accessible to a wide range of readers. People of different social or regional backgrounds speaking different dialects can still read and write a common language by using the same spelling conventions. The word that a northern speaker of American English pronounces as [pɛn] (so with a vowel as in *bet*) might sound more like [pɪn] (a vowel as in *bit*) when in the mouth of a southern speaker. Since both agree that the standard spelling of this word is "pen", it becomes possible to write texts in a general way, independent of the particular pronunciations used in a given region or by a specific social group.

Related to the last point, in the USA today being able to use standard spelling is an expected consequence of being well educated. This was not the case in England in the age of Shakespeare. But today, anyone wanting to make a good impression in formal social interactions such as in job applications had better be prepared to spell words correctly. Of course, the spelling conventions that are suitable for informal settings such as text messages are quite different from those of formal letters: consider "CU L8R" (*see you later*), "ROTFL" (*rolling on the floor laughing*), "AFAIK" (*as far as I know*).

Finally, standard spelling is also important for computer software that deals with written text. Optical character recognition (OCR) software, for instance, can use knowledge about standard spelling to recognize scanned words even for hardly legible input. It can piece together the letters that it cannot read by noticing that they are next to letters that it can read, and using knowledge of spelling to fill in the gaps.

In sum, whether you hate being forced to use English spelling or whether you enjoy it, it looks like standard spelling is here to stay. Luckily, for those of us who can never remember how to spell "Massachusetts" or "onomatopoeia", or who consistently confuse "they're" and "there", technological support exists in the form of spell checkers, grammar checkers, and style checkers. For consistency, the name for the tool that checks spelling should perhaps have been "spelling checker", but the term
spell checker **spell checker** is the one most people use, so we will follow common practice. Until and unless there is a need for a tool that checks spells, no ambiguity will arise.
writers' aids   These tools, often referred to collectively as **writers' aids**, are supposed to help; ideally, they enable writers to focus on the content of the document without worrying so much about the forms. We start our exploration of language technology applications in this book with writers' aids because we assume they are familiar to everybody, and they also provide a nice platform for introducing many linguistic concepts that you will see recur in the rest of the book.

2.2   Kinds of spelling errors

In order to detect and correct spelling errors effectively, we have to know what errors to look for, and so must know what kind of misspelled and ungrammatical input to expect. This is common in natural language processing (NLP): we may have an intuitive sense of the problem – in this case, spelling errors – but the first step in developing technology is to understand the examples or data to be covered and the concepts that are relevant for capturing the properties we see exemplified by the data.

2.2.1 Nonword errors

The so-called **nonword errors** are errors resulting in words that do not exist in a language, for example when the article "the" is erroneously written as the nonword "hte".

One can characterize such errors in two ways. On the one hand, we can ask why this error happened, trying to determine the cause of the error. On the other hand, we can describe how the word that was written differs from the target word; that is, the word the writer intended but did not write down correctly.

Looking first at the **error cause**, nonword errors are usually caused either by mistakes in typing or by spelling confusions. **Typographical errors** (typos) are errors where the person probably knew how to spell the word correctly, but mistyped it. **Spelling confusions** occur when the person lacks or misremembers the necessary knowledge. A writer might, for example, never have seen the word "onomatopoeia" or might remember that "scissors" has something odd about it, but not be able to recall the details. For the record, "scissors" has at least three odd features: the use of *sc* to make the [s] sound is unusual, as is the use of *ss* to spell a [z] sound, as is the use of *or* for the suffix that is more often written *er*. In English, when you know how to say a word, you may still be a long way from knowing how to spell it correctly.

Spelling confusions based on sound are obviously a major problem; not only do we spell based on analogy with other words, but we often use typical sound-to-letter correspondences when a word is unknown. Thus, spellers may leave out silent letters (*nave* for *knave*), may replace a letter with a similar-sounding one (*s* for *c* in *deside* in place of *decide*), or may forget nuances of a rule (*recieve*: *i* before *e* except after *c*). This is not the same across all languages, however. In some languages, such as Finnish and Korean but not English, if you know how to say a word, you will be able to make a very good guess about how to spell it. We say that languages like this have a **transparent writing system**. In these languages, we do not expect to see very many errors caused by confusions about the sound-to-letter correspondence.

Errors can happen for other reasons, such as a particular keyboard layout that causes certain typos to be more likely than others. Yet, while one can hypothesize a wide range of such underlying error causes, it is difficult to obtain definitive evidence. After all, we are not generally around to observe a person's fingers or to notice that an error was caused by a cat walking on the keys. As a result, the analysis of spelling errors and the development of spell checking technology has primarily focused on a second method for classifying errors. Instead of trying to identify the underlying cause of the error, we try to describe the way in which the misspelled word differs from the target word that the writer was aiming for. There is an obvious problem with this approach if the reader cannot tell what the intended target was, but this turns out to be rare, at least given enough context.

target
modification Research on spelling errors distinguishes four classes of **target modification** errors on the basis of the surface form of the misspelled word and the likely target word:

- Insertion: A letter has been added to a word.
  Example: "arguement" (*argument*)
- Deletion: A letter has been omitted from a word.
  Example: "aquire" (*acquire*)
- Substitution: One letter has been replaced by another.
  Example: "calandar" (*calendar*)
- Transposition: Two adjacent letters have been switched.
  Example: "concsious" (*conscious*)

You may feel that this way of describing errors is quite mechanical. We agree that the underlying causes described a few paragraphs ago are more interesting for understanding why errors arise. But we will see both in the following discussion and when we introduce techniques for automatically identifying and correcting errors in Section 2.3.2 that viewing errors in terms of target modification is a very useful perspective in practice.

Classifying errors in terms of target modification allows us to identify the most common kinds of insertions, deletions, substitutions, and transpositions that people make. By looking at long lists of examples of actual errors, it then also becomes possible to infer some likely error causes. When finding many substitutions of one specific letter for another, the mistyped letter is often right next to the correct one on a common keyboard layout. For example, one finds many examples where the letter *s* has been mistyped for the letter *a*, which is related to the fact that the *a* and *s* keys are next to another on a typical English QWERTY keyboard. We can, of course, also turn this correspondence around and use the information about keyboard proximity to calculate the likelihood of particular substitutions and other error types occurring. This will be

single-error
misspelling useful when we look at ranking candidates for spelling correction in Section 2.3.2 .

Looking at where such errors arise, we can distinguish **single-error misspellings**, in which a word contains one error, from **multi-error misspellings**, where a single

multi-error
misspelling word contains multiple instances of errors. Research has found upwards of 80% of misspellings to be single-error misspellings, and "most misspellings tend to be within two characters in length of the correct spelling" (Kukich, 1992). The two observations naturally are connected: both insertion and deletion errors only change the length of a word by one character, whereas substitution and transposition errors keep the length the same.

The insight that writers primarily make single-error misspellings within two characters in length of the correct spelling means that spell checkers can focus on a much smaller set of possible corrections and therefore can be relatively efficient. A related observation further narrowing down the search for possible corrections is that the first character in a word is rarely the source of the misspelling, so that the misspelled word and the correct spelling usually have the same first letter.

Note that these trends are based on data from good writers of native speaker English, so will not be fully applicable to other populations, such as nonnative speakers or people with dyslexia. Because traditional spell checkers are built on the assumption that the writers are native speakers, they are not good at correcting nonnative errors. Fortunately, it can sometimes help to know that we are dealing with nonnative speakers: there are specific types of spelling errors that are characteristic of people learning English as a foreign language. For example, it is common to use an English word that looks like a word from their native language. An **false friend** example of such so-called **false friends** or **lexical transfer** would be the common **lexical transfer** use of "become" in place of "get" by German-speaking learners of English – an error that arises since the German word "bekommen" means "get" in English. Chapter 3 discusses the use of computers in foreign language teaching and learning in more detail.

Typos are not caused by confusions or missing knowledge, but by mistakes in the execution of the writing process. These include misspellings caused by overuse, underuse, or misuse of the space bar. **Splits** are errors caused by hitting the **split error** space bar in the middle of a word, turning a single word into two words, such as "quintuplets" becoming "quin tuplets". This is overuse of the space bar. Although determining where a word starts and where it ends, so-called **tokenization**, is a **tokenization** tricky issue for languages other than English (and even sometimes in English), most spell checkers assume that the string that needs to be checked is contained between two spaces. (See Section 3.4 for more on tokenization.) Thus, split errors are often difficult to correct, because the checker cannot tell that the adjacent strings are intended as part of the same word. On the other hand, **run-ons** are **run-on error** errors that are caused by underuse of the space bar between two words, turning two separate words into one, such as "space bar" becoming "spacebar". Finally, there can be errors where the space between words is present, but not in the correct place, as can happen if you write "atoll way" instead of "a tollway". This is going to be especially hard to correct if, as here, the results of the mistake turn out to be real words.

2.2.2   Real-word errors

We just introduced the idea that errors can result in real words, making them more **real-word error** difficult to detect. Normally, when the result of an error is a nonword, an automated system can detect the error by trying to look up the word in a dictionary: if the word is not found, it may very well be the result of a spelling error. But this will not work for errors that result in real words, because the results will probably be listed in the dictionary. Human readers can often detect that something is wrong by inspecting the surrounding context of the word. There are three different kinds of real-word errors, each involving an appeal to context, but differing in the extent and nature of that appeal. As the appeal to context becomes more elaborate, the task of detecting the error becomes progressively more difficult.

local syntactic error First, there are **local syntactic errors**. Generally speaking, syntactic errors are errors in how words are put together in a sentence: different parts of speech are in the wrong places in a sentence or the wrong grammatical forms are used. Local syntactic errors are errors where the syntactic violation is detectable by looking within one or two words in the sentence. In sentence (3), for example, a possessive pronoun (*their*) is in the place where a noun phrase (*there*) should be, and this can be determined by the presence of the verb "was" that immediately follows it.

(3) * <u>Their was</u> a problem yesterday.

asterisk (*) In order to make explicit that this is an example of an ungrammatical sentence, we mark it with an **asterisk (*)**. This is a common convention in linguistics – and also alerts editors and typesetters to the fact that the error in the example is intended, rather than something to be corrected for publication.

long-distance syntactic error The second kind of real-word error we need to discuss here are **long-distance syntactic errors**, which are more difficult because they involve syntactic violations spread out over many more words. In sentence (4), for instance, there is a problem with subject–verb agreement, but it is spread out over five words.

(4) * The <u>team</u> that hits the most runs <u>get</u> ice cream.

Finally, there are semantic errors. These are errors in meaning: the sentence structure is grammatical, but the problem is that the sentence does not mean what was intended. In (5), "brook" is a singular noun – just like the presumably intended "book" – but it does not make sense in this context.

(5) He checked out a <u>brook</u> from the library.

It is not always easy to decide whether an error is a spelling error or an error in grammar. Example (4), for instance, could be thought of as a real-word spelling error in which the typist simply omitted the *s* of *gets*, or it could be thought of as a problem with subject–verb agreement, which is a grammatical error. Without knowing what is going on in the mind of the reader, it is hard to know which explanation is better. In example (3), on the other hand, it seems obvious that the writer was trying to produce *There*, so it is safe to classify this as a real-word spelling error.

2.3 Spell checkers

interactive spell checker Having explored the types of errors, we can now look at how to detect and correct spelling errors automatically. In general, we could design either an **interactive spell checker** or an **automatic spelling corrector**. Interactive spell checkers try to detect errors as the user types, possibly suggesting corrections, and users can determine for themselves the value of the corrections presented. Automatic spelling correctors, on the other hand, run on a whole document at once, detecting the errors and automatically correcting them without user assistance. Such correctors are never 100% accurate, so they are less desirable for the task of assisting in writing a document. When the "correction" that the system chooses is the wrong one, it will stay in the document unless the user notices and undoes the change. Note that many existing spell checkers actually make auto-corrections – which can sometimes lead to inadvertent and undesirable corrections.

Most of us are familiar with interactive spell checkers, and they will be the focus of our discussion here. Spelling correction involves the following three tasks, in increasing order of difficulty. First, there is **nonword error detection**, the task of finding strings in a text that are not words. For some purposes, simply detecting a misspelling is enough for the writer, who can then fix it by hand. Sometimes, however, we require the second task, **isolated-word error correction**. As the name implies, the goal of this task is to correct errors or suggest corrections, but without taking the surrounding context into account. For example, a corrector could correct "hte" to "the". Because it does not look at context, however, such a checker could not change "there" when it is used incorrectly in place of "their". For these errors, we need **context-dependent word correction**, the task of correcting errors based on the surrounding context. For instance, "too" used as a numeral will be corrected to "two" when it is surrounded by a determiner and a plural noun (e.g., *the too computers*).

nonword error detection

isolated-word error correction

context-dependent word correction

2.3.1 Nonword error detection

Dictionary methods
The simplest way to detect nonwords is to have a dictionary, or spelling list; if the word is not in the dictionary, it is a misspelling. While this is a good idea in general, there are several issues to consider in constructing a dictionary and looking words up in the dictionary.

First, one must realize that a dictionary is inherently incomplete, due to the productivity of language. New words are continually entering the language, such as "doh", while at the same time, old words are leaving. For example, in Shakespeare's time, "spleet" ("split") was a word and thus correctly spelled, while today it is not. Foreign words, differently hyphenated words, words derived from other words, and proper nouns continually bring new words to a language. A dictionary can never be exhaustive.

Even if we could include every word, however – including all proper nouns – it is not clear that this would be desirable. Including the proper last name "Carr" may result in not finding the misspelling in "The Great American Carr Show". A writer does not use every possible word in existence, and no two writers use exactly the same set of words. Should each person then have their own private dictionary?

The answer is both yes and no. For the majority of writers, we can narrow down a dictionary by considering only words that are "common". Rare words are likely to become confused with actual misspellings, and so they should not be included. For example, "teg" is a word ("a sheep in its second year"), but most English writers do not know or use this word. So, if it is found in a document, it is probably a misspelled form of, for instance, "tag" or "beg". The few writers who do intend to use "teg" will probably not mind if the spell checker flags it.

We can also focus on specific populations of users by utilizing separate dictionaries for particular domains. For the average user, "memoize" is a misspelling of "memorize", but for computer scientists it is a technical term. We can take this to the level of the individual user, too. Many spell checkers allow users to update their own personal dictionaries, by adding words or spelling rules. The free checker Hunspell (http://hunspell.sourceforge.net/), for instance, allows users easily to change the dictionary they use.

Turning to the internal parts of a dictionary, a general issue for dictionary construction is whether or not to include inflected words as separate entries. For example, should "car" and "cars" be stored separately? Or should "car" be stored as a single entry, indicating its part of speech (noun) and that it is regular; that is, it takes the standard -s plural ending?

The choice is one of efficiency and where to allocate the work. If they are separate entries, then the lookup mechanism is straightforward, but there is an increase in the number of words. If inflected words are not stored as separate entries, on the other hand, then there are far fewer lexical entries, but we have to strip the affixes (prefixes and suffixes) from the words before looking them up. Furthermore, one has to handle exceptions to affix rules in some systematic way, possibly by separate entries for "ox" and "oxen", for instance. And we have to prevent overgeneralizations of affix rules: there must be a special note on "ox" that it is irregular, so that "oxs" or "oxes" will not be accepted as correct spellings.

When dealing with thousands of words, looking up those words becomes nontrivial; each word has to be stored somewhere in computer memory, and finding where the word is takes time. Thus, an efficient storage and lookup technique is also needed – just as efficient storage is needed for webpages (see *Search engine indexing* in Section 4.3.4). Words could be stored alphabetically, and each word encountered could be searched for, but the words in English are not evenly distributed over the entire alphabet: for instance, the number of words that start with *x* is much smaller than the number of those that start with *s*. Computer scientists study and develop various ways to distribute word entries evenly in memory, in order to, for example, more quickly find words in the middle of the *s* section.

N-gram methods

What might be surprising is that, to some extent, words can be determined to be misspelled without using an explicit dictionary. One technique uses *n*-gram analysis. A **character *n*-gram**, in this context, refers to a string of *n* characters in a row; for instance, *thi* is a 3-gram (or trigram). Note that *thi* is a possible trigram of English (*this*), whereas *pkt* is not. Thus, one can store all possible *n*-grams for a certain *n* and a given language in order to determine whether each new string encountered has only valid *n*-grams. The set of valid (or likely) *n*-grams can be collected from a long piece of text, assuming that it has few or no misspellings.

<!-- margin note: character n-gram -->

N-gram analysis is more popular for correcting the output of optical character recognition (OCR) than for detecting writers' errors. This is due to the fact that OCR errors are more likely to result in invalid character sequences. Still, the technique is useful to examine, because it shows us how to detect spelling errors using very little knowledge or computational resources.

Specifically, one can use 2-grams (bigrams) and store them in a table. This can be done with positional information included or not. A **nonpositional bigram array** is an array, or table, of all possible and impossible bigrams in a language, regardless of the bigram's position in a word, as shown in Figure 2.1.

...	k	l	m	...
k	0	1 (*tackle*)	1 (*Hackman*)	...
l	1 (*elk*)	1 (*hello*)	1 (*alms*)	...
m	0	0	1 (*hammer*)	...

Figure 2.1 Excerpt of a nonpositional bigram array

A **positional bigram array**, on the other hand, is an array of possible and impossible bigrams for a particular position in a word, such as a word ending. Figure 2.2 illustrates this, with 1 indicating possible and 0 impossible.

...	k	l	m	...
k	0	0	0	...
l	1 (*elk*)	1 (*hall*)	1 (*elm*)	...
m	0	0	0	...

Figure 2.2 Excerpt of a positional bigram array (word ending)

Thus, *kl* is a possible bigram in English (e.g., *knuckles*), so it is in the nonpositional array (Figure 2.1), but it is not a valid word ending and so is not in the positional bigram array for word endings.

To detect errors, the spell checker first breaks the input word into bigrams and labels them with their positions. Then it looks up the bigrams in the nonpositional array for the given language. If *any* of the bigrams is missing from the array, it knows that the word has been misspelled. If all the bigrams were present, it goes on to check the positional bigram arrays. If it finds all the bigrams in the correct positions, the word is probably good. But if any of the checks fail, that means that one of the bigrams is out of place, so the input form is probably an error.

2.3.2 Isolated-word spelling correction

Taking nonword errors that have been detected, isolated-word spelling correction attempts to correct a misspelled word in isolation; that is, irrespective of surrounding words. Notice that one cannot expect 100% correctness from isolated-word spelling correctors. When humans were given the same task – correcting nonwords without knowing the context – their accuracy was around 74%.

In general, there are three main steps for a spell checker to go through in correcting errors: (i) error detection (described above); (ii) generation of candidate corrections; and (iii) ranking of candidate corrections. Isolated-word spelling correction deals with effective generation and ranking of candidate corrections. Such a task is useful in interactive spelling correctors, where a human makes the ultimate decision, because the higher up in the list the correct spelling is, the more quickly the user can approve the correction.

Generation of candidate corrections

Rule-based techniques generate candidate corrections by means of written rules, which encode transformations from a misspelling to a correct spelling. For example, a rule will look for the misspelling "hte" and generate "the" as a potential correction, or perhaps the only possible correction. Such rules can be highly effective, especially for high-frequency errors like "hte", where the intended word is clear. There are two downsides to rule-based generation of candidates, however.

The first is that someone has to write the rules, and they may not capture all the spelling errors humans might make. There have been advances in computational linguistics allowing for automatic derivation of rules, but a second problem remains: the rules are often very narrow and specific, such as the "hte" rule mentioned, which covers only one single misspelling of "the". A separate rule has to be written for "teh" and, as mentioned, generally only high-frequency errors are covered.

A second technique for generating candidates is actually an old method that was developed for working with variant names in US census data. Similarity-key techniques store words (correct spellings) with similar properties in the same bucket. That is, words with similar spellings or similar sounds and of about the same length are put together into one slot. When a misspelling is encountered, the similarity key for it is automatically calculated, and the bucket of similar but correctly spelled words is retrieved.

For example, in the SOUNDEX system, one of several well-known similarity-key systems, the word "nub" would be assigned the code N1: an N for the first letter, a 0 (zero) (which is later eliminated) for the vowel, and a 1 for a bilabial (*b, p, f, v*). The words "nob", "nap", and so on will also be in this bucket. If we encounter the misspelling "nup", we retrieve bucket N1 – which contains "nub", "nob", "nap", and other words – as our set of potential corrections.

Ranking of candidate corrections

Once the list of candidate corrections is generated, we want to rank these candidates to see which is the best. Again, we will look at two basic ideas.

Methods that use probabilities give us a mathematically precise way of indicating which corrections we want a checker to choose. But where do the probabilities come from? If we could directly measure the probability that one word will be typed when another is intended, and do this for every possible pair of words, we could use the probabilities as a way of ranking candidates. Unfortunately, because there are so many possible words, and a correspondingly large number of probabilities, this approach is not practical. It would take too long and use too much computer memory. Fortunately, it turns out that there is an effective approximate approach based on character-level **transition probabilities** and character-level **confusion probabilities** of *individual characters*. The idea is to use character-level statistics to build an adequate approximation to the word-level confusion statistics that we would ideally like but cannot obtain.

transition probability

confusion probability

Transition probabilities represent the probability of one character following another; for instance, the probability of *q* being followed by *u* in English is essentially 100%. Transition probabilities are used to model how likely it is that a character has been inserted or deleted. Confusion probabilities, on the other hand, represent the probability of one character being substituted for another; for example, using the standard English QWERTY keyboard, the chance of an *m* being typed for an *n* is higher than a *q* being typed for an *n* because *m* and *n* are nearby on the keyboard (and are similar phonetically). Starting with the misspelling, we use probabilities of insertions, deletions, substitutions, and transpositions to find the correct spelling in our candidate set with the highest probability (see the discussion on distance measurements below). We refer to this as the correction that **maximizes the probability**; that is, it is the most likely correction given the misspelling. We will take a close look at the mathematics behind this in Under the Hood 11.

maximize probability

Similarly, to rank candidate corrections, we can assign each a distance value telling how far off it is from the misspelling. A specific instance of this is called **edit distance**, which measures how many operations – insertions, deletions, substitutions, and (sometimes) transpositions – it would take to convert a misspelling into the correct spelling. (Transpositions are often not used in calculating edit distance and instead are treated as two substitutions.) The candidate with the minimum edit distance is the top-ranked one, where by **minimum edit distance** – often referred to as **Levenshtein distance** – we mean the minimum number of operations it would take to convert one word into another. For example, for the misspelling "obe", the word "oboe" has a distance score of one (insertion of *o*), while "hobo" has a score of two (insertion of *h*, deletion of *e*), so "oboe" is the better choice.

edit distance

minimum edit distance

Levenshtein distance

Of course, a word like "robe" also has a distance score of one, so to give a ranking with no ties, we need to add more information. This is where we can combine the edit distance method with the probabilistic method mentioned above. Instead of giving a value of one for each operation, we can use probabilities to determine which operations are more likely. For example, a greater edit distance would be given to substituting *q* for *n* than would be given to substituting *m* for *n*.

The minimum edit distance problem is technically challenging. The problem is this: there are many different sequences of edit operations that change a misspelling into a word. For instance, it is possible, although strange, to derive "oboe" from "obe" by deleting *o*, changing *b* to *o*, inserting *b*, and finally inserting *o*, taking four steps. Worse, there are hundreds of sequences that do this in five steps: one is to start by deleting *o*, then change *b* to *o*, then insert *b*, then insert *a*, and finally change *a* to *o*. It is pretty obvious that the *a* was a pointless diversion, but not immediately obvious how to fix this systematically.

Both human beings and computers can solve this problem, but they do so in different ways. Human beings can often use intuition to seek out and follow a single promising possibility. They can even solve a harder version of the problem in which all the intermediate stages are real words. Computers do not have intuition, so it works better for them to pursue multiple alternatives simultaneously. Fortunately, they are very good at the bookkeeping required for **dynamic programming** systematically working through a range of possibilities. The technique that makes this efficient is called **dynamic programming**, which is explained in detail in Under the Hood 3.

Under the Hood 3
Dynamic programming

The minimum edit distance problem is to decide how many edit operations are needed in order to transform a misspelling into a candidate correction. It is an example of an important class of problems that look hard but turn out, when correctly viewed, to have exceedingly efficient solutions. *Dynamic programming* is the technique that makes this possible.

The reason minimum edit distance looks hard is that there are very many different sequences of edit operations that need to be considered. However, by breaking up the problem into smaller subproblems, it is possible to find so many opportunities for saving time and space that the problem becomes feasible. The key idea is to avoid solving the same subproblem over and over again. This can be done by solving each subproblem once, then storing away the answer in case it is needed again. For an in-depth discussion on calculating minimum edit distances, see Chapter 8 of Mitton (1996), on which we base this discussion.

To set up the problem, we need to ensure that there is a finite number of steps involved. How could we end up with an infinite number of steps? We saw a hint of the problem in the discussion of *oboe* above. There we saw that there is a five-step path involving a diversion via *a*. Matters are actually far worse than this: we can also do it in six steps. We again start by deleting *o*, then change *b* to *o*, then insert *b*, then insert *a*, change *a* to *b*, then finally *b* to *o*. Or in seven, by converting the *b back* into an *a* before turning it into an *o*. In fact, since we can make the pointless diversion as long as we want, there are an *infinite* number of different ways of doing the conversion. Enumerating all these possibilities is not just inefficient, it is actually impossible. We need to set up the problem to avoid this pointless and infinitely repetitive enumeration of silly possibilities.

So, we want the algorithm for edit distance calculation to satisfy two requirements:

1. Letters cannot be changed back and forth a potentially infinite number of times.
2. The number of changes we consider should be reasonable. In fact, we will show that the number of changes we need to consider is proportional to the product of the sizes of the two words being compared. This is definitely efficient enough for spell checking, because words are typically quite short (40 characters is a really long word). If the sequences were much longer, as happens when comparing strands of DNA in biology, we might need a still more clever algorithm.

In other words, we never want to deal with a character in either word more than once. With our basic operations, it is obvious that we could get the desired result by deleting each character in the first word and then inserting each character of the second word. This establishes an upper bound on the number of edit operations we need. Mathematically, we can state this upper bound as *length*(*word1*) + *length*(*word2*). In other words, if we compare a three-letter word like "tap" to a misspelling like "step", we know that the edit distance cannot be more than seven. In fact, if you think a little more, you will be able to find a better upper bound on the number of operations needed. We will explain this tighter upper bound at the end of this section.

To calculate minimum edit distance, we set up a directed, acyclic graph, where a *graph* – which is a mathematical object that models relationships between items – is represented by a set of nodes (circles) and arcs (arrows). Arcs capture relationships between nodes; *directed* means that the arcs have a direction to them, pointing from one node to another, and *acyclic* means that there are no loops – we cannot return to a node once we have left it.

We will set up the graph as shown in Figure 2.3. Horizontal arcs correspond to deletions; vertical arcs correspond to insertions; and diagonal arcs correspond to substitutions (including the option that a letter is substituted for itself). We leave out transpositions here, although the graphs can be extended to allow them.

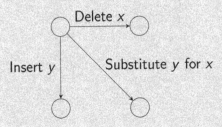

Figure 2.3   The basic set-up of a minimum edit distance graph

(Continued)

Under the Hood 3
Dynamic programming
(Cont'd.)

Let us start by assuming that the user types in "fyre." Given that "fry" is one of the possible corrections, we want to calculate how far away "fry" is. In other words, we want to calculate the minimum edit distance (or minimum edit cost) from "fyre" to "fry." As the first step, we draw the directed graph in Figure 2.4. The worst case of first deleting every letter in "fyre" and then inserting every letter of "fry" would be achieved by starting in the upper left, taking every arc across the top, and then following the arcs down the right-hand side.

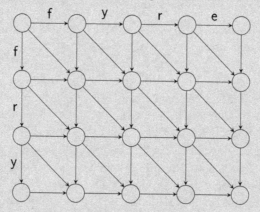

Figure 2.4   An initial directed graph relating "fry" and "fyre

What is missing from the graph are identifiers for the nodes. If we add an identifier to each state, as we do in Figure 2.5, that will allow us to define a topological order. A topological order means that the nodes are loosely, but not completely, ordered.

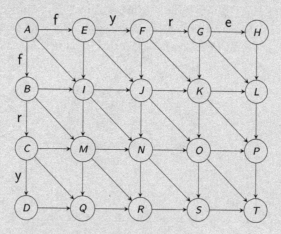

Figure 2.5   The directed graph, topologically ordered

In Figure 2.5, for example, node I comes after nodes A, B, and E, but there is no ordering between nodes C and I: there is no way to get from C to I or from I to C. The crucial property of this topological ordering, as we will see below, is that at every node, all the incoming arcs come from nodes prior in the ordering.

In order actually to calculate a distance, we need to add the costs involved to the arcs. In the simplest case, the cost of deletion, insertion, and substitution is one each (and substitution with the same character is free), as shown in Figure 2.6. In other words, there is a distance of one for any nontrivial operation. For example, from node A to node I, we substitute *f* for *f* with a cost of zero, and from I to J, we delete *y* with a cost of one.

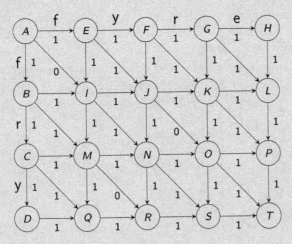

Figure 2.6 The directed graph with costs

Now, we are ready to get into dynamic programming. We want to find the path from the start (A) to the end (T) with the least cost. How do we do that efficiently?

We will start with a simple but inefficient way of doing it:

1. Follow every path from start (A) to finish (T).
2. See how many changes we have to make for each path.

This is very time-consuming, however. There are too many different paths to check. We would have to check the path A→I→J→O→S→T and then separately check the path A→I→J→O→P→T, and so on.

But note that these paths have much in common! In fact, based on this insight, we should instead reuse results, which is exactly what dynamic programming does:

(Continued)

Under the Hood 3
Dynamic programming
(Cont'd.)

1. Follow the topological ordering.
2. Calculate the least cost for each node:
   - Add the cost of an arc to the cost of reaching the node this arc originates from.
   - Take the minimum of the costs calculated for all arcs pointing to a node and store it for that node.

The key point is that we are storing partial results along the way, instead of recalculating everything every time we compute a new path. For example, let's say that we have already processed the nodes A–H and stored the minimum cost at each of those nodes. We are now at node I and need to examine all three incoming arcs (from nodes A, B, and E). Node A has a cost of zero; node E has a minimum cost of one; and node B also has a minimum cost of one. We add the cost of each node to the cost of each incoming arc, as displayed in Figure 2.7.

Source to Target	Cost at Source	+	Cost of Arc	=	Total Cost
A to I	0	+	0	=	0
B to I	1	+	1	=	2
E to I	1	+	1	=	2

Figure 2.7 Calculating the cost into node I

The least cost of these three incoming arcs is the one from node A, with a cost of 0. So we store 0 as the minimum cost at node I. This corresponds to the fact that the paths going through nodes B or E are useless for us to arrive at node I: they cost too much, and from this point onwards we can ignore those paths, keeping only the cheapest one. Now, any time node I is needed, we give the cost of 0, and we never have to recalculate its cost.

In this way, the minimum cost at every node is computed, following the ordering from A to T. At node T, we calculate costs in the same way. You can verify that node O has a minimum cost of 1, node P a minimum cost of 2, and node S a minimum cost of 2. Each of the arcs (O→T, P→T, S→T) has a cost of 1, and so the final cost at node T will be 2, taking the path coming from O. Since T is the final node in the graph, this means that 2 is the minimum cost between "fyre" and "fry".

Dynamic programming avoids infinite repetition, because it looks costs up in a table rather than recomputing them. It also satisfies the stronger requirement to avoid all unnecessary repetition, because each intermediate result is entered into the table exactly once. The number of letter–letter comparisons needed is exactly the size of the table, which is the product of the lengths of the source and target string, so we also satisfy the second requirement that the cost of the computation be in reasonable proportion to the size of the problem.

The better upper bound that we mentioned earlier is a simple one. Let us decide to work on transforming the longer word into the shorter word. First we replace all the letters of the shorter word with the corresponding letters of the longer word, then we insert the leftover letters from the longer word. To illustrate this, imagine that the shorter word is "take" and the longer word is "intake". The old upper bound said that we might need $4+6=10$ operations. The new upper bound says that we should first replace "take" with "inta", then insert "ke", for a total cost of six. We say that the new upper bound is tighter than the old one. The total number of operations required by the new, tighter upper bound is the length of the longer word.

Obviously, the real minimum cost path for this example is first to insert "in", then match up "take", for a minimum cost of two. Dynamic programming will indeed find this path. The upper bound is still useful, because it can be calculated using nothing more than the length of the words. If a node has a cost greater than the upper bound, it cannot possibly contribute to the minimum cost path, so we could design a slightly cleverer version of the minimum cost algorithm that avoids filling in nodes that would cost more than the upper bound. The answer would still be correct, and some time and effort would be saved, at the expense of making the algorithm more complicated. It is usually better to keep algorithms simple, because complicated ones are more likely to contain bugs, but in this case, especially if we are dealing with a language with very long words, the extra complexity might be warranted.

2.4   Word correction in context

The problem of context-dependent word correction is that of detecting and correcting errors that result in existing words, the real-word errors we first mentioned in Section 2.2.2. For example, the use of "There" in "There house is nice" is wrong, but it is still a word. The problem is not the word itself, but the particular way in which it is used. We say that the word does not fit the context.

This kind of spelling correction is closely related to **grammar checking**. Consider **grammar checking** "The teams was successful": here there is a grammatical error, because the subject "teams" is plural while the verb "was" is singular. Again, the words used are wrong in context. Without looking further, we cannot be sure whether the writer intended "The teams were successful" or "The team was successful", but we know that something is wrong with the sentence.

In the first case of the misspelled "there", we know that the word "there" is not a possessive, yet this is the function it has in the sentence. In order to know that this is a misspelling, we have to do some grammatical analysis, and some reasoning about what the writer probably intended. Indeed, it could be that the writer actually meant to say either "Their house is nice" or "The house there is nice". To detect, classify, and correct these issues we will need to do some guessing, and we want this guessing to be well informed and based on evidence. Thus, we will treat context-dependent word correction and grammar correction together here. Both are important, as 30–40% of spelling errors made by writers result in real words.

2.4.1   What is grammar?

grammar Before we investigate how to correct grammar errors, we have to ask ourselves what we mean by **grammar**. Traditionally, linguists have focused on **descriptive**
descriptive **grammar**, which refers to a set of rules for how speakers of a language form well-
grammar formed sentences. For our purposes, this is a good start, and we will return to different definitions of grammar in Section 2.5.

Basing our discussion in this section on Mihaliček and Wilson (2011), we define grammar in terms of rules, but when we talk about the *rules* of a language, what do
syntax we mean by that? To explain this, we need to introduce **syntax**, the study of how grammatical sentences are formed from smaller units, typically words. Some of these concepts will also resurface when analyzing learner language in Section 3.4.3.

Sentences in human language are organized on two axes. These are linear order
linear order and hierarchical structure. The idea of **linear order** is that languages can vary word order so as to convey different meanings. Thus, in English "John loves Mary" is not the same as "Mary loves John". Not all languages use linear order in exactly the same way: for example, in Czech, Russian, and German the presence of richer word endings makes it possible to vary word order slightly more freely than we can in English. In linguistics, the study of word endings and other changes in word forms is called
morphology **morphology**. Nevertheless, linear order is a guiding principle for organizing words into meaningful sentences, and every human language uses it to some extent.

The other guiding principle for sentence organization is hierarchical structure, or
constituency what is called **constituency**. Words are organized into groupings, and intuitively, these groupings are the *meaningful units* of a sentence. Take the sentence in (6), for example. It seems like "most of the ducks" forms a unit, and this intuition is backed up by the fact that we can replace it with other, similar phrases, like "people who have won the Super Bowl".

(6) Most of the ducks play extremely fun games.

When we break a sentence down further, we find that these meaningful groupings, or phrases, can be nested inside larger phrases of the same or different type: for example, "extremely fun" is a part of "extremely fun games". When we put all those
syntactic tree phrases together, it is useful to view them as a **syntactic tree**, as we see in Figure 2.8.

While this tree captures the intuition that words group into phrases, more can be
tree node done with the labels on the **tree nodes**. It is not helpful to use uninformative names

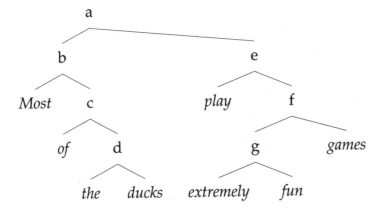

Figure 2.8   A labeled tree

such as *a*, *b*, and so forth. What linguists do is to add categorical information, to tell us something about the *kinds* of phrases there are. For example, "most of the ducks" and "extremely fun games" are the same type of phrase, and "of the ducks" is something else entirely, in that substituting it for one of the other two expressions does not result in a grammatical sentence.

If you go further in the study of syntax, you will encounter sharp debates about specific aspects relating to how words and phrases really work. What we are presenting here is the basic terminology and ideas that all linguists use, especially those linguists who primarily *use* syntax (as opposed to researching it), as many computational linguists do.

Thus, we examine word and phrase categories. Since phrases are built from words, we start with word categories: **lexical categories** are simply word classes, or **parts of speech**. The main ones are verbs (*run, believe, consider*), nouns (*duck, government, basketball*), adjectives (*bad, potential, brown*), adverbs (*heavily, well, later*), prepositions (*on, at, into*), articles (*a, the, this, some*), and conjunctions (*and, or, since*). [lexical category] [parts of speech]

We can use two main criteria to tell what a word's part of speech is. The first criterion is the word's **distribution**: where it typically appears in a sentence. For instance, nouns like "mouse" can appear after articles, like "some" or "the", while a verb like "eat" cannot. The second criterion is the word's morphology, the kinds of prefix/suffix a word can have. For example, verbs like "walk" can take an "-ed" ending to mark them as past tense; a noun like "mouse" cannot. Words that share a similar distribution and a similar morphology are put into the same lexical category. Linguists use categories that are finer grained than the familiar parts of speech, but they still talk about nouns, verbs, adjectives, and so on, and mean roughly the same as an educated nonlinguist does. (These concepts are discussed more fully in Section 3.4.2, in the context of learner language, where such evidence can diverge.) [distribution of a word]

Moving from lexical categories to **phrasal categories**, we can also look at distribution. For the sentence in (7), we can replace the phrase "most of the ducks" with "a bear"; "Barack Obama"; "many a dog"; or "people who have won the Super Bowl". All of these phrases contain nouns as their key component, so we call them noun phrases, abbreviated as NP. [phrasal category]

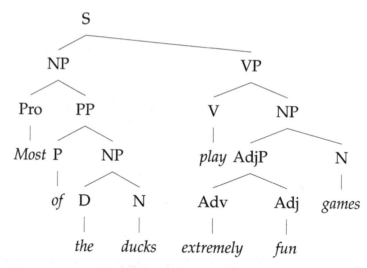

Figure 2.9 A tree with linguistically meaningful labels

(7) Most of the ducks swam a lap.

Being able to replace a phrase with another is a test of replaceability, and it is one **constituency** of several different **constituency tests** to determine which sequences of words **test** make up constituents. At any rate, if we give each phrasal category a name and an abbreviation, we can now draw a more complete tree, as shown in Figure 2.9.

The trees we draw are systematic. For example, a determiner (D) and a noun (N) often make up an NP, while a verb (V) and adverb (Adv) on their own can **phrase** never make up an NP. We use **phrase structure rules** to capture these common- **structure rule** alities and to describe a language. Phrase structure rules (PSRs) give us ways to build larger constituents from smaller ones. For instance, the top subtree in Figure 2.9 corresponds to the rule S → NP VP. This rule indicates both hierarchy and linear order. The hierarchy aspect is that a sentence (S) constituent is composed of a noun phrase (NP) and a verb phrase (VP). The linear order is indicated by the order of mention of the labels on the left-hand side: the NP must precede the VP. In the tree, we can also see structures for prepositional phrases (PP) and adjective phrases (AdjP).

Every tree node in a syntax tree is built out of a corresponding phrase structure rule. The left-hand side of the rule corresponds to the parent, and the labels on the right-hand side of the rule correspond to the subtrees nested below the parent.

Syntax trees and phrase structure rules are really two sides of the same coin. You can build a syntax tree by piecing together a set of phrase structure rules, and you can also go the other way, reading off the phrase structure rules that are used in a particular syntax tree. For instance, if we have the rule set in Figure 2.10, we can give an analysis to "the young boy saw a dragon". The analysis is shown in Figure 2.11.

context-free A grammar, then, is simply a collection of such rules. Grammars with rules of **grammar** the form shown here are referred to as **context-free grammars**. A grammar that

Lexicon:
Vt → *saw*
Det → *the*
Det → *a*
N → *dragon*
N → *boy*
Adj → *young*

Syntactic rules:
S → NP VP
VP → Vt NP
NP → Det N
N → Adj N

Figure 2.10 An English grammar fragment, including rules for words

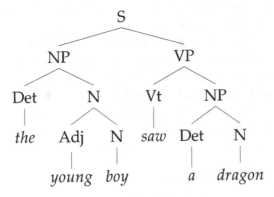

Figure 2.11 Analyzing "the young boy saw a dragon" using the given grammar fragment

accurately describes a language is able to model all and only those sentences that actually appear in the language. It is very useful to try to build such grammars for human languages, but the complexity of human language makes it unlikely that anyone will ever manage to build a complete grammar for the whole of a human language. Instead, we build **grammar fragments**. These are simplified working models of a human language. Like other working models, they can serve several purposes. In this book, grammar fragments are important because they may be built into spelling and grammar checkers. For other linguists, they may be just as important as a tool for checking out scientific ideas about how human language works in general. If an idea works in a grammar fragment, maybe that idea reflects what is really going on in the mind of a human speaker. To prove that, detailed experimental or theoretical work would be needed, but a grammar fragment is a good start in the same way that a balsa-wood model in a flotation tank is a good start on the design of an oil tanker. In this book,

grammar fragment

model   when we talk about a **model,** it is always a mathematical or computational model: an abstract system designed to capture key aspects of how we believe language to work.

So far we have relied on intuition to introduce the idea of phrase structure rules. We are now ready to do the formal mathematics. These rules have to follow a particular structure. Each rule must have a left-hand side (LHS), which is a single **nonterminal**   **nonterminal** element, and nonterminals are defined as (phrasal and lexical) categories. So, NP is an acceptable LHS, while "John" is not. Secondly, each rule must have a **terminal**   right-hand side (RHS), which is a mixture of nonterminal and **terminal** elements, where terminal elements are defined as actual words (*terminal* because they are the final nodes in a tree). So, "Det Noun" or "Noun *and* Noun" are acceptable RHSs.

You may be wondering why we call this a *context-free grammar*. The answer has to do with the fact that each rule is designed to be independent of the others. These rules can be used wherever the category on their LHS occurs. Rules cannot be further restricted to apply only in some places and not others. So, for example, you cannot have a rule specifying that PP → P NP is applicable only when there is a verb phrase (VP) above the PP. The real reason for this is complexity: by having simple rules that apply everywhere, you get the ability to reason modularly about what is going on. (For more information on this topic, see Under the Hood 4.)

A grammar composed of these rules has several properties that are useful for **generative**   modeling natural language. First, the grammar is **generative**; it is a schematic strategy that characterizes a set of sentences completely. Secondly, as mentioned, the **hierarchical**   rules license **hierarchical** structure. Thirdly, and crucially for natural languages, the rules allow for potential **structural ambiguity,** where a sentence can have more than **structural**   one analysis. This is clearly needed when we examine sentences like (8), which can **ambiguity**   have multiple meanings. In this case, "more" can either group with "intelligent" (9a) or can modify "leaders" (9b).

(8) We need more intelligent leaders.
(9) Paraphrases:
    a. We need leaders who are more intelligent.
    b. Intelligent leaders? We need more of them!

recursive   Finally, the rules are **recursive**: recursion is the property that allows for a rule to be used in building up its own substructures. In example (10), for instance, NP is reapplied within itself, thus allowing for phrases such as [NP [NP [NP *the dog*] *on the porch*] *at my feet*].

(10) NP → NP PP

Most linguists believe that recursion is an important defining property of human language. For this reason, experiments that aim to tease out the similarities and differences between human and animal communication often focus on recursion.

Parsing

Using these phrase structure, or context-free, rules, we want to get a computer to **parse**   **parse** a sentence; that is, to assign a structure to a given sentence. Some parsers are

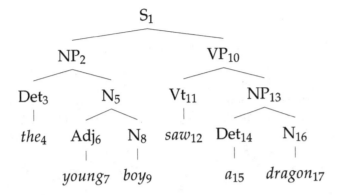

Figure 2.12 Trace of a top-down parse

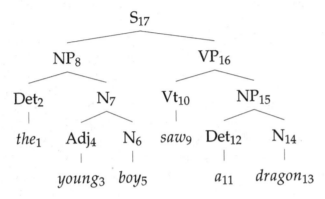

Figure 2.13 Trace of a bottom-up parse

bottom-up, which means that they build a tree by starting with the words at the **bottom-up** bottom and working up to the top. Other parsing techniques are **top-down**; that is, they build a tree by starting at the top (e.g., S → NP VP) and working down. **top-down**

To give a rough idea of how a parser works, let's start with the rules found in Figure 2.10 and attempt to parse "the young boy saw a dragon".

A top-down parse starts with the S category – since the goal is to have a sentence (S) when the parse is done – and expands that to NP VP. The next step is to try expanding the NP, in this case into Det N, as that is the only possibility in this grammar. A trace of the order of rules can be seen in Figure 2.12. If there are multiple possible NP rules, the parser can consider them one at a time and then **backtrack** **backtrack** if a particular NP expansion does not work out.

Instead of starting with the goal of S, the bottom-up way of parsing starts with the very first word, in this case "the", and builds the tree upwards. Based on the lexicon, Det is the only category that fits for "the", so this is added to the tree next. On its own, Det cannot form any higher category, so the next word (*young*) is considered, which is an adjective (Adj). This continues upwards, as seen in Figure 2.13.

This is only a brief sketch of how parsing proceeds to analyze a sentence given a grammar. In general, there are many parsing techniques; pointers are provided in the *Further reading* section at the end of the chapter.

Under the Hood 4
Complexity of languages

We discussed context-free grammars earlier, and these can be used to process natural languages and to assist in error detection. But what we did not justify was that context-free grammars are: (i) all we need (we call this being sufficient) and (ii) nothing more than we need (necessary). In other words, maybe there are simpler ways of analyzing language? On the other hand, maybe context-free grammars are incapable of capturing all natural language phenomena?

What we are discussing is linguistic complexity, or the limits of what a particular type of grammar can do. Intuitively, the idea is that the phenomenon under discussion might be too complex to fit into the framework that we have for characterizing it. But what exactly do we mean by being too complex? To answer this, we need to sketch some formal language theory. In formal language theory, we *define* a language as a set of acceptable sentences (albeit an infinite set). This is a technical use of the word *language*, not the everyday one, but it turns out that there is a close parallel between the mathematical reasoning that we can do about formal languages and the scientific reasoning that we want to do about natural, human languages. In the same way, there is a formal definition of what a grammar is, and a mathematical description of exactly what it means for a language to be characterized by a grammar.

Formal grammars, such as context-free grammars, differ in terms of which formal languages they can and cannot describe. Loosely, what we are going to say is that a formal grammar is more powerful than another if it can draw finer distinctions among formal languages. Instead of relying on informal intuitions about power and complexity, we can use mathematics. The point of the move to mathematics is to gain clarity by learning to view our scientific questions in an abstract way. For many of us, this is a scary thing to do. Fortunately, in the case of formal language theory, the results of doing the abstract thinking are so valuable, and so obviously relevant to language, that overcoming the initial discomfort is worthwhile.

Formal grammars and languages are therefore useful tools in coming to grips with the issues around the complexity of natural languages. You should think of formal language theory – with its precise definitions for what a grammar is, what a language is and what mathematical operations are allowed – as a working model of aspects of the way in which natural language behaves. Real languages are obviously messier than this, but the models are still useful.

For example, we can write a context-free grammar to capture the following kinds of center-embedded structures in English:

(11) a. The frog is happy.
   b. The frog **that the princess saw** is happy.
   c. The frog **that the princess that the prince liked** saw is happy.

At some point, these sentences become difficult to understand, but in theory we can have an arbitrary number of sentences embedded within other sentences in English. (As a side point, we can also remove "that" and get a valid sentence.) The relevant context-free rules might look as in (12).

(12) a. $S \rightarrow NP\ VP$
   b. $NP \rightarrow NP\ S$

It turns out that context-free grammars are more powerful than regular grammars, such as those used to write regular expressions, as in Chapter 4. (Note that in regular grammar and regular expression we are using *regular* in a technical sense.) There is no way to write a regular expression that can capture an arbitrary number of center embeddings. Thus, it seems like we need to use context-free grammars at least for natural language syntax.

We have said that context-free grammars are more powerful than regular grammars. This is not the end of the matter: there are even more powerful grammar formalisms, capable of describing yet more complex formal languages, namely context-sensitive grammars. It turns out that context-free grammars cannot capture what are called cross-serial dependencies. With center embeddings, as shown above, we have a noun phrase subject that is associated with a verb phrase; in all three sentences, "the frog" and "is happy" go together. When we look at it this way, we see that the last sentence has a structure akin to *abccba*, as shown in (13) (which is a repeat of (11c)). (This tells us that we can use context-free grammars to write palindromes, too!)

(13) The frog$_a$ that the princess$_b$ that the prince$_c$ liked$_c$ saw$_b$ is happy$_a$.

Cross-serial dependencies, on the other hand, are of the form *abcabc*. They are called *cross-serial* because, for *a* to match up with *a*, it has to cross over the dependency between the two *b*s. If we imagined English to have cross-serial dependencies, we would expect (11b) to be rewritten as in (14).

(14) The frog$_a$ the princess$_b$ is happy$_b$ saw$_a$.

This clearly does not happen in English, but does it happen in other languages? Perhaps surprisingly, the answer is yes. In Swiss German, for example, verbs and their direct objects cross. We can see this in example (15), where

(Continued)

Under the Hood 4
Complexity of languages
(Cont'd.)

"em Hans" ("Hans") is the object of "hälfed" ("helped"), and "huus" ("house") is the object of "aastriiche" ("paint"). At least some languages, then, need more powerful grammars than context-free grammars.

(15) ... mer em Hans es huus hälfed aastriiche.
    ... we Hans$_a$ the house$_b$ helped$_a$ paint$_b$
    "... we helped Hans paint the house"

2.4.2   Techniques for correcting words in context

Grammar-based word correction

With a syntactic model of language, what we have is a model of grammatical language. Therefore, we can use a parser to find where the grammar breaks down. When a parser fails to parse a sentence, we have an indication that something is grammatically wrong with the sentence. Here we are more concerned with identifying that there is a grammatical error, such that a native speaker could figure out exactly what the problem is. In the context of language tutoring systems (LTSs), discussed in Chapter 3, additionally the nature of the error needs to be specifically pointed out to the learner.

relaxation-based technique   There are a variety of general approaches for dealing with ill-formed input, and here we will discuss relaxation-based techniques. **Relaxation-based techniques** for detecting grammar errors relax the parsing process to allow errors. The parser is altered in some way to accept input that it would normally reject as erroneous. This might involve relaxing the parsing procedure so that what would normally result in a parsing failure is allowed to continue building a parse tree, noting where in the parsing the relaxation took place. Alternatively, one might write grammar rules that

mal-rule   predict types of failures (i.e., **mal-rules**); for example, a rule might be expressly written to allow a first-person singular subject to combine with a third-person singular verb, indicating the construction as erroneous.

Although this way of writing grammars can be highly effective, it is not without problems. First, grammars have to be written by hand by trained experts. Both the training and the grammar writing can be time-consuming and intellectually demanding. Even the simple context-free formalisms developed so far are subtle enough to call for sustained thought and careful reasoning, since the consequences of writing a particular rule may be wide-ranging and subtle. This is even more challenging when we consider that the rules we saw in Section 2.4.1 were a simplification of what grammar writers usually do. In practice, grammars are usually augmented

with **linguistic features** to encode properties such as agreement. S→NP VP, for **linguistic**
example, becomes S[PER *x*, NUM *y*]→NP[PER *x*, NUM *y*] VP[PER *x*, NUM *y*], **feature**
where PER and NUM stand for "person" and "number", and *x* and *y* are variables,
where every occurrence of the same variable is assumed to represent the same value.
This is good because it reduces the number of very similar rules that have to be
written, but potentially bad because the extra power increases the risk that the
grammar writer will get confused and make a mistake. On the other hand, if you are
a particularly patient, orderly, and careful thinker, you may find that you are good
at writing grammars, in which case you might have a future doing so.

Secondly, there are grammatical constructions that are rarely used, and we have
to decide whether to include these rules in our grammar. For instance, should we
have rules to cover "the more, the merrier", where no verb is used? Finally, as with
dictionaries, grammars are likely to be incomplete. Not only are there new words to
deal with, but people also continue to create novel expressions and turns of phrase.
So if you do find work as a grammar writer, you will probably find that you have
taken on a long-term obligation to maintain the grammar as new words and
phrases appear.

Error pattern-based word correction

Grammar-based techniques attempt to detect all errors in a text. However, since
grammars are a fair amount of work and since people are more concerned about
eradicating the most common errors, we can save time by focusing on only a subset
of errors without using a full grammar.

A very simple technique for detecting and correcting grammatical errors is simply
to write rules that spot an error pattern and alter it. For example, a rule could match
the pattern of "some" or "certain" followed by "extend", and change "extend" into
"extent". Even a small set of such error pattern rules can be used to build a grammar
corrector that can work as well as some commercial software. The disadvantage,
again, is that the rules have to be handwritten, and they will be necessarily incomplete, as people make new errors (and new kinds of errors) all the time.

Note that these rules are typically **regular expressions** (see Section 4.4), which **regular**
means that we are no longer capturing all of language completely. To learn more **expression**
about this, see Under the Hood 4. Likewise, the next technique also does not attempt
to model language completely.

Probability-based word correction

Complementing the rule-based techniques described in the previous sections, statistical techniques can be used to detect and correct words in context, be it real-word
spelling errors or grammatical errors. One such technique is to use *n*-grams of words
to tell us what are likely and unlikely sequences of words. By *n*-gram we mean
sequences of elements: in the context of spell checking in Section 2.3.1, we used
sequences of characters, but here we use sequences of *words*. A simple statistical
bigram grammar corrector would use the probability of one word following
another to determine whether an error has been made. For example, "conducted

be" is not a likely word bigram in English, but "conducted by" is. We will base our discussion here on Wilcox-O'Hearn, Hirst, and Budanitsky (2006).

Real-word spelling correctors that use *n*-grams typically use trigrams of words. Before we get to how trigrams are employed let us look at the overall scheme: (i) For each word in a sentence (real-word or misspelling), a set of candidate corrections, or spelling variants, is obtained. (ii) A set of candidate corrections for the *sentence* is obtained by changing exactly one word in the original sentence to a spelling variant. (iii) The sentence with the highest probability is selected. This probability calculation is where trigrams are used, as will be discussed in a moment.

Let's walk through an example, given in (16).

(16) John came <u>form</u> the house.

(i) We first find all candidates for each word, typically real words that are one operation away. For "came", this will be "come", "lame", "cane", etc.; for "form", we will have "from", "dorm", etc. (ii) Taking these candidates, we generate candidate sentences, as in (17), by changing one and only one word. (iii) Finally, we find the sentence from this set with the highest probability.

(17) a. John <u>come</u> form the house.
      b. John came <u>from</u> the house.
      c. John come form the <u>hose</u>.

The probabilities are obtained by breaking the sentence down into trigrams and then multiplying the probabilities of each trigram. For the ultimately correct sentence, we will multiply the probabilities in (18), which correspond to the trigrams "John came from", "came from the", and "from the house", in addition to including START and END tags to model the likelihood of particular words starting or ending a sentence.

(18) $P(\text{came}|\text{START}, \text{John}) \times P(\text{from}|\text{John}, \text{came}) \times P(\text{the}|\text{came}, \text{from}) \times P(\text{house}|\text{from},$
      $\text{the}) \times P(\text{END}|\text{the}, \text{house})$

To get these probabilities, we have to go through a corpus and count up how often different trigrams occur. A major problem with such techniques is that it is hard to estimate the probabilities of all possible trigrams from a corpus, given that language **data sparsity** is infinite. This is an issue of **data sparsity**: no matter how much data we use, there will always be something we have never seen before. Data sparsity is a core problem in much of statistical natural language processing, where the behavior is guided by the data one has seen. Learning from a larger corpus can help alleviate the problem, although it does not completely solve it. However, this presents another issue: the number of observed trigrams will be large (e.g., 20 million), so the data structures used need to be efficient. With a large corpus and efficient data structures in place, the method is intuitive, easy to implement, and effective at suggesting error corrections.

machine   *N*-gram techniques for grammar checking are a form of **machine learning**, where
learning a computer learns in what contexts a word might be misspelled. Machine learning

involves a computer program learning from data such that it can apply what it learns to a new task (see more in Chapter 5 on document classification). Another, similar set-up is to view the context-dependent spelling correction task as a **word disam-** **biguation** task: we want to find which of a set of words is the correct word in a given context. We base much of the following discussion on Golding and Roth (1999).

Instead of using sets of candidates based only on spelling differences, these techniques use **confusion sets** consisting of words that are potentially confounded with one another in any relevant property. For example, a set could contain the words "there", "they're", and "their", and the task of the system is to figure out which of the words was meant in a given context. The advantage of such confusion sets is that the words do not have to be similar looking: "amount" and "number", for instance, can make up a set of words that are commonly confused. The disadvantage of these confusion sets is that someone has to define them in advance.

The task for the machine, then, is to learn which member of a confusion set is the most appropriate in a particular context. To do this, we break down the surrounding context into different **features**. Common kinds of features are context words and collocations. **Context words** capture a broad semantic context because they are simply words within a certain distance of the word in question. For example, it is useful for the spelling corrector to know whether "cloudy" appears within the surrounding ten words if the confusion set we are dealing with is composed of "whether" and "weather". Collocations, on the other hand, capture a very local context – essentially *n*-gram information. With the same set of "whether" and "weather", for instance, a collocation might be the word in question followed by "to" and a subsequent verb (e.g., *whether to run*).

We will not discuss the actual machine learning mechanisms here, but the idea is that the computer learns which contextual features tend to go with which member of the confusion set. When a new text is encountered with a member of the confusion set, the machine checks to see whether that word is the best one from the set in this context.

Meaning-based techniques

Many real-word errors result in a word that does not seem to fit the meaning of the rest of the sentence or paragraph. We refer to this as being **semantically inappropriate**. For instance in example (19) given by Hirst and Budanitsky (2005), the word "hole" does not fit very well with "sincere."

(19) It is my sincere <u>hole</u> that you will recover swiftly.

The word "hope", on the other hand, fits rather well with surrounding words like "sincere". This leads to a two-step procedure for identifying semantically inappropriate words:

(i) Find words that are semantically unrelated to their surroundings.
(ii) Find a candidate correction that is a better semantic fit in the sentence.

Margin notes:
word disambiguation

confusion set

feature

context word

semantically inappropriate

For this to work, we then require two things: a way to identify words that are semantically unrelated to their surroundings, and a way to obtain a set of candidates for correction. We already discussed in Section 2.3.2 how to obtain candidate cor-

semantic rections, so we just have to define **semantic relatedness** between words; that is, how
relatedness far apart they are. In other words, we want to know which words are likely to appear in the same topic; relevant here are synonyms (e.g., *couch* and *sofa*), antonyms (e.g., *good* and *bad*), and any sort of meaningful relationship (e.g., *penguin* and *Antarctica*) (see also Sections 3.3 and 7.6).

semantic One way to define semantic relatedness is to use a **semantic hierarchy**, such as
hierarchy WordNet (http://wordnet.princeton.edu/). A semantic hierarchy defines relationships between words, such as: a "hatchback" is a type of "car", which is a type of "vehicle". For English, at least, WordNet is an impressive resource that lays out the relationships between many different words and concepts (and more information on it can be found in the *Further reading*). Roughly speaking, we can use the distance between two words in WordNet to tell us how semantically related they are: "hatchback" and "boat" are somewhat related, in that both are "vehicles", but "hatchback" and "terrier" are not particularly related, as the only commonality is that they are "physical objects".

As a side note, the techniques we have been discussing are very similar to techniques
word sense used for a related task, that of **word sense disambiguation (WSD)**. In that task,
disambiguation a system takes a semantically ambiguous word like "bank" and attempts to determine
(WSD) which sense the word has in a given context (e.g., a financial institution vs. the sloped land next to a river). Hierarchies like WordNet are useful for defining the senses.

Under the Hood 5
Spell checking for web queries

Spell checking is generally seen as a useful task for editing documents, but we really need spell checkers any time we have to enter input. One prominent area that benefits from quality spell checking is in improving web queries, as these are prone to misspellings. For example, the search engine Google lists approximately 600 different spellings that people have tried in searching for "Britney Spears" (http://www.google.com/jobs/britney.html), and around 10–15% of search queries contain errors. We will present discussion and examples from Cucerzan and Brill (2004) as one way of approaching the problem.

Correcting the queries for search engines is difficult because we have to be able to handle frequent and severe spelling errors, proper names, new terms (*auto-complete*, *shrek*), and so on; see Table 2.1 for examples. In addition techniques that are designed for correcting real-word errors in writing often use a large window of context, but queries are usually very short.

As one example to combat this problem, we can take a potentially misspelled query and iteratively transform it into more likely queries. To determine a

Table 2.1   Yahoo! Top 20 misspellings in 2007

On May 23, 2007, Erik Gunther of Yahoo! listed the 20 top search misspellings from its search logs, with the corrected versions listed in parentheses. Note that, except for "Tattoo" and "Genealogy", these are all proper names. Furthermore, many of the people were relatively unknown before 2006.

1. Wallmart (Wal-Mart)
2. Rachel Ray (Rachael Ray)
3. Amtrack (Amtrak)
4. Hillary Duff (Hilary Duff)
5. Katherine McPhee (Katharine McPhee)
6. Britany Spears (Britney Spears)
7. Geneology (Genealogy)
8. Jaime Pressley (Jaime Pressly)
9. Volkswagon (Volkswagen)
10. Wikepedia (Wikipedia)
11. William Sonoma (Williams-Sonoma)
12. Tatoo (Tattoo)
13. Travelosity (Travelocity)
14. Elliot Yamin (Elliott Yamin)
15. Kiera Knightley (Keira Knightley)
16. Kelly Pickler (Kellie Pickler)
17. Brittney Spears (Britney Spears)
18. Avril Lavinge (Avril Lavigne)
19. Rianna (Rihanna)
20. Jordan Sparks (Jordin Sparks)

query's likelihood and thus what it should be corrected to, we can use query logs. A query log lists all of the queries that people have entered at one time or another to a search engine (see also Section 4.3.4 for search engine details). For example, "albert eintien" appears 3 times in one query log, while the correct "albert einstein" appears 4,834 times. Query logs are useful, despite the fact that many of the queries are misspelled. The main assumption is that the correct spelling will be more frequent than any similar-looking incorrect spelling, and this turns out to be generally true.

To make this clearer, let us walk through an example of how the system works, where the user types in "anol scwartegger", as shown in Figure 2.14. As a first step, "anol" is changed into "arnold" and "scwartegger" into "schwartnegger", because "arnold schwartnegger" appeared more often in the query logs than "anol scwartegger". Thus, it is a more likely query, and furthermore, it is still fairly similar to the original query, in terms of edit distance. On the next two iterations we find even better queries, finally arriving at the correct spelling of this name. The misspelling did not really resemble the last name at first, which is why it took several iterations to find it.

The algorithm takes two steps: (i) The set of all *close alternatives* for each word in the query is computed. We look at word unigrams and bigrams from the logs, in order to determine what counts as a close word, and a weighted edit distance (as we have already discussed) is used in processing. (ii) From the sequence of alternatives that we have, we search for the most likely alternative string.

(Continued)

Under the Hood 5
Spell checking for web queries
(Cont'd.)

With this algorithm in place, we are able to make many useful corrections. For example, we can correct queries that are sensitive to context, as in (20): "crd" changes differently depending on the previous word. We can also correct known words into better queries, as in (21). (All examples are from Cucerzan and Brill, 2004.)

(20) a. "power crd" → "power cord"
     b. "video crd" → "video card"
     c. "platnuin rings" → "platinum rings"

(21) a. "golf war" → "gulf war"
     b. "sap opera" → "soap opera"

                          "anol scwartegger"
              →   "arnold schwartnegger"
              →   "arnold schwarznegger"
              →   "arnold schwarzenegger"

Figure 2.14 Iteratively transforming a query

2.5   Style checkers

Earlier, when we discussed the question of what grammar is, we said that we were interested in *descriptive grammar*: how the language is actually used. For many prescriptivism writing purposes, however, we are also interested in **prescriptivism**: how one is supposed to use a language. For example, many of us were instructed never to end a sentence with a preposition. When writing a paper or any formal document, many people want to have these rules in place. When writing a less formal document, these rules may not be followed.

style checkers   Thus, we distinguish **style checkers** from grammar checkers. Style checkers can check for violations of a particular style, such as that prescribed by MLA standards. The constructions may still be English, but are simply unacceptable for the purposes of the current document. For example, one might want to have a style checker find singular uses of "data", such as "the data is", if the style dictates that it should be plural.

In terms of technology, style checkers work as grammar checkers do; they just identify different constructions. For instance, style checkers might flag the use of too many passive constructions, which are usually disliked in "clear" writing, or they might disallow split infinitives (e.g., *to boldly go*). As with grammar checkers, style checkers might only examine a small window of context; often, a passive construction with many words between the "be" verb and the passive participle will go undetected as a passive (e.g., *was very readily and quickly detected*).

Checklist

After reading the chapter, you should be able to:

- Give two reasons why standard spelling is useful.
- Describe the difficulties of real-word spelling.
- Describe what goes into making a spell checking dictionary.
- Explain some methods for generating and ranking spelling corrections.
- Give the two guiding principles for building sentences in a language.
- Understand the basic properties of phrase structure rules and context-free grammars.
- Understand the different kinds of techniques for correcting words in context and how they use syntactic and/or semantic information.

After reading the Under the Hood sections, you should be able to:

- Explain why dynamic programming methods are efficient.
- Provide an example of how context-free grammars are insufficient as mathematical descriptions of human languages.
- Explain how web spell checking can use a small amount of context to make spelling corrections.

Exercises

1. **ALL**: Select your favorite spell checker and type in a number of misspellings.
   (a) In terms of edit distance, how far off can your misspellings be and still have the correct spelling suggested?
   (b) Select your second favorite spell checker and perform a comparison of their performances. For each of your misspellings, which spell checker has a better ranking? Can the misspellings be more or less far off?

2. In Section 2.3.2, we talked about the SOUNDEX system for generating candidates for correction.
   (a) **ALL**: Develop your own SOUNDEX-like system for grouping similar words into buckets by working out what rules you need to map a word to the appropriate bucket. Can your rules handle transposition errors?

(b) **CS:** If you're a programmer, implement your SOUNDEX rules. Make sure that each of the following sets of words is mapped to the same bucket:
   (i) Catherine, Kathryn, Katherine
   (ii) principal, principle
   (iii) eye, I, aye

3. **ALL:** A user types in "folg" when they meant to type "frog." Draw the directed graph and describe how minimum edit distance is calculated.

4. **MATH:** Describe how such a graph could be redrawn to allow for transpositions.

5. **ALL:** Consider again the *n*-gram grammar-correction techniques from Section 2.4.2. Would these techniques be appropriate for web spell checking? For learner language? Why or why not?

6. **ALL:** Select your favorite spell checker and evaluate its effectiveness by designing a **test suite** of sentences with spelling errors. A test suite is simply a list of cases that are used to test the effectiveness of a system. Include 10–20 errors and some nonerrors, too.
   (a) What is the purpose of each error? In other words, what is each type of error attempting to test about the spell checker's capabilities?
   (b) Of the number of words flagged by the checker as errors, how many (what percentage) are actually errors? (This measures **error detection precision**.)
   (c) Of the errors you introduced, how many (what percentage) does the spell checker flag? (This measures **error detection recall**; precision and recall are discussed more in Section 4.3.2.)
   (d) Of the suggestions the checker makes, how often (what percentage of the time) is the first correction the correct, intended word? (This measures **error correction precision**.)

Margin terms: test suite; error detection precision; error detection recall; error correction precision

Further reading

For a good (if slightly dated) overview of spell checking techniques, see Kukich (1992), which has a similar structure to this chapter and presents many of the facts on which we relied (e.g., human agreement rates for isolated-word spelling correction). Mitton (1996) is a somewhat more recent book that provides a good overview of both the types of errors people make and how to correct them. For those who are more computationally inclined, the LingPipe software suite contains a tutorial of spelling correction (Alias-i, 2009), including relating spell checking to the noisy channel model and walking through some programming code that corrects web queries (http://purl.org/lang-and-comp/lingpipe).

We relied on many references for this chapter. To see more about storing probabilities, see Kernighan, Church, and Gale (1990); for more on types of errors, Damerau (1964) provides some early analysis. Mangu and Brill (1997) discuss automatically deriving spelling rules.

The SOUNDEX system was developed in Odell and Russell (1918) (note that this was almost a century ago!). Wing and Baddeley (1980) provide evidence of the percentage of real-word spelling errors.

For more information on what grammar is, one can consult any introductory linguistics textbook, such as Mihaliček and Wilson (2011). If you are interested in parsing techniques, you can consult chapters 12–14 of Jurafsky and Martin (2009), which also contains pointers to more advanced works.

A very readable description of formal language theory and complexity can be found in Chapter 16 of Jurafsky and Martin (2009). A comprehensive formal treatment of the topic can be found in Hopcroft, Motwani, and Ullman (2007).

While many of the papers on techniques for correcting words in context are somewhat challenging to read, given the amount of computer science background they assume, Wilcox-O'Hearn, Hirst, and Budanitsky (2006) has a great deal of useful discussion about n-gram grammar correctors, as well as the general task of context-sensitive spell checking, that many readers will find understandable and enlightening. If desired, one can also check out earlier papers such as Mays, Damarau, and Mercer (1991) and Verberne (2002). Likewise, the introduction of Hirst and Budanitsky (2005) provides a good overview of the challenges facing such correctors. Leacock *et al.* (2010) provide a very readable introduction to the task of grammatical error detection, focusing on its uses for ESL learners, but also presenting, for instance, some discussion of how the Microsoft Word grammar checker works.

For rule-based grammar checking, Naber (2003) originally used 56 rules to achieve good performance. This later developed into the open source software Language Tool (www.languagetool.org/).

If you want to explore word sense disambiguation, there is a wealth of papers and resources, such as those associated with the SemEval workshops (http://www.cs.york.ac.uk/semeval/). A survey paper aimed at a general audience is McCarthy (2009). WordNet is more fully described in Fellbaum (1998) and can be freely found at http://wordnet.princeton.edu/.

More on machine learning techniques can be found in Golding and Roth (1999), Mangu and Brill (1997), and Jones and Martin (1997); note, however, that these papers require some formal or computer science background to read.

3

Language Tutoring Systems

Computers are widely used in language classes to help students experience a foreign language and culture. They deliver videos and podcasts, texts and multimedia presentations, and they can host chat rooms and online lessons where learners interact with native speakers. Many students also log on to complete computer-based exercises and tests on the web. Yet, the typical tests and drills with true/false and score feedback are only pale approximations of what a good teacher can provide as feedback, and indeed such systems do not really use the special capabilities of the computer to analyze language in an important way. In this chapter, we discuss how computers can help provide foreign language learners with a richer, more personalized, and more effective learning experience.

3.1   Learning a language

You probably don't remember learning your first language or having anyone teach it to you, yet here you are reading this book. Students learning a second language experience a situation very different from that encountered during **first language acquisition**. Babies and young children seem to need no instruction in order to pick up their native language, and this process certainly does not require computer skills from any of the participants. This remarkable human capability has been a hot issue in the science and philosophy of language since the very beginning of scholarship. Researchers strongly disagree with each other on how much of the ability to learn a language is **innate**, and how much simply **emerges** from experience, and these arguments do not look likely to be conclusively resolved any time soon. It is clear,

first language acquisition

innateness

emergentism

Language and Computers, First Edition. Markus Dickinson, Chris Brew and Detmar Meurers.
© 2013 Markus Dickinson, Chris Brew and Detmar Meurers. Published 2013 by Blackwell Publishing Ltd.

though, that our innate biological endowment and our ability to learn from a rich social and physical environment both play imporant roles.

However it works, children can learn a language just by using it and being exposed to it in the course of everyday life. At the beginning of their lives, babies can already cry to express displeasure and make other sounds to signify pleasure. They start to play with making sounds soon after, and at about six months typical babies are beginning to use sequences of consonants and vowels such as *bababa*, a stage referred

babbling to as **babbling**. They then quickly start learning words by their first birthday and can form simple two-word utterances by the time they turn two. Children then make use of more and more of the language structure, so that by the age of three they can already voice and understand sentences of surprising complexity. In the next nine or ten years of childhood, more and more words and complex language structures are

stages of first acquired, with some structures such as passive sentences being added relatively late,
language around nine or ten years of age. These typical **stages of first language acquisition**
acquisition are essentially the same across all languages and cultures, and they apply, with some individual variation, to almost all children. If a child can hear, has a normal social life, and is otherwise healthy, language acquisition is almost automatic. Because of this, health professionals pay careful attention to language development in assessing the general health and welfare of a young child.

Interestingly, if they grow up in an environment in which more than one language is spoken, children can also acquire several languages at the same time. This is, for example, often the case when one parent speaks one language and the other parent another, or in environments where multiple languages are being spoken, which is the norm in many countries outside the USA and Europe, for instance in Africa

native speaker or the Indian subcontinent. A child thus can be a **native speaker** of multiple first languages, acquiring each of them without requiring explicit instruction.

Consider in contrast what it is like to learn a language as an adult, a situation
second language generally referred to as **second language acquisition**. Even after living in a foreign
acquisition country for a long time, listening to and talking in a foreign language there, adults do not automatically acquire a second language. In line with that general observa-
language tion, research since the 1990s has shown that **language awareness** as an awareness
awareness of the forms, functions, and regularities of a given language is important for an adult
article learner to acquire that language successfully. For example, the use of the **articles** "the" and "a" in English is quite difficult to learn, especially for foreigners whose native language does not make use of articles, such as Chinese or Russian. Learning
mass noun the distinction generally requires awareness of classes such as **mass nouns**, a class of nouns that cannot be counted (e.g., "rice", which would lead to ungrammatical
generic use sentences such as "Please give me three rice"), and of **generic uses** of nouns (e.g., "lion" in "The lion generally lives in Africa"). In a sense, this is also reflected in the fact that we typically learn foreign languages in school instead of just being able to tune in to a foreign language radio or television station to pick it up – even though such exposure to a foreign language can support foreign language instruction, which gets us back to the starting point of using computers to help learners experience a foreign language and culture.

What are the particular needs of second language learners? We mentioned that they benefit from foreign language instruction to become aware of language forms and regularities, yet the time a student learning a foreign language can spend with an instructor or tutor typically is very limited. As a consequence, work on form and rules is often deemphasized and confined to homework, so that the time with the instructor can be used for discussions, role-playing, and other communicative activities. The downside is that the learner has relatively few opportunities to gain language awareness and receive insightful **individual feedback** on their writing. **individual** Indeed, the British National Student Surveys identified the lack of prompt feedback **feedback** as an important concern for higher education in general: "students are notably less positive about assessment and feedback on their assignments than about other aspects of their learning experience" (Williams and Kane, 2008).

This situation seems like an excellent opportunity for developing computer-assisted language learning (CALL) tools to provide dedicated, individual feedback on assignments written by the learner. CALL tools can also make users aware of particular aspects of foreign language texts, such as the particular ways in which ideas are expressed, the forms in which specific words need to be used, or the order in which words have to appear. In the following, we discuss how computers are used to support those aspects of a foreign language and take a closer look at the nature of the analyses this requires.

3.2   Computer-assisted language learning

As a starting point, computers can be used to explicitly store the knowledge about words or the grammar of a foreign language necessary to complete a specific exercise. For example, Figure 3.1 shows the first part of a web-based quiz targeting the use of prepositions in English.

He lives ___ Main Street, doesn't he?
- ○ at
- ○ on
- ○ in

Slashing government spending ___ a depressed economy depresses the economy further.
- ○ in
- ○ at
- ○ with

Thomas Jefferson died ___ the Fourth of July.
- ○ during
- ○ at
- ○ on

Figure 3.1   A web-based multiple-choice quiz

multiple-choice exercise

distractor

Such **multiple-choice exercises** found on many language learning websites can work well for practicing or testing specific choices of forms or meanings. The person creating the exercise includes so-called **distractors** as incorrect choices in addition to the correct answer. Good distractors will generally be of the same class as the correct choice, such as another preposition in the exercise above.

frame-based CALL system

Computers are a good medium for delivering language exercises because they allow immediate feedback and, more generally, because they can respond in a more flexible way than is possible using pencil and paper. In a **frame-based CALL system**, the answers given to an exercise by a student are matched against a set of correct and incorrect answers that are explicitly specified by an instructor in a so-called frame. In addition to true/false feedback, the frame can include more elaborate feedback for each of the choices. For example, for the option "in" of the first exercise in Figure 3.1, one could specify the feedback: "False. While the preposition 'in' can be used for cities, it cannot be used for streets as in this example."

fill-in-the-blank (FIB)

cloze exercise

gap-fill exercise

It is not necessary for multiple-choice exercises to be presented as lists of check-boxes. Some systems instead allow the student to respond by clicking on a hotspot in a graphic; or use pull-down menus listing the choices; or **fill-in-the-blank (FIB)** texts, where a word in a sentence is erased and the learner must type in the missing word – also referred to as **cloze exercises** or **gap-fill exercises**.

fallback case

canned text response

In addition to the set of expected answers and the feedback to be provided, such cloze exercises need to provide a **fallback case** to respond to any unexpected input. For instance, if a learner types "Help me!" in a FIB exercise targeting prepositions, the fallback option may provide the feedback: "You entered 'Help me!', which is not a preposition in English. Please enter a preposition." Such computer responses are also called **canned text responses**. It is often appropriate for the canned message to incorporate material that is based on what the user said, such as the phrase "Help me!" entered by the user above. This is often a good idea, because it can make the system seem responsive. In the chapter on dialog systems (specifically, Section 6.7) we will see an extended example of how this can be used to create the impression of natural dialog.

It is easy to see that there will be limits to what can be done by explicitly listing all answer choices and the feedback messages to be displayed for them in a language learning exercise. We are about to discuss those limits, and what can be done to overcome them. But first, let us consider what an excellent automated tutor could do in response to learner input, in addition to providing feedback. Like a good teacher, it could provide remedial exercises for students having problems, but allow students doing well on an exercise to move on to more challenging exercises and materials.

sequencing of instruction

Indeed, such dynamic **sequencing of instruction** is found in some present-day frame-based CALL systems.

linear CALL system

In their most basic variants, **linear CALL systems** pose a question as part of an exercise, accept an answer from the student, and then inform the student as to whether or not the answer was correct (as well as any more detailed feedback stored for the choice made). Regardless of the correctness of the answer, linear systems then proceed to the next question.

In **branching CALL systems**, on the other hand, the sequencing of the exercises depends on what the student does. For example, if for a given exercise the student provides a correct response, the system continues with a slightly harder question; if the student provides an incorrect response, the system next presents a simpler question and might suggest additional reading material explaining the specific issue at hand. The hope is that this flexible sequencing will allow each student to receive instruction that is precisely tailored to their individual needs. This kind of flexible sequencing is also used in **computer adaptive testing (CAT)**. Once again, the choice of items is affected by the previous answers given by the test taker. But this time, the goal is different: if the system can make sure that strong students do not spend time on questions that are much too easy for them, and weak students do not spend time on questions that are much too hard for them, fewer questions will be needed in order to get an accurate assessment of each student's ability. If you have taken computer-delivered standardized tests, you may have experienced this strategy in action. Once again, this kind of adaptivity is really only feasible if the test is delivered electronically.

A general problem with frame-based CALL systems is that their knowledge is very specific. They do contain the frames, the pre-envisaged correct or incorrect answers that the student might enter, and the feedback that the system should provide for these answers, but they do not contain any generally applicable knowledge of language. This limits their flexibility. Since they do not really analyze language, the best they can do is match the string of characters entered by the student against strings of characters stored as potential answers to the exercise. If the response matches an expected answer, whether right or wrong, the system can trot out the prescribed action. But if the response is unexpected, the system will have to fall back on default responses, many of which are unlikely to be very helpful. If the system could analyze language in a deeper way, it might be able to find a more appropriate response. In the next sections, we will give more detail on what is needed in order to overcome these limitations of frame-based systems.

(marginal notes:) **branching CALL system**

computer adaptive testing

3.3 Why make CALL tools aware of language?

While CALL systems can successfully handle exercises of the type discussed in the previous section, the fact that traditional CALL systems cannot analyze language means that everything needs to be spelled out explicitly when the teacher designs the exercise – all options for answering it and the feedback the system should provide for each one. For instance, take a basic fill-in-the-blank exercise such as the one in (22).

(22) Today is November 5. What is tomorrow's date?
      Tomorrow is _____.

Possible correct answers include the ones shown in (23), plus many other ways of writing down this date in English.

(23) a. Nov., the 6th
      b. the sixth
      c. November, the sixth
      d. 11/06
      e. 06. 11.
      f. 6. Nov.

Combined with the many different ways one could misspell any of these options and the large number of incorrect answers a learner might enter for this blank, even for such a trivial question we obtain a very long list of possible correct and incorrect answers. To enable a CALL system to react to such answers, as part of the exercise one would have to list each of those options explicitly together with the feedback the system should provide for it.

Consider other dates, say "October 10", "Oct., the 10th", etc. Clearly, the many different options for writing down dates in English are available for any date you pick. Instead of having to explicitly list every option for every date, what we need is a general way to refer to a given date in all the possible, predictable ways of writing it down in English. In computational linguistics, the related task of identifying dates, **named entity recognition** addresses, or names of people or companies in a text is referred to as **named entity recognition**. It has received much attention since recognizing all the different ways to write the same name is, for example, also important for search engines and other information-retrieval applications.

At this point, one may well object that the different ways of writing down dates or names are not particularly interesting language aspects for learners of English. Yet, the need to be able to refer to classes instead of individual strings arises in language much more broadly than just for dates and other named entities. Consider, for example, the fill-in-the-blank exercise in (24), modeled on a German exercise in Trude Heift's E-Tutor system.

(24) John works in New York City, but his family lives in Boston. On the weekend, he drives home. Fortunately, John has a new_____.

The different options for filling in this blank correctly go far beyond differences in writing things down. For one thing, languages typically offer many words for expressing a given meaning – for instance, for the exercise in (24), the English language includes many words to talk about vehicles. Among the possible correct **synonym** answers, there are **synonyms**; that is, words that mean the same (at least in certain **lexical semantic** contexts), such as "car" and "automobile". And as we discuss in the context of **relation** machine translation in Section 7.5, there are various other **lexical semantic relations** between words. In our context, another relevant lexical semantic relation is hypo-**hyponym** nymy; this is the option of picking a more specific term, a so-called **hyponym**, such as "pick-up", "SUV", or "hybrid car" in place of the more general term "car", the **hypernym** **hypernym**. Finally, though the people designing exercises generally try to avoid this, there may also be multiple different meanings that make sense for a slot in a given exercise; for instance, in (24) the context would also be compatible with inserting "yacht", "personal jet", or even "car radio" – and for each one of these, various semantically related words could be used.

Clearly, specifying all such related words as options in the frame of an FIB exercise would involve a great deal of work – and this is work that would have to be repeated for every new exercise, even though these lexical semantic relations are encoding a general property of the language, not something specific to a given exercise.

The situation is similar when we consider that a single word in a language can **citation form** show up in different forms. For English, a word such as "bring" has a **citation form** or **lemma** "to bring"; this is the canonical form under which it can also be found in **lemma** a dictionary. In a text, the same word can appear in various forms, such as "bringing", "brought", "bring", or "brings". The different word forms and their function are investigated in morphology as a subfield of linguistics.

Many languages include an even richer inventory of forms than English. For example, you may know from studying Spanish that verbs surface in complex conjugation patterns. Just looking at the present tense of one of the verbs meaning "to be" in Spanish, one finds the six forms "soy", "eres", "es", "somos", "sois", and "son" – and this is only one of over a dozen other tenses and moods. If we want to specify an exercise frame in a CALL system to provide different feedback for different forms, we would have to spell out the many different forms for each exercise – even though this clearly is a general property of the language which we should be able to encode once and for all, instead of having to spell it out for each exercise frame.

For exercises where the learner can enter more than single words, we face an additional problem since, depending on the language, words are combined in different orders and forms to create sentences. This aspect of language is studied in the subfield of syntax, which identifies different word-order possibilities and the forms in which words have to appear in these different patterns (see Section 2.4.1). From our perspective of exploring how difficult it is to specify explicitly all options in the frame of a CALL exercise, the various word-order possibilities result in additional, systematic variation. For example, consider the FIB exercise in (25) targeting phrasal verbs, where both of the orders in (26) are possible.

(25) John, the radio is much too loud. Please _____ !
(26) a. turn down the radio.
     b. turn the radio down.

While for English word order is relatively rigid, for **free word-order languages** such **free word-order** as the Slavic languages, sentences typically offer a wide range of possible word **language** orders. This is systematic and thus should be expressed by mechanisms capturing language generalizations instead of expanding out all possibilities as part of the frame of a CALL exercise.

So far, we have considered the question of how we can make use of linguistic generalizations to specify compactly the expected correct or incorrect answers, instead of spelling out all forms and word orders by hand in the frame of a given exercise. We still have to specify in the frame what we expect to find in the response, but we can do this more compactly if we can rely on natural language processing (NLP) tools to generate or recognize the wide range of morphological forms and word orders for us. In other words, we can compactly specify the different form options by which language can encode a given meaning, but we still need to provide some specification of the intended answer to ensure that the learner actually provided a meaningful answer to a given exercise.

In ending this discussion, let us note that there are things we can say about the form in general, independent of the exercise. For example, we can refer to parts of speech and require that every sentence should contain a verb; then, we can connect that requirement to feedback reporting when a verb is missing. For such rules, the particular exercise to which they are applied is no longer relevant, apart from the fact that the exercise requires a sentence as the answer. If this idea of using rules sounds familiar, you are right: it is the approach of rule-based techniques to grammar checking that we mentioned in Section 2.4.2; it is used in the grammar and style checkers found in common wordprocessing software today.

3.4   What is involved in adding linguistic analysis?

Now that we have seen why it is useful to capture generalizations about language instead of hand specifying them for each activity, we need to take a closer look at what is involved in realizing this idea.

3.4.1   Tokenization

If we want to get to generalizations about words, such as the lemmas or parts of speech mentioned in the previous section, as the very first step we need to find the words. In Chapter 1, we saw that text in a computer is encoded on a character-by-character basis. So, a text is simply a very long list of letters. To process such text, as a first step language technology generally needs to identify the individual words,
token   more generally referred to as **tokens**. This step is referred to as tokenization or **word segmentation** and a number of different approaches have been proposed for **word**   this task. This may surprise you. After all, what is hard about starting a new word **segmentation**   whenever there is a space?

The first issue that comes to mind is that the writing systems of many languages do not actually use spaces between the words. For example, in Chinese a word consists of one or more Chinese characters, the so-called *zi*, and characters are written next to one another without spaces to separate the words. In Section 1.2.3, we saw that in the logographic writing system of Chinese, the characters are generally associated with meanings (as opposed to with sounds, as in alphabetic systems). Differences in segmenting the long string of characters into words thus will directly influence the meaning. Take for example the two character string 要害. If we segment

*布什	在	谈话	中指	出
Bush	at	talk	middle-finger	out

布什	在	谈话	中	指出
Bush	at	talk	middle	point-out

"Bush pointed out in his talk"

Figure 3.2 A potential overlapping ambiguity in Chinese

it as two words of one character each, it means "will hurt"; if we segment it as a single word consisting of two characters, it means "vitals". Which tokenization is chosen depends on the context – much like the context determines whether an occurrence of the English word "bank" refers to a financial institution or a river bank. Such a segmentation problem, where two or more characters may be combined to form one word or not, is referred to as a **covering ambiguity**.

> covering ambiguity

A second kind of tokenization problem is **overlapping ambiguity**, which refers to cases where a given character may combine with either the previous or the next word. Lu (2007, p. 72) provides a clear illustration of this ambiguity with the string 布什在谈话中指出. Depending on whether the second to last character 指 is part of the last word or the word before that, the meaning of the sentence changes significantly, as illustrated by Figure 3.2 (even though in Chinese only the second segmentation option is a grammatical sentence).

> overlapping ambiguity

You may consider yourself lucky that the writing system used for English makes it so much easier to determine what the words are by simply starting a new word whenever there is a space. But even for English, life is not that simple. After all, "inasmuch as" and "insofar as" would then be split into two tokens and "in spite of" into three – but to process them further or even just to look them up in a dictionary, clearly identifying them as a single token would be most useful! For an even more common case, let us begin with a simple sentence such as (27a), where starting a new token for every word is straightforward.

(27) a. I got my car fixed yesterday.
    b. I got my flu shot yesterday.
    c. I got my salary yesterday.

But then we see (27b) on the lapel sticker of someone in the street – and we do not run away thinking we met a criminal bragging about his first killing! We immediately interpret "flu shot" as a single token, parallel to the occurrence of "salary" in (27c), despite the fact that it contains a space. Naturally, this is very much language dependent, as a **compound noun** such as "flu shot" is, for instance, written without spaces as "Grippeimpfung" in German. So spaces should presumably be allowed in some English tokens, which immediately raises the question of when exactly a tokenizer should identify words that include spaces and when not.

> compound noun

The opposite problem is posed by strings such as "I'm", "cannot", or "gonna". None of these tokens contains a space, but we know that "I'm" is nothing but a short form, **contraction** a so-called **contraction**, of "I am". Similarly, "gonna" occurs in the same places and is interpreted in the same way as "going to". And a word such as "dunno" (which might well appear in an English text to be processed, even if some people would rather ignore such forms) seems to be equivalent to "do not know". So, does it make sense to treat them as one token in the contracted form and as two or three tokens in the form including a space? Clearly, treating the two variants in such a radically different way would complicate all later processing, which would not be necessary if we, for instance, tokenized "I'm" as two tokens "I" and "'m". This naturally raises the general question of when exactly a tokenizer should split up English strings that do not contain spaces into multiple tokens.

In sum, to tokenize an English text, there are some general strategies, such as starting a new token whenever we encounter a space or punctuation symbol, and there are more specific segmentation cases where tokens can contain spaces and where multiple tokens result from a string lacking spaces. The automatic tokenizers used today thus typically contain long lists of known words and abbreviations, as well as a number of rules identifying common subregularities (these are generally finite-state rules; see Under the Hood 7 for a discussion of finite-state technology).

3.4.2 Part-of-speech tagging

Once we have identified the tokens, we can turn to obtaining the general classes of words we are looking for, such as the part-of-speech (POS) classes that, for example, make it possible to identify that the sentence a learner entered into a CALL system is
meta-linguistic lacking a finite verb and to provide the general **meta-linguistic feedback** message "The
feedback sentence you entered is missing a verb", independent of the particular requirements specific to a given activity.

But what are parts of speech and where does the evidence for them come from? Essentially, parts of speech are labels for classes of words that behave alike. What counts as alike naturally needs to be made more precise, and one essentially finds
distribution three types of evidence for it. The first is **distribution**, by which we refer to the linear order with respect to the other tokens; that is, the slot in which a word appears. For example, in the sequence "John gave him ball", the slot between "him" and "ball" is the distributional slot of a determiner such as "the" or "a".

When designing automatic POS taggers, distributional information is typically collected in the form of statistics about which POS sequences are likely to occur, parallel to the n-gram statistics we saw in the discussion of language models in Under the Hood 2. To be able to observe possible POS sequences, one naturally needs a corpus that is already annotated with POS tags. Such corpora with so-called
gold-standard **gold-standard annotation** are generally created using significant manual effort to
annotation annotate or correct the annotation. To obtain gold-standard corpora of the size needed to train current POS taggers (and supervised machine learning approaches

in general – see Chapter 5) thus requires large, long-term projects. Correspondingly, they so far only exist for less than 10% of the roughly 6,000 human languages (which poses a significant challenge to the development of NLP tools for underresourced languages).

The second type of evidence is the one we use every time we look up a word in a dictionary. For some words, **lexical stem lookup** provides an unambiguous part-of-speech category. For example, "claustrophobic" is only listed as an adjective. Yet, many words are ambiguous and belong to more than one part-of-speech class. For example, the word "can" occurs as an auxiliary in "The baby can walk.", as a full verb in "I can tuna for a living.", and as a noun in "Pass me that can of beer, please!" Even a word like "some", which at first glance one might think unambiguously is a determiner (e.g., *some cars*), is also found used as an adverb (e.g., *The cut bled some.* or *You need to work on it some.*) or pronoun (e.g., *Some like it hot.*). **lexical stem lookup**

Another problem of lexical lookup arises from the fact that there are words that are not in the lexicon. Even if we tried very hard and got the world's best dictionary resource, there still would be words not listed there, since new words are added to the language all the time. For instance, words such as "googling" or "facebooked" clearly do not occur in texts from the 1980s (see also Section 2.3.1). All automatic POS taggers make use of lexical information. That lexical information typically is collected from the POS-annotated gold-standard corpora in the training phase, which records the distributional information mentioned above.

The third type of evidence for classification of words into parts of speech presents itself when we take a closer look at the form of words, their morphology. Certain markings, such as **suffixes** added to the end of stems, encode information that is only appropriate for particular parts of speech. For example, -*ed* is a suffix indicating a past-tense marking of words as, for example, in "walked" or "displayed". Thus, if we find a word such as "brachiated" in a sentence, even if we know nothing about this word or its context, we can infer based on the -*ed* suffix that it is likely to be a past-tense verb. **suffix**

Apart from **inflectional suffixes** indicating information such as the tense or agreement markers (e.g., the -*s* found on verbs in the third-person singular), other potential sources of information include **derivational affixes**, such as -*er*, which is used to turn verbs into nouns (e.g., *walk – walker, catch – catcher, love – lover*). In automatic POS taggers, suffix analysis is often included in a **fallback step**. Whenever a word has not been seen before in the training data, so that no lexical or distributional information is available for that word, **suffix analysis** is performed to determine the most likely part of speech, for example using handwritten rules. If none of the suffix rules applies, as a last resort POS taggers generally assign the most common option, usually a noun tag. **inflectional suffix** **derivational affix** **fallback step** **suffix analysis**

While distribution and morphology already came up in the discussion of guiding principles for part-of-speech analysis in Section 2.4.1, in the CALL context we are considering in this chapter, a complication arises from the fact that we are dealing with a so-called **interlanguage** written by students with one native language while they acquire another, foreign language. That complication confirms in an interesting **interlanguage** way that indeed we are dealing with three independent sources of evidence which we are using to determine the part-of-speech class of a word. Consider the following two sentences written by Spanish learners of English (from the NOCE corpus, Díaz Negrillo *et al.*, 2010):

(28) a. ... to be **choiced** for a job ...
      b. RED helped him **during** he was in the prison.

In (28a), the word "choiced" distributionally appears in a verbal slot, and morphologically it carries a verbal inflection (*-ed*), whereas lexically the stem "choice" is a noun (or adjective). And in (28b), the meaning of the sentence is fine, but "during" distributionally is a preposition, which cannot appear in the distributional slot of a conjunction. POS-tagging approaches to learner language thus need to be extended to take into account such potentially mismatching evidence.

3.4.3   Beyond words

Naturally, there are many abstractions and generalizations about language that can be used in concisely characterizing and providing feedback to learner answers in CALL systems. Another typical area in this context is grammar – in a sense that is quite different from boring and dry rule books. It is more related to the regularities you can observe in, say, chemistry, when you ask yourself what happens if you combine two given substances. Certain molecules can combine; others don't; a particular order is needed for them to be able to combine; and sometimes an additional element, a catalyst, needs to be present for a combination to be possible. Or in music, there are clear generalizations about the way you can combine musical notes in chords or when setting music. For those who like neither chemistry nor music, just think of the good old days when you may well have played with LEGO bricks – and again, only certain forms fit together in a particular order, independent of what it is that you actually want to build. So that is what grammar is about when it comes to using language.

    Grammar as studied in the linguistic subfield of syntax captures the same kind of generalizations for language. We already mentioned some of the basic generalizations

word order that syntax makes in Section 2.4.1. These include generalizations about **word order**. For example, in a typical English sentence, the subject precedes the verb and the object follows it. There also are generalizations about which elements have to appear together; for example, if the verb "devour" occurs in a sentence, it must be accompanied by a particular kind of an object, a noun phrase, to avoid ungrammatical sentences

selection such as "John devoured recently." Here, the generalization is that a verb can **select** (or subcategorize) the category of elements that can or must accompany it.

    Other generalizations in the area of syntax deal with the forms in which words need to appear to be able to occur together. For example, a subject can only appear

agreement together with a verb if they share so-called **agreement** features, a generalization that is necessary to rule out ungrammatical sentences such as "I walks." In other situations, when the generalization involves one element telling another what to look like, we typically speak of **government**. For example, a verb such as "hug" **government** requires its object to occur in the accusative case, to ensure that we get sentences such as "Sarah hugged him" and not sentences where we instead get the nominative form of the pronoun, as in "Sara hugged he."

We discussed the techniques used for expressing generalizations about the order and form of words in Section 2.4.2 in the context of the chapter on writers' aids, so we will not repeat them here. Instead, we continue by asking ourselves what happens when we add linguistic analysis in the form of tokenization, part-of-speech tagging, and syntactic parsing and agreement checking to a CALL system. We then obtain a CALL system that is aware of language, in the sense that it can analyze and check some generalizations about language that are independent of a particular exercise.

In such language-aware systems, often referred to as intelligent computer-assisted language learning (**ICALL**), one no longer needs to explicitly specify everything in **ICALL** a frame that matches all possible learner answers to the feedback messages to be given in those cases. In ICALL systems, some of the feedback thus is based on a general analysis of language, while other feedback remains based on information explicitly specified in a given exercise – for example, without looking at the exercise materials there is no way to determine the names of the people that a question asks about.

3.5   An example ICALL system: TAGARELA

Having discussed various issues that arise in providing feedback with a computer-assisted language learning system, you probably wonder what such systems actually look like. So, in this section, we take a closer look at an **intelligent language tutoring** **intelligent** **system (ILTS)** called TAGARELA (Teaching Aid for Grammatical Awareness, **language** Recognition and Enhancement of Linguistic Abilities), an intelligent web-based **tutoring system** workbook for beginning learners of Portuguese. **(ILTS)**

The TAGARELA system offers self-guided activities accompanying teaching. It includes six types of activities: listening comprehension, reading comprehension, picture description, fill-in-the-blank, rephrasing, and vocabulary. It thus is similar to traditional workbook exercises, with the addition of audio. But it provides on-the-spot meta-linguistic feedback on orthographic errors (spelling, spacing, punctuation), syntactic errors (nominal and verbal agreement), and semantic errors (missing or extra concepts, word choice).

Figure 3.3 shows a rephrasing activity, in which the learner is given a sentence and has to rewrite it using the words provided. In this example, the learner forgot to include a verb in the answer they typed into the answer field at the bottom left of the page. The system displays a feedback message pointing out this error at the bottom right of the page. Note that just as discussed at the end of Section 3.3, a sentence missing

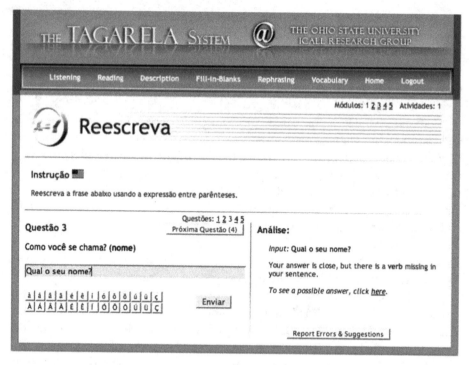

Figure 3.3   TAGARELA: Feedback on missing verb

a verb is an error the system can detect and provide feedback on solely based on knowledge about the language. In TAGARELA, this knowledge about the language is encoded in grammar rules for Portuguese, which are independent of this particular activity.

Figure 3.4 shows an example for a reading comprehension question. The feedback provided by TAGARELA for the learner response in this exercise illustrates another general type of error made by language learners, so-called **subject–verb agreement errors**, where the form of the verb does not agree with its subject.

subject–verb
agreement error

The feedback in the previous two examples was computed by TAGARELA based on the system's general NLP capability to analyze language – from identifying tokens, words, lemmas, and parts of speech to syntactic generalizations – without the need for explicit frames spelling out all potential learner answers and the feedback to be provided. Yet, we also mentioned at the end of the previous section that some of the feedback that an ICALL system provides remains based on the specific exercise. An example for such exercise-specific feedback is shown in Figure 3.5, where a text about Brazil introduces the different regions of the country and the learner is asked a reading comprehension question about it.

The learner response states that there are five cities in Brazil, even though the specific question at hand in this exercise was asking about the number of regions in that country. Making use of information specific to this exercise, the system feedback alerts the learner to the fact that the answer is not expected to be about cities but about regions.

Figure 3.4 TAGARELA: Feedback on agreement

Note that even for such feedback based on exercise-specific information, the feedback at the same time also makes use of generalizations detected by the system's NLP capabilities, by pointing out that the problem is associated with a noun. The system thus recognized the unexpected word "cidade" as belonging to the POS category of noun and used that general information obtained about the learner input in formulating the feedback.

3.6 Modeling the learner

So far, we have mentioned two sources of information that are used by computer-assisted language learning systems. We started with the explicit information in the exercises, in particular the frames that need to be specified for each exercise in a traditional CALL system. The second source of information arises from the computational linguistic analysis in an ICALL system, which is based on the general knowledge about a language and thus is independent of a particular exercise.

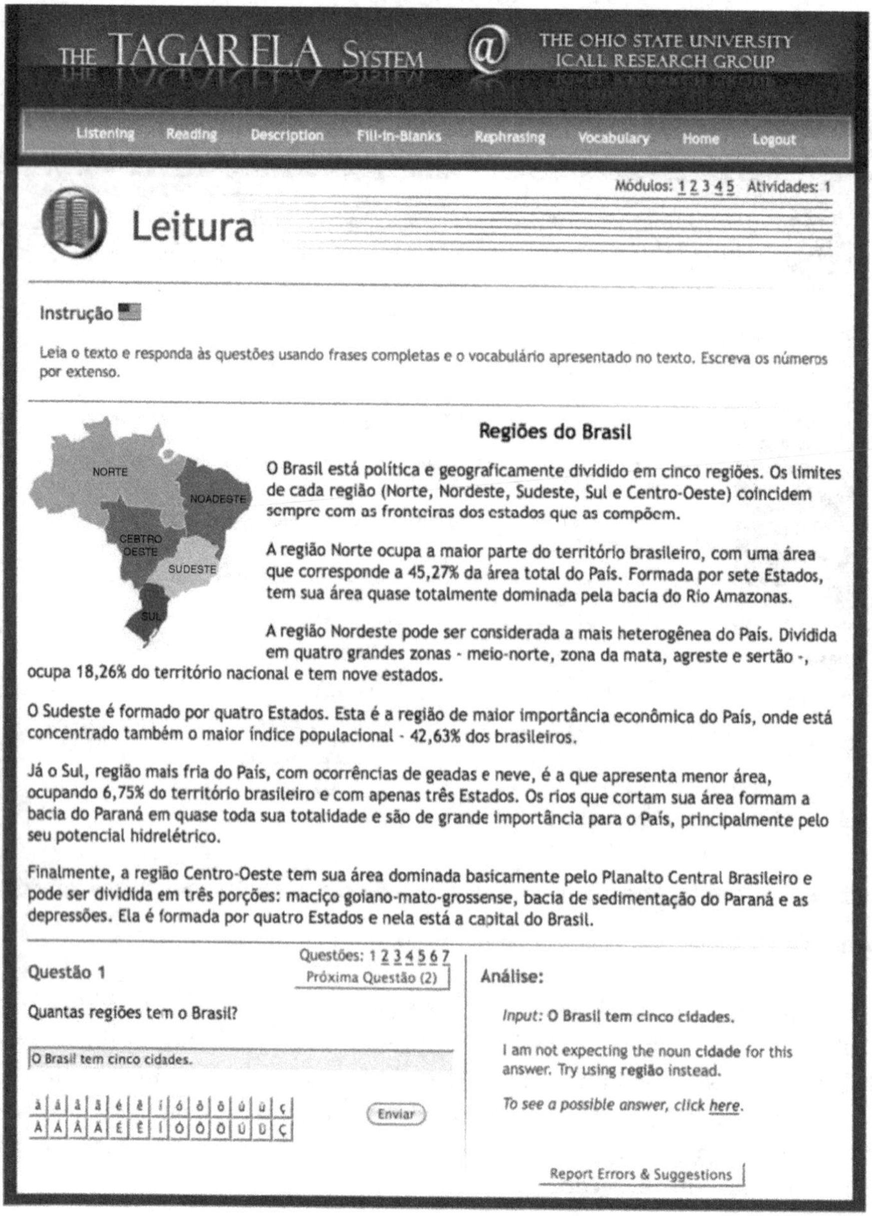

Figure 3.5 TAGARELA: Example for exercise-specific feedback

In addition to those two sources of information – the exercise and the language – it can also be important to take into account what we know about the learner. Generally learner speaking, such **learner modeling** includes two types of information. On the one modeling hand, there are learner properties that are more or less permanent, such as the gender, native language, or learning style preferences – and it is easy to see that, for example, system feedback for visual learners should be enhanced with more visual cues than for other learner types. On the other hand, there is the dynamic record of learner performance so far, essentially a history recording whether a given learner has successfully used particular words or structures before.

Both types of information about the learner are relevant when providing feedback. For example, a learner's mother tongue (or first, native language; that is, L1) strongly influences the words and constructions used and the mistakes made when learning a second language – correspondingly, one often reads about positive and negative **L1 transfer**. An example of negative transfer is the fact that many native speakers of languages such as Chinese or Czech, which do not include articles of the kind found in English, find it very difficult to use the English articles "the" and "a" properly. Correspondingly, a tutoring system should provide feedback on article misuse for learners with such native languages, whereas for other users a missing article may be a minor typo, so that feedback should instead focus on other, more relevant aspects of the learner answer. **L1 transfer**

Implicit in this last example is the fact that tutoring systems generally try to focus the feedback on the most relevant errors first, since it is known that providing all possible corrections and comments is problematic – just like most students receiving back graded homework will simply stuff it in their bag instead of reading the comments if there are massive red marks all over the place. Learner modeling provides important information for the **prioritization of feedback** needed to make learners notice the most relevant aspects specific to themselves. **prioritization of feedback**

Naturally, L1 transfer does not always cause problems; it can also help a learner in acquiring a new language. An example of positive L1 transfer is the fact that for speakers of Spanish and other Romance languages, many of the English ten-dollar words popular in standardized tests such as the GRE are comparatively easy, since they frequently have Latin roots that survived in many Romance languages.

An important difference between static learner properties such as the mother tongue and the constantly updated history of learner interaction as the second component of learner modeling lies in the way in which the learner information is obtained. Information for the more or less permanent part of a learner model typically stems from a questionnaire asking for information such as gender, mother tongue, time spent abroad, and other languages spoken in the family, as well as from tests providing information on the learner's general cognitive or more specific language abilities. For the second component of learner modeling, on the other hand, the system needs to draw **inferences** from the learner's interaction with the system. Let us take a closer look at what is meant by inferences here and why they are needed. **inference**

One could simply record everything the learner enters in exactly the way it is entered. However, all this would help detect is whether the learner has entered a particular answer before, which would allow the system to provide specific feedback for a single, very specific case of minor relevance. To be able to make more use of recording past learner performance, just like in the discussion of analysis and feedback in the first part of the chapter, it is necessary to abstract away from the surface of what the learner entered into the system to the more general linguistic properties and classes of which the learner answer provides evidence. For example, one may want to record whether a learner answer contains a finite verb and whether it showed correct subject–verb agreement. Once we have observed learner answers that include instances of a particular linguistic class or relation, we can infer that the learner has mastered this aspect of the language to be learned and deprioritize

sequencing of feedback on it in the future. Where the tutoring system supports this, learner models
teaching may also be used to **sequence the teaching material** appropriately, for example
material by guiding learners to additional material on concepts they apparently have not mastered yet.

language testing   It is far from trivial to determine when such inferences are valid. Just like in the context of **language testing**, in the intelligent tutoring context **construct under-**
construct **representation** can hinder the recording of a particular ability in a learner model.
under- In other words, the exercises the student is completing need to provide enough
representation evidence of a particular language ability if we want to record and update the record of what the learner can do in the learner model. To ensure valid inferences, it also is not enough only to consider the learner answers themselves. Instead, we also need to include information on the exercise the learner was completing and the strategies learners may employ to succeed in such a task. For example, a particular learner answer may simply have been copied by the learner from the text they

lifting were answering a question about, which is known as **lifting** – and such an answer naturally does not provide good evidence of mastery of the linguistic material it includes. To be able to interpret learner answers in terms of what they allow us to

learner infer about the learner's abilities, an intelligent tutoring system thus also needs to
strategies take into account **learner strategies** such as lifting or avoidance of structures about which the learner is unsure.

Concluding our exploration of language tutoring systems and the role the analysis of language needs to play within them, the use of NLP in language teaching and in education in general is one of the application areas that is just starting to take off. Following in the footsteps of the first few intelligent language tutoring systems in real-life use today (E-Tutor, Robo-Sensei, TAGARELA), the coming years will bring a much wider range of exercise types with more adaptive feedback and increased use of virtual environments. The first interactive robots used for language teaching are already appearing on the scene. Based on what we discussed in this chapter, it is clear, however, that one aspect will stay the same in all such uses of computers in language learning: for these systems to be able to react to learner input in an intelligent way, going beyond a small number of pre-envisaged frame specifications, it is crucial for the systems to be able to step back from the specific learner answer at hand to more abstract linguistic representations. These representations support system feedback and interaction with a wide range of learner responses. The key to success lies in combining generalizations about language with aspects specific to the given activity and information about the particular learner and their interaction history.

Checklist

After reading the chapter, you should be able to:

- Distinguish first from second language acquisition and point out some of the differences between them.
- Understand why feedback is particularly useful in a second-language context.
- Sketch what frame-based CALL systems are and where information about language is encoded in them.
- Explain which aspects of language make it hard or impossible to specify frames.
- Give examples of how different words and phrases can be used to express the same or related meanings.
- Exemplify what makes tokenization difficult, even for some English cases.
- Explain why abstractions and generalizations about language are useful in the context of a CALL system and provide some examples.
- Distinguish the different types of evidence that play a role in the classification of words into parts of speech.
- Describe syntactic generalizations that are captured in a grammar and give examples of errors in sentences that those generalizations allow us to detect.
- Give an example of how linguistic generalizations are used in ICALL systems in both analysis and feedback.
- Indicate how modeling the learner is relevant for an ICALL system.

Exercises

1. **ALL:** In learning their first language, young children frequently produce forms such as "I **goed** to school yesterday.", "I **catched** it.", or "The **mens** repaired it." How would you characterize what is going on in those cases?

2. **ALL:** Try to find some real-life examples of the general pattern you identified in the first exercise by browsing the Child Language Data Exchange System (CHILDES) started by Brian MacWhinney. You can browse the American English transcripts at (http://purl.org/lang-and-comp/childes).

   For example, line 124 of the transcript at (http://purl.org/lang-and-comp/childes-ex) shows "I falled down again." In which sense is this similar to the cases discussed above? Can you find other examples of this pattern? Are there other, related patterns you can see recurring in the transcripts?

3. **ALL:** Consider the learner language examples such as those from the first and second exercises above. Which of those will have an impact on part-of-speech tagging and which won't?

   To answer this, run a part-of-speech tagger on some learner sentences or entire texts from the CHILDES repository. You can use one of the free online tagging services, such as (http://purl.org/lang-and-comp/claws) or (http://purl.org/lang-and-comp/cogcomp-pos).

What do these part-of-speech taggers do for words used by learners that are not words in native English? Think about the different sources of evidence (distribution, morphology, lexicon). How does the fact that these are sentences written by language learners affect the overall performance of the tagger?

4. **ALL:** We mentioned multiple-choice exercises as a common CALL activity, for which all linguistic knowledge is directly encoded in the activity. Start a web browser and do a search for multiple choice language exercises. Explore the pages you find to see which language topics such multiple-choice exercises are used for. Why are those topics well suited to this exercise type?

    Are there any differences between the exercises offered for learners of English and those for learners of Spanish (e.g., on the pages found by a search for Spanish multiple choice exercises)?

5. **ALL:** Many of the web pages identified by the search in the previous exercise also include exercise types other than multiple choice. Which kind of exercises do you find on those pages? Where do you think the knowledge to evaluate and provide feedback to those activities is encoded? Which kind of feedback do they provide? Are these canned responses?

6. **ALL:** We discussed that tokenizing Chinese poses significant problems, but even for English there are difficult cases. What problems do sentences such as the following pose for tokenizing in English?

    (29) (a) There is no prima facie reason why a vacation in Italy is better than a hike to the North Pole.
          (b) Did you see the jack rabbit near the bridge?
          (c) It arrived without a scratch, in spite of my fears.
          (d) However, it may soon turn into a hundreds-of-billions-of-yen market.

7. **ALL:** A typical kind of lexical L1-transfer error made by language learners is known as a **false friend**. What kind of error is this? Find examples on the web and discuss different ways in which such false friends arise.

    As discussed in the text, L1 transfer is not always a problem for language learners, it can also be helpful. Consider which words a Spanish native speaker would find easy or hard when learning English and give examples.

Further reading

A general overview of the use of NLP in the context of language learning is provided in Meurers (2012). A detailed discussion of ICALL projects, including a historical overview and a characterization of the techniques used, can be found in Heift and Schulze (2007).

Two prominent collections of research articles on *intelligent language tutoring systems* are Swartz and Yazdani (1992) and Holland, Kaplan, and Sams (1995). Most of the research on *learner modeling for intelligent tutoring systems* does not deal with learning languages but other subjects, such as mathematics. However, the work of Susan Bull (http://purl.org/lang-and-comp/susan.bull) provides a good overview of the topics and issues discussed in connection with learner modeling for intelligent language tutors. Amaral and Meurers (2008) explain the need to extend learner models of ICALL systems beyond linguistic knowledge.

To get an idea of what intelligent language tutoring systems look like, you can find descriptions of the German E-Tutor system and the exercise types it offers in Heift (2010). More discussion of such systems and how they relate to real-life language teaching can be found in Amaral and Meurers (2011).

4

Searching

4.1 Introduction

In writing the introduction to this chapter, one of the authors wanted to use an example taken from a scene in the movie *Mission: Impossible*, involving a character searching for important information on a computer. Ironically, the author was unable after 15 minutes to find a description of this scene on the internet. It seemed like he was going to have to track it down by watching the movie again. (Luckily, this turned out not to be the case, as discussed below.)

What is the problem here? We know what the name of the movie is and can find all sorts of facts about it (it stars Tom Cruise, came out in 1996, and so on); we know the scene involves searching on a computer; and we know that the internet houses a wealth of information and random movie facts. We know exactly what we are looking for, so why is it so difficult to find what we want?

Unfortunately, the phrase `mission impossible` is so famous that it is used for a variety of purposes (e.g., a book title *Protection against Genocide: Mission Impossible?*); the movie features several scenes involving computers, most of which are more famous; and searching for anything related to searching turns up links to web search engines with other results for the movie. Although this example may seem trivial, it is genuine, it corresponds to a real information need, and it reveals some of the problems that can arise when we search the internet.

Consider what the options are for finding the information we want:

- Keep searching online, hoping that the right combination of search terms will turn up the results.

Language and Computers, First Edition. Markus Dickinson, Chris Brew and Detmar Meurers.

- Go to specialist sources, such as movie databases, discussion boards, and lists of movie gaffes. If the information there is well organized, it might be obvious how to find what you need.
- Find a book that discusses the influence of computers in modern cinema.
- Talk to friends who may have seen the movie.
- Watch the movie (note that for other search problems – such as tracking down in which cities you can find a statue of a rabbit on a rock – "cheating" like this is not an option).

There is no single right answer: if you have friends who are movie buffs, asking is good; if you are patient about working through reams of search engine results, that will work; if you are pretty sure you have seen the information in a particular book and more or less know where it is, that may be quickest. For the present problem, a suggestion to look for `mission impossible script` was what eventually led to finding the reference.

We all know that there are many possible ways to obtain a piece of information, from more traditional resources, such as books and newspapers, to more recent resources like the web and various databases. Finding the information in a hurry, however, is not always a straightforward task, as the example above illustrates. You have to know what resources are available, and how to search through those resources. This chapter provides an overview of different types of searching and different kinds of resources.

written text   We will focus on searching in **written texts**, but you might also be wondering about the possibility of searching through speech. After all, it would be extremely useful and time-saving to be able to find a particular sentence spoken in an interview, especially if no transcript exists, but only a recording or audio file. Unfortunately, this type of searching is not readily available with current technology.

While this might be a bit disappointing, searching in speech may not be far away. It is already possible to detect the language of a spoken conversation and to detect a new topic being started in a conversation, and it is possible to use speech recognition to provide automatic, if fallible, closed captioning of videos.

structured data   We are going to start our tour of searching with a look at so-called **structured data**. The characteristic of structured data is that it is very orderly. There are **fields**
field   such as author and title that will certainly be present in every entry. Because care has been taken to bring all the data into a uniform format, it can often be searched very easily.

This type of data is found in every library database that we know of, for example. For instance, there is an entry in the World Cat Library Database for "The White Star timetable, South Island of New Zealand: the official guide of the White Star Tourist Services Ltd., 1924–25", and we are told its author: "White Star Tourist Services", language: "English", and that it includes advertising.

Structured data is extremely useful. If you know you need information on "duck-billed platypuses", for instance, it will help to look through "zoology" and "animal" topics. The problem with structured data, of course, is that the structure needs to be created and imposed on the data. This takes work, which for many centuries had to be done by librarians, filing clerks, and other human beings. Somebody had to enter all that stuff about the New Zealand bus timetable. Thus, we have much more **unstructured data** available, most strikingly in the form of the millions of files on the internet. A number of search engines allow us to search for information over the web, for example Google.

unstructured data

After examining structured databases, we will turn to so-called **semi-structured data**. Not every document will have the same structure or format as every other document, and fields may vary substantially from document to document. For example, in a database of internet movie reviews, some reviews might be based on a four-star system and others on a five-star system. The data contains useful categorizations, but the user may have to work harder to extract information. As we will discover, so-called *regular expressions* are useful for this type of searching.

semi-structured data

Finally, we will turn to smaller, more focused collections of data, using text corpora (i.e., collections of text) as our example. The advantage of using focused databases means that searching can also be more focused, for example in the form of looking for linguistic patterns. Additionally, there is a benefit to small size, which is that a small team of humans can add very rich and detailed special-purpose information about the document. We will illustrate this possibility by showing how linguists use **corpus annotation**.

corpus annotation

4.2 Searching through structured data

A library catalogue is an excellent example of structured data. To find articles, books, and other library holdings, a library generally has a **database** containing information on its holdings, and to search through this, each library generally provides a **database frontend**. For the exercises in this chapter almost any library will do, so long as it has an online search interface, as most now do. Alternatively, you can use WorldCat (http://www.worldcat.org), which is available to anyone with internet access and indexes libraries all over the world. We cannot promise that you will see exactly the same search features for every library, but what we describe here is fairly typical.

database

database frontend

A library catalogue is highly structured. Each item is associated with a fixed set of fields – the author, title, keywords, call number, and so on associated with an item. You can select which field you want, and search for the occurrence of **literal strings** within that field. If you know that a book was written by someone with a last name of "Haddock", which is not a very common name, an AUTHOR search in a library catalogue may produce a tight set of results that you can easily look through. Doing the same with a simple internet search for the word "Haddock" might produce a much larger and less manageable collection of results, since the search engine would have no way of knowing that you are looking for a book and its author.

literal strings

At the core of a database search is the task of searching for strings of characters. The literal strings entered as **queries** are composed of characters, which of

query

course must be in the same character-encoding system (e.g., ASCII, ISO8859-1, UTF-8) as the strings stored in the database.

Online library catalogs have existed for decades, and some were designed to work with old-fashioned Teletype terminals, which did not have lower-case letters. So you may find that your query is quietly converted to upper case before being submitted as a search. It could even be that the accents and diacritics on queries written in foreign languages are dropped or otherwise transformed. If this happens, it is because the software designers are trying to help you by mapping your queries onto something that has a chance of being found in the database.

special character   Database frontends provide different options for searches, allowing more flexibility than simply searching for strings, including the use of **special characters**. For example, some systems such as WorldCat allow you to abbreviate parts of words. A typical
wildcard   special character is the **wildcard**, often written as `*`; this symbol is used to stand in for a sequence of characters. For example, the query `art*` might find "arts", "artists", "artistic", and "artificial". There may also be other characters that stand in for a single character or for a particular number of characters, and, in fact, the exact effect of a wildcard may vary from system to system – some only apply at the ends of words, some are restricted to less than five characters, and so on. While special characters are useful and are sometimes the only option you have, we will later see more principled ways of searching with regular expressions (Section 4.4).

Boolean   **Boolean expression** operators allow you to combine search terms in different
expression   ways. The use of `and`, `or`, and parentheses provide the basics. For example, (30a) finds items with both the word "art" and the word "therapy" used somewhere, while (30b) finds anything containing either word, thus returning many more documents. The operator `and not` functions similarly, but allows words to be excluded. For example, if a search on `art` is returning too many books about art therapy, one could consider using a query like (30c). When using more than one operator, parentheses are used to group words together. The query (30d) eliminates documents about either "music therapy" or "dance therapy". With such operators, we can be fairly specific in our searches.

(30)   a. `art and therapy`
       b. `art or therapy`
       c. `art and not therapy`
       d. `art therapy and not ((music or dance) therapy)`

While Boolean expressions are fairly simple in their basic form, they can become overwhelmingly confusing when they are combined to form long and complex queries. There is also an ever-present risk of typing mistakes, which grows as the query gets longer. When learning Boolean expressions, therefore, it pays to test out simple queries before trying more complicated ones. When we need to build a complicated query, we do not usually type directly into the search box. Instead, we type into a text editor, write a simple version of the expression, then paste the result into the search box. If that works, we go back to our text editor, copy the query that we just ran, then create a slightly more complex version. If we mistype, we have a record of what we have done and can backtrack to the last thing that seemed to work. The exercises at the end of the chapter should help you in your progress.

4.3   Searching through unstructured data

In some respects, unstructured data presents a completely different scenario: there is no explicit categorization of the documents to be retrieved. In other respects, however, the fundamentals are the same: searching through unstructured data is closely related to doing a keyword search in structured data. What distinguishes searching in unstructured data tends to be the sheer scale of the data, with billions of webpages to search through. Some of the searches that providers can easily do with a small, structured database are difficult or impossible at web scale. The consequences of this difference in scale show up in the different operators that are typically offered, in the subtly varying behaviors even of operators that look the same, and in the different actions that users can take in order to improve their search results.

We must make one further point about structure before continuing. When we say that the data is *unstructured*, what we really mean is that no one has predetermined and precoded the structure of the data for us. We are not saying that structure is entirely absent. Consider the case of trawling the web looking for English translations of Chinese words. There is no field for a webpage labeled *English translation*, but there are many pages that display a Chinese word followed by an English word in brackets (e.g., [word]). Even better are cases with an explicit marker of a translation (e.g., [*trans.*, word]). There even exist bilingual dictionaries online with the words in column format. Certainly, there is structure in these examples. The point of calling the data *unstructured* is to draw attention to the facts that the structure is not predetermined; it is not uniformly applied or standardized; and fields, such as Chinese, English, and etymology, are not available for use in queries. If we wanted, we could process the examples, bring them into a uniform structured format, and offer the world a structured interface into our web-derived Chinese–English dictionary. And if we really wanted, we could have a team of bilingual librarians check and edit the structure to make sure that the Chinese words, English words, and other fields have all been correctly identified.

4.3.1   Information need

To discuss searching in unstructured data, we need to discuss the concept of **information need**. The information need, informally, is what the information seeker is **need** really looking for. Before this can be submitted to a search engine, it has to be translated into a query. It is often the case that the query is an imperfect reflection of the information need. Consider, for example, the case where a person is searching for a

Russian translation of "table", as shown in (31). It is obvious what the connection is between the information need and the query, which is `russian translation table`. Unfortunately, this query is ambiguous: the same query might easily be chosen by someone looking for a table, or chart, of Russian translations. Since the search engine is not able to see into the mind of the searcher, it cannot reliably tell which of these interpretations is correct, so the results will probably not be as focused as the searcher expects.

(31) a. Information need:
     one or more Russian translations of the English word "table"
    b. Possible query:
     `russian translation table`

4.3.2   Evaluating search results

The concept of information need affects how we view evaluation. One can see this in the evaluations used for the Text REtrieval Conference (TREC, http://trec.nist.gov/), for example, as illustrated in Figure 4.1. To evaluate search technology, they express the information needs in natural language and have written down queries intended to capture those needs. Human beings then compare the documents returned by the information retrieval systems with the descriptions of the information needs.

```
<top>
<num> Number: 303
<title> Hubble Telescope Achievements

<desc> Description:
Identify positive accomplishments of the Hubble telescope
since it was launched in 1991.

<narr> Narrative:
Documents are relevant that show the Hubble telescope has
produced new data, better quality data than previously
available, data that has increased human knowledge of the
universe, or data that has led to disproving previously
existing theories or hypotheses.  Documents limited to the
shortcomings of the telescope would be irrelevant. Details
of repairs or modifications to the telescope without
reference to positive achievements would not be relevant.
</top>
```

Figure 4.1   Characterization of an information need in a TREC evaluation

A document is judged relevant if it meets an information need. Systems that place relevant documents high up in the list of results are given high scores.

More specifically, TREC defines "right answers" in the following way: "If you were writing a report on the subject of the topic and would use the information contained in the document in the report, then the document is relevant" (http://trec.nist.gov/data/reljudge_eng_html). The definition is fairly open-ended, but it gives guidance for a human to evaluate whether a document is a match or not.

However, that leads to a numerical question: How many pages is the search engine getting right? For a given search engine and query, attempting to match a particular information need, we require some way to measure search engine quality. Two common measures from computational linguistics are worth examining here, as they help to outline the different ways in which search engines do or do not meet our needs (see also Section 5.4.1 in the Classifying Documents chapter). The first measure is **precision**, which can be phrased as: Of the pages returned by a search   **precision** engine, how many are the ones we want? Consider the case where an engine returns 400 hits for a query, 200 of which are related to the desired topic. In this case, precision is 50%, or 200 out of 400.

The second measure is **recall**: Of all the pages in existence on the topic we wanted,   **recall** how many were actually given? Consider the case where an engine returns 200 pages, all of which we wanted (as above), but there were actually 1,000 pages on that topic on the internet (we missed 800 of them); recall is thus 20% (200/1,000). Note that the numerator (200) is the same for both precision and recall.

Nevertheless, how can we know that there are 1,000 pages out there? In TREC, researchers used fixed collections of documents, so they were able, with effort, to know exactly how many relevant documents were in the collection. But if you are working with the whole of the internet, no one knows for sure how many relevant documents there are. Even if someone were prepared to try to count the number of relevant documents by hand, by the time they were halfway through, many relevant documents may have been added or deleted. So, in practice, while recall is a useful concept, it cannot always be calculated with any certainty. (In medical science, recall is also used, but goes by the name of *specificity*, as discussed in Section 5.4.1.)

The goal of a search engine is to provide 100% recall (so that we find everything we want) and 100% precision (so that we do not have to wade through unhelpful pages). These are often competing priorities: you can get 100% recall by returning every single webpage in existence, but this would be overwhelming. On the other hand, a search returning one webpage could have 100% precision, but at the cost of lack of coverage.

4.3.3   Example: Searching the web

The most familiar form of unstructured data is the web, which contains billions of webpages and very little in the way of categorization. To find information on the web, a user goes to a **search engine**, a program that matches documents to a user's   **search engine** search requests, and enters a query, or a request for information. In response to this query, the search engine returns a list of websites that might be relevant to the query, **evaluation of** and the user **evaluates the results**, picking a website with the information they were **results** looking for or reformulating the query.

As web pages are typically uncategorized, the main thing that search engines must rely on is the content of each webpage. They attempt to match a query to a page based primarily on words found in the document. This can be difficult, given the **lexical** common problem of **(lexical) ambiguity**; that is, a single word having multiple **ambiguity** meanings. The presence of a word like "Washington", for example, does not tell us whether this is the author of the webpage, the location of the webpage (or which exact *Washington* location), a page about the first president, a listing of all last names in the USA, and so on.

Some webpages do contain some degree of structure, which can be exploited by a **metadata** search engine. For example, web designers can offer useful information by including **metadata** – additional, structured information that is not shown in the webpage **meta tag** itself, but is available for a search engine. An example of a **meta tag** is something like `<META name="keywords" content="travel,Malta">`. This information is present in the HTML text that the web designer creates, but is not displayed by web browsers. HTML is the raw material of the internet. Some web designers use a text editor to write HTML directly; others use word processors or other authoring tools to create the webpage, then save it as HTML when it is ready for the website. If you are unfamiliar with HTML, see Under the Hood 6.

Search engine features

Most of what we say in this chapter is true of all search engines, but each search engine has its own special features designed to make life easier for the user, and these can vary. For instance, search engines may differ in the details of what they count as a word. They may differ in whether they treat words with the same stems (e.g., *bird* and *birds*) as the same, or as different. They may treat words with differing capitalization (e.g., *trip* and *Trip*) as the same or not. And, of course, any of the four **capitalization** possible ways of combining **capitalization** and **stemming** is a possibility. Search engines use a simple criterion to decide about these and other options: they analyze **stemming** search behavior and try to predict whether a policy will help searchers.

Most current search engines do collapse upper- and lower-case letters together. We just tried a search for BLUEFISH on a famous search engine, and it produces exactly the same results as a search for bluefish. They do not seem to do the same for stemming: our search for fish does not produce the same results as for fishes. We can be pretty sure that this policy is not accidental, but is based on careful observation of what seems to work well for the majority of search users. What works for the majority may not be perfect for the minority, however. For example, searches for Tubingen, Tübingen and Tuebingen all produce the same search results, even though only the second two are correct spellings of the German city of "Tübingen". The search engine apparently has a policy of mapping English characters to relevant non-English characters, because it knows that this will help people not used to

German. People who are used to German may be confused by this behavior, and those who are trying to use web search to study the ways in which people tend to type German words will definitely hate the policy.

Additionally, search engines have user-selectable options, and they differ in which **options** they support in the query. For example, Google allows users to request results written in a particular (human) language. Most web pages do not explicitly declare what language they are written in (they could do this, using metadata, but they usually do not), so the search engine has to make an informed guess (see Chapter 5 on Classifying Documents for ideas about how this might be done).

Search engines also try to present their results in a convenient way. For example, search engines can offer ways to **cluster** pages – in other words, to group similar results together. Instead of presenting a long list of very similar results, the search engine can show the user one representative of each of the important clusters. For example, a search for `tricks` currently produces five top-level results: a cluster for bar tricks, another cluster for magic tricks, an encyclopedia definition of a hat trick, a similar definition of a trick-taking game, and finally an Urban Dictionary entry for various slang usages of the term. The first two are genuine clusters, with a representative page, and little links to other members of the cluster. The last three are somewhat special, because the search engine in question knows that search users often have information needs that are satisfied by encyclopedia and dictionary entries. Because the web lacks explicit structure, the search engine once again has to make an informed guess about which pages are similar. The decisions about how to satisfy search users will be made on the basis of careful experimentation, data collection, and analysis. The rapid progress of modern search engines is due in large measure to the fact that search engine companies have learned how to automate this work, making it possible to apply the scientific method, in real time, to the complex and changing desires of search users.

Ranking of results
Perhaps most importantly, search engines differ in how search results are ranked. As we hinted when discussing clusters, a search engine's success depends on how it **ranks** the results that are returned in response to a query. When a search query has been entered, the webpages matching this query are returned as an ordered list based on guesses about each page's **relevance** to the query. But how can a search engine, which does not understand language, determine the relevance of a particular page?

There are a number of general factors that search engines can use to determine which webpages are the most likely responses to a query. First, there is comparison of the words in the document against the words in the query. Clearly, pages that mention the words in the query are likely to be better than ones that do not. Pages that mention the query words a lot are probably even better. And pages that mention query words near the top of the document, or even in a title, may be best of all. Search engines deal with this by weighting words according to their position, the number of times that they appear on the page, and so on. Highly weighted words strongly affect the ranking of the page, less highly weighted words have a lesser effect. Depending on the nature of the page, words mentioned in its metadata may need to receive a special

[margin notes:] search engine option · cluster · ranking · relevance

weight: either high, if the search engine believes the metadata to be trustworthy, or very low, if the search engine judges that the metadata is an attempt to mislead it. (See the section on *Search engine indexing* for more details on how words are used.)

Estimating a page's *quality* can be much more sophisticated and is usually done by counting the number of links to and from a page because these are an effective measure of how popular a page is. There is a balance to be struck here: an engine that relied entirely on popularity estimates might make it nearly impossible to find pages that are either new or relevant only to a small minority of search users. We will discuss this more in the section on *How relevance is determined*. Relatedly, search **click-through** engines can measure how often users click on a result, called the **click-through** **measurement** **measurement**; the more users who click on a link, the more likely it is that the page at the other end of the link is of interest.

4.3.4   How search engines work

While using a search engine is usually straightforward, you may have noticed some curious functionality sometimes. For example, a search engine such as Google returns a list of results and provides a brief excerpt from the webpage; an example of searching for `indiana  linguistics` is provided in Figure 4.2. Occasionally, when you click on a link, the page is gone or the content is radically different.

Department of Linguistics: Indiana University

Lauri Karttunen was awarded the Linguistics Department's Distinguished Alumni Award on April 23. Dr. Karttunen received his Ph.D. in Linguistics from ...
www.indiana.edu/~lingdept/ - Cached - Similar

Figure 4.2   A Google search result for `indiana  linguistics`

It would be nice to know why these links die: What is going on in the background to make this happen? To understand this, we need to know that most of the work associated with satisfying a query is done ahead of time, long before the user has even thought of carrying out the search.

Specifically, it works like this: at some point in time, the engine crawls the web, following links and finding every webpage it can. It stores a copy of all web pages (this takes a lot of space, which is why search engines need huge data centers), and it also creates an **index** **index** of all the pages it crawls. This index is used to provide efficient access to information about a large number of pages (e.g., Google currently searches over 1 *trillion* pages, http://googleblog.blogspot.com/2008/07/we-knew-web-was-big.html). The search engine determines the relevance of each page using only the record of the page's contents **snippets** that is stored in the index. The index is also used to construct the so-called **snippets**, the little extracts that are provided along with the search results. There is no guarantee that the page is still there: all that the engine really knows is that the index contains information about the way the page looked at the moment the index was built.

The indices of real-world search engines are pretty complicated, and they do far more than simply maintaining a list of words. They will also track the position of words on a page, note whether the words are in the title, contain information about the metadata and its trustworthiness, and so on. Nevertheless, the basic ideas are simple, and it is to these that we now turn.

Search engine indexing

Search engines need to store data in a way that enables them to have efficient access to it later on. Think about it: if you have one trillion pieces of information, you cannot store them just anywhere and hope to find what you want quickly; the pages need to be indexed, so that the search engine can find what it needs quickly later on. Conceptually, this is similar to the index at the back of a book: it helps us find terms quickly. In this section, we are going to examine the basics of how to index data, basing our discussion on Manning, Raghavan, and Schütze (2008).

To begin with, as a search engine crawls the web, it builds a **term-by-document matrix**. The term-by-document matrix shows which terms (i.e., words) appear in which documents (in this case, webpages). We can get a sense of what happens by looking at part of a term-by-document matrix for a few mystery novels in Figure 4.3. We use words here, but lemmas or stems may also be used.

	Affair at Styles	Secret Adversary	Sherlock Holmes
Poirot	1	0	0
Sherlock	0	0	1
adventure	1	1	1
exceedingly	1	0	1
strychnine	1	0	0
subsided	1	0	1

Figure 4.3 Excerpt from term-by-document matrix for mystery novels

In Figure 4.3 terms are listed in the left-hand column, and for each novel (e.g., Agatha Christie's *The Mysterious Affair at Styles*), a 1 denotes that the word appears in that document, and a 0 denotes that it does not.

In this process, common words may be left out; these are often referred to as **stop words**. This means that words like "I" or "the" are not always included in the index or subsequently in searching. There are two benefits to this: first, it saves time and effort if you ignore words and do not need to store them; secondly, these words are uninformative, because they appear in almost every document, and are very unlikely to make a difference to judgments about the relevance of a particular document.

Recall that this matrix building is done offline; that is, before the search engine is queried. Thus, we can afford to do extra work to make the search process efficient. Specifically, we can take the term-by-document matrix and derive a representation that is faster for page lookup, namely what is called an **inverted index**. If we assume that every document has a unique ID, in this case a number (e.g., *Secret Adversary* = 2), then we can see an example of part of an inverted index in Figure 4.4. Each term now points to a list of documents in which it appears. This is a very efficient structure: if the query contains the word `strychnine`, for example, a single access into the inverted index gives us a list of all the documents in which that word appears.

Poirot	→1, 4, 13, 15, 45, ...
Sherlock	→3, 111, ...
adventure	→1, 2, 3, 4, 5, 9, 15, ...
exceedingly	→1, 3, 11, 25, ...
strychnine	→1, 15, 60, ...
subsided	→1, 3, 12, 13, 25, ...

Figure 4.4 Excerpt from inverted index for mystery novels

When someone searches for `adventure AND strychnine`, we need to combine information from two different lines of the inverted index. This is quite straight-forward: simply take the **intersection** of the two document lists to which "adventure" and "strychnine" point. In this case, the intersection will certainly contain at least documents 1 and 15, and possibly others not shown in Figure 4.4.

intersection

For even more complex queries, there are steps that can be taken to ensure that query processing is efficient. Consider if someone searches for `poirot AND adventure AND strychnine`. In this case we have to intersect three lists. We know that the result of intersecting three lists is the same as first intersecting two lists, then intersecting the result with the third list. It is up to us to decide which two lists should be handled first, and which list should be left until last. This choice is not going to affect the final result, but can it affect the efficiency of the process of getting to the result?

To answer this, we need to understand that the task of intersecting lists takes longer the longer the lists are. For example, "adventure" has a long list of documents, as mystery novels seem frequently to reference adventures. If we take another frequent word, such as "murder", the result will be another long list, and it is likely that their intersection will be lengthy, too; that is, they have much in common. But "strychnine" is less common, and "poirot" tends only to appear in Agatha Christie books, so these lists are shorter. For efficiency, we can intersect the shortest lists first. This will probably be effective, because the intersection of two short lists is likely to be short. Thus, internally, the search engine looks at the query words, finds the length of their document lists, and reworks the query to specify the order of operations. In this case, for example, `poirot AND adventure AND strychnine` becomes `(poirot AND strychnine) AND adventure`. Strictly speaking, this strategy does not guarantee optimal efficiency, because it could turn out that the intersection of two lists that are short but very similar will be longer than the intersection of two other lists that are long but very dissimilar. Nevertheless, in practice, the strategy of doing the shortest lists first is a very good one, and saves a great deal of time and effort.

Under the Hood 6
A brief tour of HTML

HTML stands for *Hyper-Text Mark-up Language*, and it is what webpages have often been written in. Regardless of whether it is HTML or some other web mark-up language, an important concept in viewing webpages is that what you see is not identical to what the web programmer wrote. The page is written in a web mark-up language, and web browsers choose how to display what is written. For example, the HTML code may specify that some text is a header, but the specific font size and shade of bolding can vary across browsers.

If you go to a webpage and select *View Page Source*, you will see the raw HTML. It resembles English, but has extra features. For example, looking at the English Wikipedia page (http://en.wikipedia.org/wiki/Main_Page), we find an excerpt of the source code shown in Figure 4.5. This is what lies underneath the page; when displayed in the Safari browser, we find links to *Arts, Biography*, and *Geography* pages in the upper right-hand corner of the page.

As can be seen, the code is composed of different HTML tags, which are found between angled brackets, for example `<li>`, which marks a list item. For every opening bracket (e.g., `<li>`), there is a closing bracket (e.g., `</li>`). You can see how to alter text in Figure 4.6.

Many HTML tags have obvious effects on the display of the page, but some have more subtle effects. Most browsers display the content of the `<TITLE>` tag not on the page itself, but rather in the title bar of the window within which the page appears. Even more strikingly, the contents of the `<META>` tags are there solely to give passing web crawlers information about the content of the page.

```
<td style="width:11%; font-size:95%;">
<ul>
<li><a href="/wiki/Portal:Arts"
     title="Portal:Arts">Arts</a></li>
<li><a href="/wiki/Portal:Biography"
     title="Portal:Biography">Biography</a></li>
<li><a href="/wiki/Portal:Geography"
     title="Portal:Geography">Geography</a></li>
</ul>
</td>
```

Figure 4.5 An excerpt of web source code from English Wikipedia (accessed July 13, 2009)

(Continued)

Under the Hood 6
A brief tour of HTML

(Cont'd.)

These tags should have no effect on the display whatsoever. Other tags exist to give the browser nonbinding advice about how to display the content. It is up to the browser to decide whether to follow this advice.

HTML also gives you the tools to create links to other webpages. The < A > tag (short for *anchor*) does this, so you can find HTML code such as < a href = "http://ling.osu.edu" >Click here</a>. Any person or program that understands HTML will be able, by finding all the < A > tags, to trace the links that lead away from this page. We will see the usefulness of this shortly.

```
<p>We'll throw in some <b>bold</b>, <i>italicized</i>,
    and <u>underlined</u> text.</p>
```
We'll throw in some **bold**, *italicized*, and underlined text.

Figure 4.6 Basic HTML tags

How relevance is determined

Now that we know a little more about what goes on in the background, we can begin to look at how search engines are able to match queries to content on webpages with a high degree of precision. And we have the tools to understand how search engines can group pages into meaningful clusters.

As mentioned, search engines use many different kinds of information to determine webpage relevance. One method in particular has become increasingly **PageRank** influential over the years, and it is referred to as **PageRank**. This algorithm was developed by Larry Page and Sergey Brin and was used as the basis of their start-up company in the late 1990s: Google. It relies heavily on the idea that when a person bothers to make a link to some other page, the page is probably somehow noteworthy, at least for the person making the link.

We will sketch out the ideas behind the PageRank algorithm here, by looking at a particular example of page linking. Consider Figure 4.7, where each square represents a webpage. In this case, pages X, Y, and Z all link to page A. The question is whether these links are any better or worse than those that link to page B, shown in Figure 4.8.

The way PageRank determines which pages are better is to reason about the relationship between links and popularity. If a site has a large number of incoming links, it must be well-known, and this could be because people like it.

Thus, we calculate importance based on popularity, where popularity is estimated based on how many sites link to a website and how popular each one of those is. In order to compare how popular website A is compared to website B, we can add up how popular each incoming site is. It might help to think of the situation like this:

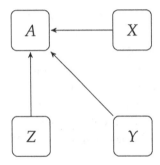

Figure 4.7 Weblinking: X, Y, and Z all link to A

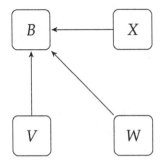

Figure 4.8 Weblinking: V, W, and X all link to B

each site that links to A gets to vote for A, and each of them gets a different number of votes based on how popular each of them is.

If you are bothered by the idea that Google is based on a popularity contest, you can replace the word *popular* with the word *authoritative* in the discussion above. And if you do not like that, you can just use the term *PageRank* instead. The algorithm does not care what we call our measure of quality, only that every page has a score, and that the score of a page is related to the score of the pages that provide its incoming links.

To see how the calculations are done, consider Figure 4.9. Here, X casts 15 votes for A, Y casts 10, and Z casts 20. This may make intuitive sense, but we are stuck with

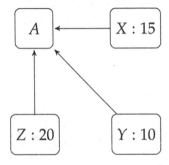

Figure 4.9 Pages with weights

an immediate problem: the website A now has 45 votes, and that is clearly too many. After all, the most popular incoming site only had a score of 20. This way of adding will lead to ever-increasing popularity scores.

We want a solution that distributes votes from pages in a sensible way. The solution PageRank uses is to spread out each page's votes through all the pages to which it links. Viewing this as a voting process, it means that each webpage must split its votes among all the pages to which it links. In Figure 4.10, for example, the webpage X has 15 votes, and it links to 3 pages. Thus, it casts 5 votes for each of those pages.

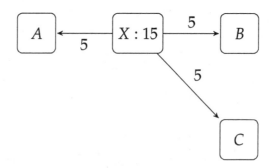

Figure 4.10   Dividing the weights

Let us assume, then, that after spreading votes out among their different webpages, A's final score is 12. Which leads us to ask: 12 of what? What does it mean to have a score of 12? Is that good or bad?

Truth be told, scores on their own do not mean much. We need to compare the score to other websites to determine a relative rank. If website B's score is 10 and A's is 12, we can say that A is preferred, and we may want to call it *authoritative*. If, when the search engine analyzes the words on the pages, two pages seem to be equally relevant in their content, then the page rank score can be used to determine which webpage is placed nearer to the top of the results list.

To sum up so far, there are two main factors to consider when calculating a ranking for a website based on its weblinks: links coming into a website, and links going out of a website. The formula (at least for Google) captures these properties. It can be seen in (32) for webpage A with three pages linking to it: we use $R(X)$ to mean the *rank of page X* and $C(X)$ to refer to the *number of pages going out of page X.*

(32) $R(A) = \dfrac{R(X)}{C(X)} + \dfrac{R(Y)}{C(Y)} + \dfrac{R(Z)}{C(Z)}$

Let us make sure that this formula represents what we want it to. First, we add up the scores of the different pages coming into A (e.g., $R(X)$) because, in order to know how popular A is, we need to know how popular everyone else thinks it is. Secondly, we divide each score by the number of pages going out of X, Y, and Z (e.g., $C(X)$)

because we are spreading out their weights among all the pages to which they link. And this tells us how popular a site is, one factor used in ranking results.

4.4   Searching semi-structured data with regular expressions

As mentioned in the introduction to this chapter, *semi-structured data* contains some categorization, but is not fully structured. Wikipedia entries and the Internet Movie Database (http://www.imdb.com) are good examples: since users add much of the content, the way the sites are structured and categorized varies from user to user. Yet there is structure there, even if it takes a little more work to uncover.

Looking at the Internet Movie Database, let us compare the pages of two different actresses, namely Nancy Cartwright and Yeardley Smith, who are the voices for Bart and Lisa Simpson, respectively, from the popular television show *The Simpsons*. (If you are unfamiliar with *The Simpsons*, we fear that you may also not know what a television is.) On October 27, 2011, the page for Nancy Cartwright listed her as *Nancy Cartwright (1)* since there are multiple actresses with that name, yet Yeardley Smith had no such designation; implicitly, it is *Yeardley Smith (1)*. Additionally, Yeardley Smith's bio page listed a *Mini Biography*, while Nancy Cartwright's bio page only listed *Trivia*.

Looking at their biography/trivia information, consider how the information is written down, as illustrated in Figure 4.11.

Spouse
Daniel Erickson   (18 May 2001 – 8 September 2008) (divorced)
Christopher Grove   (1990 – 1992) (divorced)

Trade Mark
Best known as the voice of "Lisa Simpson" on the TV show "The Simpsons" (1989)

Figure 4.11   Some snippets of trivia about Yeardley Smith

Note, first of all, that if we are searching for dates, they come in different formats with different information: "1990" vs. "18 May 2001". It is likely that there are also dates listed on imdb in the format "May 18 2001" or "May 18, 2001". Secondly, note that there is no field for *voice* (at least on the bio page), just as there is often no information distinguishing an actor's role as a lead role, supporting role, or cameo – yet the information is often there to be had.

Or consider this snippet of trivia about Nancy Cartwright: "Attended Ohio University from 1976–1978 as an interpersonal communication major and was awarded the Cutler Scholarship for academic excellence and leadership." What if we want to find out where different actors went to school? We would have to find patterns such as X University, Y College, or University of Z, as well as misspelled variants of these. Then, there are references such as this one from Parker Posey's bio: "Parker attended high school at R. H. Watkins High School in Laurel, Mississippi, and college at the prestigious SUNY Purchase." Here, "university" is only found as a *U* within an abbreviation. If we also wanted to search for an actor's major, we would have to search for studied X at Y, majored in X, a(n) X major, and so forth. In both cases, we are describing a search not just for specific strings, but for *patterns* in the data.

We are starting to see the need for searching over more complex patterns of words and text. Think also about the following scenarios: (i) In a large document you want to find addresses with a zip code starting with 911 (around Pasadena, CA); you clearly do not want to also find emergency phone numbers in the document. (ii) You want to find all email addresses that occur in a long text. You cannot just search for a few words; you need to specify patterns.

Any time we have to match a complex pattern, regular expressions are useful. A regular expression is a compact description of a set of strings. So, a regular expression can compactly describe the set of strings containing all zip codes starting with 911 (in this case, the regular expression is /911[0-9][0-9]/, which is explained below).

Regular expressions have been extensively studied and their properties are well known (see Under the Hood 7 on finite-state automata and their relation to regular **formal language** expressions). In **formal language theory**, language is treated mathematically, and a **theory** set of strings defines a language. For instance, English is defined as the set of all legitimate English sentences. As in other formalisms, regular expressions as such have no linguistic content; they are simply descriptions of a set of strings encoding a **natural** **natural language** text. While some patterns cannot be specified using regular **language** expressions (see Under the Hood 4 on the complexity of grammar), regular expressions are quite suitable for our purposes.

Regular expressions are used throughout the computer world, and thus there are a variety of Unix tools (grep, sed, etc.), editors (Emacs, jEdit, etc.), and programming languages (Perl, Python, Java, etc.) that incorporate regular expressions. There is even some support for regular expression usage on Windows platforms (e.g., wingrep). The various tools and languages differ with respect to the exact syntax of the regular expressions they allow, but the principles are the same. Implementations are very efficient so that large text files can be searched quickly, but they are generally not efficient enough for web searching.

4.4.1   Syntax of regular expressions

We can now turn to how regular expressions are used to describe strings. In this section we will discuss the basics of the syntax, and in the next section we will walk through the use of regular expressions with one particular tool. Note that while some of the symbols are the same as with basic search operators (e.g., `*`), as outlined in section 4.2, they often have different meanings. Unlike search operators – whose definitions can vary across systems – regular expressions have a mathematical grounding, so the definition of operators does not change.

In fact, regular expressions can consist of a variety of different types of special characters, but there is a very small set of them. In their most basic form, regular expressions have strings of literal characters; examples include `/c/`, `/A100/`, `/natural language/`, and `/30 years!/`. In other words, we can search for ordinary strings just as we would expect, by writing them out. One note on putting regular expressions between forward slashes: this is a common representation, but in the next section we will see that each application has its own way of referring to regular expressions.

To allow for different possibilities, we can add **disjunction**. There is ordinary disjunction, as in `/devoured|ate/` and `/famil(y|ies)/`, which allows us to find variants of words – "devoured" and "ate" in the former case, and "family" and "families" in the latter – and there are character classes, defined in brackets, to specify different possibilities. `/[Tt]he/`, for example, matches either "The" or "the"; likewise, `/bec[oa]me/` matches "become" or "became". Finally, we can specify ranges, as in `/[A-Z]/`, which matches any capital letter. For our earlier problem of finding all zip codes starting with "911", then, we can specify `/911[0-9][0-9]/`, which nicely excludes "911" when followed by a space.

In addition to disjunction, we can use **negation**, to specify characters that we do not want to see. We use the character class notation (`[...]`), with `^` denoting that it is not this class. For example, `/[^a]/` refers to any symbol but a, and `/[^A-Z0-9]/` indicates something that is not an uppercase letter or number.

Regular expressions begin to display their full range of power in the different **counters** available. These counters allow us to specify how often an item should appear. First, we can specify optionality through the `?` operator; `?` means that we can have zero or one of the previously occurring item. For example, `/colou?r/` matches either "color" or "colour". Secondly, we have what is called the Kleene star (`*`), which allows for any number of occurrences of the previous item (including zero occurrences), for instance `/[0-9]* years/`. The third and final counter is very similar, but it stands for one or more occurrences of the previous element and is represented by `+`. So `/[0-9]+dollars/` requires there to be at least one digit, but possibly more.

Another operator that allows us to specify different possibilities is the period (`.`), a wildcard standing for any character. Thus, the query `/beg.n/` designates that there can be any (single) character between "beg" and "n" (*begin, began, beg!n*, etc.).

Because we have defined special uses for a variety of characters, we also want a way to search for those actual characters. For example, how can we search for a question mark (?) when it has a special meaning? To do this, we use **escaped characters**, which allow us to specify a character that otherwise has a special meaning, and we notate this with a backslash: `\*,\+,\?,\(,\),\|,\[,\]`.

disjunction

negation

counter

escaped character

Table 4.1　Summary of Regular Expression Operators

Operator	Notation
1. Parentheses	(…)
2. Counters	? , *, +
3. Literals	a, b, c, …
Escaped characters	\ ?, \ *, \ [, …
Wildcard	.
4. Disjunction	|, […]
Negation	[^…]

operator precedence With a variety of different operators, there can sometimes be confusion about which operator applies first. But there are rules of **operator precedence,** just like in arithmetic, where, for example, in evaluating $4 + 5 \times 6$, we obtain 34 because multiplication has precedence over addition. Likewise, there is a precedence for regular expressions, as summarized in Table 4.1. From highest to lowest, this precedence is: parentheses, counters (*+?), character sequences, and finally disjunction (|). So if we see, for example /ab|cd/, this matches either *ab* or *cd*, because character sequences have precedence over disjunction. (If disjunction had higher precedence, we would match *abd* or *acd*.)

4.4.2　Grep: An example of using regular expressions

To illustrate fully how regular expressions work, we are going to walk through a tool used on a variety of platforms to find sequences in text. This tool is called grep, and it is a powerful and efficient program for searching in text files using regular expressions. It is standard on Unix, Linux, and Mac OSX, and there also are various translations for Windows. The version of grep that supports the full set of operators mentioned above is generally called egrep (for extended grep). By the way, grep stands for "global regular expression print."

We list a variety of examples below. For each, we assume a text file f.txt containing, among other strings, the ones that we mention as matching. The purpose of grep or egrep is to return the lines that contain a string matching the regular expression.

Strings of literal characters　egrep 'and' f.txt
matches lines with:
and, Ayn Rand, Candy, standalone, …

Character classes:　egrep 'the year [0-9] [0-9] [0-9] [0-9]' f.txt
matches lines with:
the year 1776, the year 1812a.d., the year 2112, …

Escaped characters: `egrep 'why\?' f.txt`
matches lines with:
`why?, ...`
but does not match lines with:
`why so serious, ...`

Disjunction (|): `egrep 'couch|sofa' f.txt`
matches lines with:
`couch, w sofa, couched, ...`

Grouping with parentheses: `egrep 'un(interest|excit)ing' f.txt`
matches lines with:
`uninteresting, unexciting`
but does not match lines with:
`uninterested, super-exciting`

Any character (.): `egrep 'o.e' f.txt`
matches lines with:
`ore, one, sole, project, ...`

Kleene star (*): `egrep 'sha(la)*' f.txt`
matches lines with:
`sha, shala, shalala, ...`
but does not match lines with:
`shalaaa, shalashala, ...`

One or more (+): `egrep 'john+y' f.txt`
matches lines with:
`johny, johnny, johnnny, ...`
but does not match lines with:
`johy`

Optionality (?): `egrep 'joh?n' f.txt`
matches lines with:
`jon, john, jones, ...`

This should give you a flavor for regular expressions and a good sense of what they can accomplish. We have a few exercises at the end of the chapter to get you more acquainted with regular expressions, but to use them in your daily life, you should look for a tutorial online or exercises in a book, as regular expressions take practice to master. Although they may be new to you, regular expressions are useful in a variety of purposes, including searching for linguistically interesting patterns, an issue we turn to below. There are thus a range of regular expression resources to play with!

Under the Hood 7
Finite-state automata

Regular expressions are closely related to finite-state automata (FSAs). In this section we will explain what finite-state automata are and show how the connection can be made to regular expressions.

To get a sense of what FSAs are and how they correspond to strings, we can start with an example. Figure 4.12 shows a finite-state automaton that matches a single letter *a*. It has two states (1 and 2) and one edge that links them. This edge is labeled with the letter *a*. There is a start arrow marking state 1 as initial and special formatting (a double circle) marking state 2 as final. The idea of a finite-state automaton is that it matches all the paths that can go from the initial state to the final state. This automaton is especially boring: it only has one path, and the only sequence it can match is the single letter *a*.

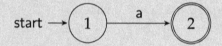

Figure 4.12   A first automaton

We say that the automaton generates the language corresponding to the paths. The language generated by the simple automaton in Figure 4.12 is just as boring: the sequence containing a single letter *a* is in the language, and everything else is not. (Recall back in Section 4.4 that we can talk about languages as being sets of strings.) We relax this a little in Figure 4.13, which allows *b* and *c* as well as *a*. This automaton is still pretty dull, and so is the language that it generates (three different one-letter strings).

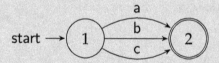

Figure 4.13   A second automaton

The next automaton (shown in Figure 4.14) is less dull. What has happened here is that we have made an edge, labeled with *a* that loops around as many times as necessary, making *a*'s, then finishes off with a choice of *a*, *b*, or *c*. This is powerful, because it describes an infinite (but still possibly dull) language consisting of all the strings that start off with a sequence of *a*'s and finish with at least one of either *a*, *b*, or *c*. This language can also be described by the regular expression /a*(a|b|c)/.

It turns out to be useful to think of regular expressions as a *notation* for finite-state automata. That is, when we write down a regular expression, it is a

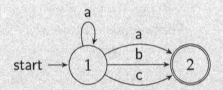

Figure 4.14   An automaton with a loop

precise description of some finite-state automaton. Going the other way, if you have an FSA, you can write it down as a corresponding regular expression. This allows us to use finite-state automata as a way of being mathematically precise about what regular expressions mean. We say that finite-state automata provide the semantics for regular expressions. In computer science and linguistics, when talking about *semantics*, you can think of the term as a synonym for *mathematically precise meaning*.

Thus, every finite-state automaton can be associated with a set of strings that it accepts. One of the simplest automata has two states (1 and 2) and a single arc, labeled with the letter *a* running from 1 to 2, just as in Figure 4.12. This automaton, which we will call *x*, accepts *a* and nothing else. The set of strings that it accepts is therefore {*a*}. Another simple automaton is the one with two states 1 and 2, a single arc running from 1 to 2, this time with the label *b*. This automaton, which we call *y*, accepts *b*, the sole member of the set {*b*}.

Now that we have two automata, *x* and *y*, we can think about combining them. We can do this in two ways: in parallel or in sequence. If we take the first option, we create an automaton with two states, as before, but with two arcs, each running from 1 to 2, with one of the arcs labeled *a* and the other labeled *b*. This new automaton, which we can give the name *x* times *y*, corresponds to the language {*a*, *b*}. Obviously, we could keep adding arcs between 1 and 2, creating automata that accept more and more single letters; Figure 4.13 shows the case for three letters. If we instead choose to combine *x* and *y* in series, we get a three-state automaton, with states 1, 2, and 3, one arc between 1 and 2, and one between 2 and 3. We can then, for example, make *x* . *y* (*x* concatenated with *y*), which has the label *a* on the arc between 1 and 2 and the label *b* on the arc between 2 and 3, as in Figure 4.15. This accepts just one two-letter string: the single member of the set {*ab*}.

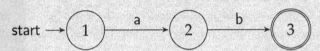

Figure 4.15   An automaton with three states

We could also make *y* . *x* with the label *b* on the arc between 1 and 2 and *a* on the arc between 2 and 3. Generalizing this, it is easy to see how to build automata that accept strings of length 3, 4, 5,

(Continued)

ntics

Under the Hood 7
Finite-state automata
(Cont'd.)

and greater, and how to add labeled arcs so as to accommodate more symbols, such as all the lower-case letters a–z.

As automata involve movement, it may help to think of traveling by plane and to view an automaton as your flight path. In this case, the states of the automaton correspond to airports and the arcs correspond to flight routes between the airports. If you have flown, you know that at every airport you are asked for a new boarding pass, with a new "label" indicating your next destination. You reach your destination only if you are able to present the right boarding passes in the right sequence. This is illustrated in Figure 4.16: to go from Indianapolis (IND) to Atlanta (ATL) to Orlando (MCO), you start in IND, and if you have a boarding pass to Atlanta, you are allowed to go to ATL. Any other boarding pass and your trip fails. Likewise, you next need a boarding pass to Orlando to make it to MCO. Roughly speaking, this is how a finite-state automaton works; instead of boarding passes, though, we try to match strings.

Returning to our automata examples, the simple two-state automaton with

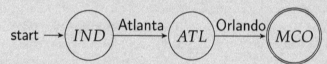

Figure 4.16   Viewing an automaton as a flight path

which we started is not the simplest, after all. There are also automata with just one state. Such automata only make sense if their single state is both an initial (starting) state and a final (accepting) state; that is, a legitimate end point. The simplest automaton of all has one state and no arcs and accepts exactly one string: the empty string ".

More usefully, there are also one-state automata that have arcs. For example, if 1 is both initial and final, and there is a single arc looping from 1 to 1 labeled with a – as in Figure 4.17 – the automaton accepts any sequence made up exclusively of as. These include a, aa, aaa and indeed the empty string " (which can be viewed, somewhat strangely, as a sequence of no a's at all). Notice that this automaton, while finite, accepts an infinite set of strings. There is no limit on the number of a's.

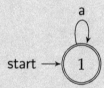

Figure 4.17   A one-state automaton with a loop

Obviously, we can add more arcs, with more labels, and make one-state automata that accept a larger range of strings. And we can combine these automata in series or in parallel to accept yet further strings. For example, it is easy to make an automaton that accepts a series of *a*s followed by a series of *b*s, as in Figure 4.18, which corresponds to /a*b*/. (Think about how you would have to change it to correspond to /a+b+/.)

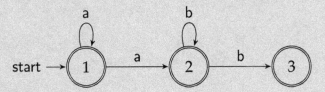

Figure 4.18   An automaton for /a*b*/

Perhaps the most important take-home point from this section is that for every regular expression you can write down, there is a corresponding finite-state automaton, and for every automaton, you can write down a corresponding regular expression. Automata are transparent (all that you need to understand are states, arcs, labels, and initial and final states), but regular expressions are more concise because they have convenient features like the * and + operators and other abbreviations. It is somewhat tiresome to write out all the arcs that are involved in the automaton that goes with a regular expression like / [A-Z] [a-z]+/, but reassuring to know that you could do it if you wanted to. It would be very reasonable for a simple implementation of regular expression matching, for example, to create and make use of the corresponding automata as internal data structures.

4.5   Searching text corpora

The final type of searching context we will examine is searching through corpora (singular form = **corpus**), which are collections of text. There are a variety of corpora available, containing the works of various writers, newspaper texts, and other genres. Once these documents have been collected and electronically encoded, we can search these texts to find particular expressions (see Under the Hood 8 on *Searching for linguistic patterns*), and the bigger the corpus, the more likely we are to find what we want. Luckily, corpora can be quite large. The British National Corpus (BNC, http://www.natcorp.ox.ac.uk), for example, is a 100-million-word collection representing a wide cross-section of contemporary written and spoken British English, and there is also a similar American National

corpus

Corpus (ANC, http://www.americannationalcorpus.org). Another example of a useful large corpus is the European Parliament Proceedings Parallel Corpus 1996–2006 (http://www.statmt.org/europarl/), which has 11 languages and 50 million words for each language.

Both the BNC and the European Parliament corpus can be searched using online web forms, and these generally allow the use of regular expressions for advanced searching. To provide efficient searching in large corpora, in these search engines regular expressions over characters are sometimes limited to single tokens (i.e., words).

4.5.1   Why corpora?

If all we want are large datasets, why not just use web searches all the time? After all, the web is the largest data source we have. While this is true, there are some downsides to using web data. To begin with, if there is any case in which we want uncorrupted data – or data that has been edited or proofread – then the web is clearly not a good source. Certainly, there is "clean" data on the web, such as newspaper websites, but we cannot easily determine the type of language being used (see Chapter 5, though, on Classifying Documents). Furthermore, there often are duplicate documents on the internet, for instance stories distributed by Associated Press and posted on multiple news websites. If we search for something and find it 10,000 times, how can we ensure that 500 of those times were not duplicates?

Consider another issue: What if we are interested in what people in the USA think about a particular topic? Which websites are written by people in America? Suffixes of website names (e.g., .edu) give some clues, but these are not foolproof, as, for example, Americans studying abroad may maintain a website hosted on their school's computer (e.g., .uk). If we want to ask what women in America say about a topic or what Southern women say about a topic, we are in a deeper quagmire using the internet, with its lack of classified webpages.

So, although bigger data is generally better, there are times we only want relevant and classified data. This is especially true if we want to make scientific generalizations on the basis of some set of data: we need to have the data collected in such a way that we know what its properties are, in order to know how any results may be generalized. Because corpora are usually carefully collected bodies of text, they allow us to draw more solid conclusions.

The Semantic Web

annotation Corpora have also been good places to find various types of **annotation**; that is, mark-up of different properties of the text. To think about what kind of annotation is useful for different tasks, let us start by considering what kind of annotation we would like to have in webpages.

We mentioned in Section 4.3.4 that the PageRank algorithm works by taking linking relationships between webpages and deducing how reliable each page is. But using weblinks is a very coarse way of determining the relationship between two pages. It would be good if humans could specify not just the fact that two webpages are related, but how they are related.

The **Semantic Web** is a recent innovation that helps address this issue by incor- **Semantic Web** porating more information about a webpage's content. The framework of the Semantic Web allows web designers to specify how concepts and webpages are related to one another. For example, a webpage can be annotated with a description like *car*. If a *hatchback* is specified as a subclass of *car*, and another webpage states that *ToyotaMatrix* represents a type of *hatchback*, then we can infer that *ToyotaMatrix* represents a type of *car*. Such hierarchical groupings can assist in determining whether a search for, for instance, the term hatchback should return the Toyota's page. A company like Toyota, Mercedes-Benz, or whoever else might be prepared to put effort into such annotation so that consumers can easily find out information about its products.

The relations we are describing form a hierarchy of data, where words are synonyms, hypernyms, and hyponyms of each other (see also Section 7.6). The OWL Web Ontology Language makes specific what kinds of relations can be defined. This allows web designers to create an **ontology**, specifying the concepts within a **ontology** world and their relationships. For marketing research firms (e.g., J.D. Power and Associates), such ontologies are important for articulating the relationships between consumer goods, especially big-ticket items such as cars. Another way of stating what the Semantic Web does is that it makes explicit some of the structure that is already present in this unstructured web data.

4.5.2   Annotated language corpora

As it turns out, mark-up conveying semantic properties is used frequently with language data, in order to annotate different linguistic properties. As just mentioned, such information can improve searching by knowing the content of a document. But annotating linguistic properties has a wider reach. Consider the fact that knowing a word's part of speech can help us differentiate between one use of a word and another (e.g., for *plant*). If we have a corpus annotated with grammatical properties such as part of speech, then this can help us build tools that can automatically mark part of speech. This gets us into **corpus linguistics**, which is the study of language and **corpus** linguistics through the use of corpus data. **linguistics**

Linguistic annotation can come in many different forms: morphological annotation (subword properties like inflection, derivation, and compounding), morphosyntactic annotation (part-of-speech tags), syntactic annotation (noun phrases, etc.), semantic annotation (word senses, verb argument annotation, etc.), and discourse annotation (dialog turns, speech acts, etc.).

Annotation is useful not just for providing information to, for example, search engines, but for training natural language processing (NLP) tools: the technology can learn patterns from corpus annotation. Corpus annotation is also useful for finding linguistic examples. Questions such as the following can be most easily answered if we have different kinds of morphosyntactic annotation, for example:

- What is the plural form of "fish"?
- Are there subjectless sentences in German?
- Is it possible in English to have something between a noun and its modifying relative clause?

Let us consider the case of **part-of-speech** (POS) annotation and look at an example of how to represent it. For POS annotation, we need to associate a POS tag with every word, as in Figure 4.19.

```
I/PRP will/MD then/RB maybe/RB travel/VB directly/RB on/IN to/IN
                            Berlin/NNP
```

Figure 4.19   POS annotation

An example of syntactic annotation is given in Figure 4.20. This is the same tree as in Figure 2.9, but represented differently. Importantly, the bracketing given here is systematic and completely text-based, so that computers can easily process it. Other annotation types include those for word sense, semantic predicate-argument structure, discourse relations, and so on.

```
(S (NP (Pro Most)
       (PP (P of)
           (NP (D the) (N ducks))))
   (VP (V play)
       (NP (AdjP (Adv extremely)
                 (Adj fun))
           (N games)))))
```

Figure 4.20   Syntactic annotation

Under the Hood 8
Searching for linguistic patterns on the web

Most of this chapter has been dedicated to issues related to searching for particular content. Since many of you are likely interested in language and its properties, we are going to turn to an issue of interest to linguists: using corpora to find interesting linguistic patterns and their frequency of usage. For example, we might have questions like these to investigate:

- To what extent is a new word or construction entering the language (e.g., *phishing*) and who is using it?
- How are adjectives ordered with respect to each other in English (e.g., do color words follow other adjectives)?
- Is it more common to say one term or another, such as "strong accent" vs. "thick accent"?

Annotated corpora help us address these questions, but we might also wonder: Is it possible to search the web to get an idea of what is happening in the language? After all, search engines on the internet provide a vast amount of data that could have some bearing on linguistic searching.

Let us say that I want to help a friend learning English to see some of the quirks of English. So, I tell my friend that "thick accent" is a better phrase in English than "strong accent". But then I second-guess myself. Is "strong accent" actually acceptable?

One way I can get a sanity check on my intuitions is to compare their uses on the internet. Searching Google (February 11, 2008) I find 87,200 hits for "strong accent" and 141,000 for "thick accent". So, while there seems to be a slight preference for "thick accent", both appear to be in use. Investigating when they are used, of course, will require some closer inspection – for example, "strong accent" is often a music term – but these numbers give me a good starting point.

As another example, take the case of how we order adjectives in English. Quality adjectives are said always to precede color adjectives, and thus "little red car" is acceptable, but "red little car" sounds somewhat odd. We check this and find 8,860,000 hits on Google for "little red" and 120,000 hits for "red little" (February 11, 2008). So, I feel comfortable telling my English-learning friend to take note of this property.

Again, we also need to do qualitative analysis to make sure that these cases are exactly what we think they are. Why, for example, do we get any cases of "red little" at all? As it turns out, many of these cases have some other factors at play; for instance, a book title like *Little Red, Little Blue* is one of the top results for "red little". This shows that search engines can only be used for very coarse linguistic analysis.

While using a search engine to deduce linguistic patterns can give you very broad ideas of how people use language, it must be approached with caution. For one thing, as we have discussed, it is important to know how the words you searched for are actually being used. Further, it turns out that search engine counts are not always 100% reliable.

Take the following example (June 20, 2011):

(Continued)

Under the Hood 8
Searching for linguistic patterns on the web
(Cont'd.)

- A search for `markus` on Google returns 291,000,000 pages.
- A search for `dickinson` on Google returns 61,000,000 pages.
- A search for `markus OR dickinson` returns 413,000,000 pages.

You are not misreading that. Even though the last query should return no more than 352,000,000 pages – the combined set of pages from the first two queries – it returns many more. And in previous searches two years before, the disjunctive search returned the fewest hits.

There are many possible reasons for web counts demonstrating odd behavior – such as the possibility that Google is storing multiple, slightly different copies of its databases – but the upshot is that you should not use web counts for much more than a sanity check.

Checklist

After reading the chapter, you should be able to:

- Describe the pros and cons of searching in structured and unstructured data.
- Form well-thought-out Boolean queries.
- Describe how search engines rank results and index pages.
- Understand and use regular expressions.
- Know what annotated language corpora are and why they are useful.

Exercises

1. **ALL**: For each of the following, describe how you would approach the search problem. Be sure to outline which resources you would use (e.g., library catalog, a particular online structured database, etc.), as well as those you would not, and discuss the rationale.
   (a) Finding the whereabouts of an old friend with a common name (e.g., *Tim Lee*).
   (b) Finding general information on what the Lincoln–Douglas debates were.
   (c) Finding a general quote, or quotes, from the Lincoln–Douglas debates that will support a theory that Abraham Lincoln was not completely anti-slavery.
   (d) Finding a particular quote from the Lincoln–Douglas debates that you can only partially remember.
   (e) Finding quotes from the Lincoln–Douglas debates that have their origin in the Bible.

2. **ALL:** What do you think the relationship is between how much *prior knowledge* you have about a topic and the amount of *structure* you require in the database you search through?

3. **ALL:** Imagine that there are 11 books in a library with the following subject fields:

    1) rock paper   7) rock paper scissors
    2) rock scissors   8) rock paper bomb
    3) rock bomb   9) rock scissors bomb
    4) paper scissors   10) paper scissors bomb
    5) paper bomb   11) rock paper scissors bomb
    6) scissors bomb

    Looking at the list of queries below, which of the subject numbers do they match? For example, rock AND bomb matches 3, 8, 9, and 11.
    (a) rock OR paper OR scissors
    (b) rock AND (paper OR scissors)
    (c) (rock AND paper) OR (scissors AND bomb)
    (d) (rock OR paper) AND (scissors OR bomb)
    (e) rock AND (paper OR (scissors AND bomb))
    (f) ((rock AND paper) OR scissors) AND bomb

4. **ALL:** The website http://www.googlewhack.com outlines the internet game of Googlewhacking. On the site there are lists of pairs of words, without using quotation marks, which generate exactly one – that is, one and only one – result on http://www.google.com. Some previous examples are `squirreling dervishes` and `inculcating skullduggery`.
    The rules for googlewhacking are:
    *   Words must be in Google's dictionary.
    *   Google determines uniqueness; that is, the number of counts.
    *   Word lists or randomly generated text are not allowed as googlewhacks.
    Attempt to find a googlewhack, or as few hits as possible, using only two words without quotation marks. In doing so, discuss the following:
    (a) What kinds of linguistic properties are you relying on to find a googlewhack?
    (b) How are unrelated words actually related?
    (c) Will there ever be a day when obtaining a googlewhack becomes impossible? (Is that day now?)
    (d) What is the relation of this exercise to searching for content that you actually want to find?
    (e) What are your general search strategies for this challenge?
    (f) Can you use the feedback from one search to help refine your searching?

5. **ALL:** For the following scenarios, describe whether precision or recall is more important and why.
    *   Identifying cases where a cancer-curing drug has a side effect of nausea.
    *   Identifying cases where a cancer-curing drug has a side effect of death.

- Identifying cars running red lights.
- Identifying and removing weeds that look like (desired) native flowers in your garden.

6. **MATH**: When we talked about how weblinking is used to rank webpages, we mentioned how one page's popularity helps determine another's. But there's a problem: Where do we start? How can we know another page's popularity if it, too, is based on other pages' popularity?
    Assume that we initially assign every page a score of 1.
    (a) If every incoming page has the same score, namely 1, what is the new score of a webpage, based on our previous formula?
    (b) Based on your answer to the previous question, what would be the next step for giving every webpage a new score? How many steps would it take until every page had a final score? Or, another way to word it: How could you determine when you are done?

7. **ALL**:
    (a) Describe in your own words why *popularity* is a good heuristic to use for returning search results.
    (b) Provide an example where your search query results in a popular, yet incorrect, result as the first result from a search engine. What rank is your desired result?

8. **ALL**: In the section on regular expressions, we mentioned that some operators have different meanings in basic web searching and in regular expressions. Describe the difference in meaning between the wildcard * allowed in web interfaces and the Kleene star * used in regular expressions.

9. **CS/ALL**: At the book website, we have made available a text file containing a list of movie titles.
    We will walk through how to search through this document using a Mac. For Windows, you will have to use something like WinGrep, but the principles are the same. Versions of `grep` for Windows can be found in a number of places such as http://purl.org/lang-and-comp/grep1, http://purl.org/lang-and-comp/grep2, or http://purl.org/lang-and-comp/grep3.
    Open up Terminal (often found in Applications → Utilities). If `movies.txt` was saved in the directory, type `cd Downloads`. (If it was saved in another directory, substitute that directory name for Downloads to change to the right directory.)
    To view the file, type: `less movies.txt` (to quit viewing just type q).
    To use egrep, type: `egrep "REGULAR-EXPRESSION" movies.txt`
    For example, if I wanted to find all titles containing the letters *a* or *b*, I would type: `egrep "[ab]" movies.txt`
    Note that egrep returns the whole line containing the matching pattern. If you just want to see the exact part that matches, type in: `egrep -o "[ab]" movies.txt`

Write regular expressions to find the movie titles matching the following descriptions. For each one, try to write the shortest regular expression you can. Use egrep to verify that your regular expression finds the right movie titles.

(a) "the" or "The."

(b) Which movies were released between 1990 and 2000 (include both these years as well)?

(c) Which movies have numerals other than their years of release inside them? You are looking for sequel numbers like King Kong 2, and so on.

(d) *h* followed by a letter that is not a vowel.

(e) Search for movies that contain a dot somewhere inside their titles.

10. **ALL**: Assume that you have a huge text file that consists of all the content of the English Wikipedia from a particular day (http://en.wikipedia.org/wiki/Main_Page). You have a report due tomorrow on major and minor holidays of the world, focusing on ones not found in the United States and celebrated during the fall.

(a) Would regular expressions be more or less useful in this context than using the Wikipedia search box?

(b) What is more important to you in this context, precision or recall?

(c) Let us say that we attempt to search for holidays and holy days in August, and we come up with this use of egrep. What is wrong with these queries, and how could we fix them?

    i.   `egrep 'world.*August.*(holidays)?'`

    ii. `egrep 'august hol(i|y)days?'`

    iii. `egrep 'holidays|holy days in August'`

11. **MATH/CS:**

(a) Can you describe the set of strings accepted by the automaton that has a single state (*P*) that is both initial and final, but this time two arcs each looping from *P* to *P*, one of the arcs labeled with *a* and one labeled with *b*?

(b) Can you see how to make an automaton that accepts "", *ab*, *abab*, *ababab*, and so on for ever? That is, can you work out how to arrange the states and arcs so that the available routes from an initial to a final state are the ones that correspond to zero or more repetitions of *ab*?

Notice that the strings in the previous question are exactly the ones that are matched by the regular expression /(ab)*/. How can you change your automaton so that it accepts the strings defined by the regular expression /ab(ab)*/? How about the regular expression /(ab)+/?

12. **MATH/CS:** In Under the Hood 7, we discussed matching strings to finite-state automata. As it turns out, there are some string-matching tasks that are easy to state, but that neither regular expressions nor finite-state automata can do. Consider the following five sets of strings:

- Sequences following the pattern "", *ba*, *baba*, *bababa*, up to any length.
- Sequences following the pattern "", *abc*, *abcabc*, *abcabcabc*, up to any length.

- Sequences consisting of any number of *a*s followed by the same number of *b*s. The pattern is "", *ab*, *aabb*, *aaabbb*, *aaaabbbb*, up to any length.
- Sequences consisting of any number up to 10 of *a*s followed by the same number of *b*s.
- Sequences following the pattern "", *aba*, *abaaba*, *abaabaaba*, up to any length.

  (a) Three of these sets of strings have automata and regular expressions that you will probably find quite quickly and not mind writing down. Which ones are these?

  (b) One of the string sets can be matched by a regular expression and can also be associated with an automaton that accepts exactly the right strings, but neither the expression nor the automaton is something that a normal human being would enjoy writing down. Which one is this?

  (c) One of the string sets can neither be matched by a regular expression nor accepted by a finite-state automaton. Which one is this? And why does this happen?

13. **LING**: At the homepage of Mark Davies (http://purl.org/lang-and-comp/mark.davies), there are several corpora available for which he provides search interfaces. Using the Corpus of Contemporary American English (COCA) and the British National Corpus (BNC), provide evidence that American English and British English speakers either do or do not differ much in their use of "not" with auxiliaries (*have, is/are, ought to, might*), specifically in how often and when they form contractions.

14. **CS**: There are several tools available now to build web corpora; that is, bodies of text culled from the internet. One of these is called BootCaT (*Bootstrap Corpora and Terms from the Web*). Go to the BootCaT website (http://purl.org/lang-and-comp/bootcat) and download the BootCaT tools; you will also need Perl installed on your computer (although you do not need to know the details of how the programs work). Follow the site's instructions to build your own web corpus, consisting of documents related to some topic of your interest. Discuss the following:

  (a) How did you select your seed terms?

  (b) How many duplicate documents did you have in the corpus that had to be removed?

  (c) Sample 10 of the resulting documents. What are the precision and recall, in terms of being related to your domain?

  (d) What purpose could your corpus serve?

Further reading

A good, though technical, introduction to the field of information retrieval is Manning, Raghavan, and Schütze (2008), which thoroughly covers modern techniques needed for retrieving information from massive amounts of data. If you want details on

Google's PageRank algorithm *et al.* you might even want to try reading the paper that describes it (Page *et al.*, 1999).

For more information on Boolean expressions and logical thinking, you can consult a number of textbooks on basic symbolic logic. To obtain more of a focus on logic in the realm of linguistics, look for books on mathematical or formal linguistics, such as Partee, ter Meulen, and Wall (1990).

For corpus linguistics, there are also a number of good textbooks to consult, for example McEnery, Xiao, and Tono (2006), and several excellent websites, such as David Lee's extensive Bookmarks for Corpus-based Linguistics (http://tiny.cc/corpora).

Web as corpus research is growing, and if you are interested in using web data, take a look at the Special Interest Group on the Web as Corpora (SIGWAC): www.sigwac.org.uk/. You might also want to read through papers that give an overview the methodology of using the web as a corpus (e.g., Baroni and Bernardini, 2004; Baroni and Kilgarriff, 2006; Sharoff, 2006). For a word of warning about using web counts, see Kilgarriff (2007).

5

Classifying Documents
From Junk Mail Detection to Sentiment Classification

5.1 Automatic document classification

In the 1960s, if you wanted to read the news, you bought or borrowed a newspaper. If you were unwilling to spend the necessary time, you could read capsule summaries of the most important news in, for example, *Time* magazine's listings section. If you were too busy, or too important, to do even that, you could arrange for someone to read the newspapers for you and give you a summary of what you needed to know. If you were a fruit grower, you could subscribe to *Fruit Growers' News* and get targeted digests of the news that mattered to you.

But now, many newspapers and magazines offer you the chance to read their material online, often at no charge. This is a big change, because the text is now searchable, indexable, and available for reuse. As well as traditional newspapers, there are weblogs and **aggregator sites**. Aggregators pull together information from **aggregator sites** all over the web, providing a digest suitable for the target audience. Aggregators exist for tracking news about cars (www.autoblog.com), greener cars (www.green. autoblog.com), bicycles (www.cyclelicio.us), running (www.coolrunning.com), baby strollers (http://strollersandprams.com), and stationary exercise machines (www.treadmilladviser.com). Even *Fruit Growers' News* is now readily available online (www.fruitgrowersnews.com), as are countless other websites and weblogs catering to specialist interests. These can be money-making ventures if they can deliver an audience that is attractive to advertisers.

Now that text is available online, we have the opportunity to add value by using language technology to process the text. The methods we study in this chapter are all about sorting documents into user-defined **classes**, so the techniques go by the **classes**

Language and Computers, First Edition. Markus Dickinson, Chris Brew and Detmar Meurers.

document classification name of **document classification**. You might, for example, have one class for articles about cars, another (overlapping) class for articles about environmentally friendly cars, and another for articles about fruit trees. In principle, the classes can be anything you like, but in practice you only care about classes that have some commercial or scientific value.

     One of the most commercially significant uses of this technology is known as **sentiment analysis**. Another term that means much the same is **opinion mining**. The key idea is to automate the detection of positive and negative sentiments in documents. For many years companies, political parties, and pressure groups have **opinion mining** used focus groups and audience surveys to track opinions about their products, policies, and positions. Sentiment analysis technology promises to be able to automate this process, trawling the press, internet, and social media for documents that express opinions, organizing them according to the opinions that they express, **data mining** and presenting summaries of the results. This is a kind of **data mining**, one that makes especially heavy use of language technology.

     For example, if you want to find out about the general opinion of the movie *Pearl Harbor*, you can check out Metacritic (www.metacritic.com) or Rotten Tomatoes (www.rottentomatoes.com) and see multiple reviews, by both professionals and lay people. The least favorable user review makes its opinion very clear:

> Ridiculous movie. Worst movie I've seen in my entire life [Koen D. on metacritic]

This person hated it. The most positive review is equally clear:

> One of my favorite movies. It's a bit on the lengthy side, sure. But its made up of a really great cast which, for me, just brings it all together. [Erica H., again on metacritic]

However, most of the reviews for this movie are similar to Alan Scott's from the *New York Times*:

> The Japanese sneak attack on Pearl Harbor that brought the United States into World War II has inspired a splendid movie, full of vivid performances and unforgettable scenes, a movie that uses the coming of war as a backdrop for individual stories of love, ambition, heroism and betrayal. The name of that movie is *From Here to Eternity*. (First lines of Alan Scott's review of *Pearl Harbor*, *New York Times*, May 25, 2001)

While Scott's review finishes up being positive about the fabulous action sequence at the heart of *Pearl Harbor*, and very positive about *From Here to Eternity* (a different, and apparently much better, movie), it drips with sarcasm about everything else in the first movie. That is obvious to a human, but is difficult for a machine to spot. Here is another review that we enjoyed reading:

> The film is not as painful as a blow to the head, but it will cost you up to $10, and it takes three hours. The first hour and forty-five minutes establishes one of the most banal love

triangles ever put to film. Childhood friends Rafe McCawley and Danny Walker (Ben Affleck and Josh Hartnett) both find themselves in love with the same woman, Evelyn Johnson (Kate Beckinsale). [Heather Feher, from http://filmstew.com]

Most review sites use human editors to associate scores with reviews, but this is very much the kind of activity that people want to automate. Some of the automation might be quite easy: a review that dubs the film "ridiculous" and "worst" is probably negative, and one that says "favorite" and "great" is probably positive. But Scott's clever *New York Times* review reads a lot like a very positive review, until you notice that the positive comments are directed at a completely different film. And Feher's backhanded "not as painful as a blow to the head" is also likely to defeat any simple automated system.

"Painful" would be bad, "not painful" might be good, "not as painful as …" suggests that some pain is involved. "Not as painful as a blow on the head" quantifies the pain in a rather alarming way. Language is like that: the meaning twists and turns as each word is added to the next. The authors happen to find Feher's subtle deployment of this roller-coaster effect cool and funny, but it certainly is not going to be easy for a machine to handle.

Clearly, if we can rate movie reviews automatically, we can make our own versions of MetaCritic, and maybe apply the idea to a wider range of topics than is possible when humans are in the loop. But language is subtle, so we cannot be sure that this kind of automation is going to be possible.

The movie sites are interested in telling the difference between good and bad reviews, and also in assigning a numerical score – which generally makes them semi-structured data, as outlined in Section 4.4. In general, when we are interested in assigning a label (e.g., *good* or *bad*) to a document, the task is called **classification**. **classification** In this chapter, we focus on document classification, and show some of the uses to which it can be put. The most important practical examples of this technology are the junk mail filters that try to protect you from the flood of unwelcome email that would otherwise clog up your inbox. They are so good that we normally hardly notice them, but when they stop working or misbehave we realize how important they are in keeping our email interactions manageable. Other uses of the technology are call-routing systems (the systems that try to send you to the best, or perhaps cheapest, person when you phone a helpline), systems for classifying texts by topic, and systems that classify documents according to their **sentiment**. An automated **sentiment** movie review site would need a really good sentiment classifier to judge whether a **classification** review is good or bad. It might also make use of a topic classifier to scan documents and decide whether they are movie reviews in the first place.

5.2   How computers "learn"

Document classification is an example of a computer science activity called machine learning. Machine learning applies not just to language, but to any situation in which the computer is expected to "learn from experience." If we wanted, we could devote pages to discussions of whether machines can ever be said to be truly intelligent, or about the true nature of the so-called learning. We think that these discussions are interesting, and we touch on them very briefly at the end of Chapter 6, but they really belong in a philosophy class, not here.

training set   The basic set-up for machine learning is the following: we have access to a **training set** of examples; we aim to learn from these examples. For the moment, think of the examples as articles from the online version of last month's *New York Times*.

Our long-term goal is to use what we have learned in order to build a robust system that can process future examples of the same kind as those we found in the training set. Think of these future examples as the articles that are going to appear in next month's *New York Times*. Clearly, we have a problem, because future examples are not yet available.

test set   As an approximation, we use a separate **test set** of examples to stand in for the unavailable future examples. Think of these as this month's *New York Times* articles. Since the test set is separate from the training set, the system will not have seen them. If the system performs well on the test set examples, it will probably also do well on the unseen future examples.

There are several important variations on this scheme, at which we take a closer look in the next sections.

5.2.1   Supervised learning

supervised In **supervised learning** we need the training set and the test set to have been labeled
learning with the desired "correct answers." Imagine that there is a news service that provides a stream of uncategorized articles, and that a newspaper needs a system that will sort these articles into separate piles for *News*, *Sport*, *Arts*, *Business*, and *Do not use*. The first step is to make a training set and a test set by labeling a few hundred articles with the desired categories. The second step is to apply machine learning software to the labeled training set. This produces an object called a model, which summarizes what the software has learned from the training set.

The third step is to read the trained model into the machine learning software and use it to generate *predictions* for the test set. Since we are testing the model's ability to make a prediction, we do not let the software see the correct answers for the test set examples. If the software is working well and the model is good, the predictions will often be accurate. We discuss precisely how to measure accuracy in Section 5.4. It is unlikely that the model will be perfect, but it may well be good enough for our purposes. The fourth and final step is to deploy the trained model on unseen examples. It uses what it has learned to sort the articles into the necessary piles. This kind of learning could be the basis for an automated system. A newspaper might have a national news section, a local news section, a business section, and a sports section. The learning goal would be to allocate each article to the correct section. In a real-world application, there will usually be someone who is responsible for checking the results before the paper is printed, because there will almost certainly be some mistakes, no matter how good the machine learning method is.

5.2.2 Unsupervised learning

In **unsupervised learning**, we assume that there are no prespecified categories. **unsupervised** Imagine that the newspaper still has a stream of uncategorized articles, but now the **learning** task is to organize the articles into piles in such a way that **similar** articles occur in the same pile. In this setting, the piles are often called clusters, and the process of organizing the articles into clusters is called **clustering**. Clustering can be used to **clustering** sort articles into groups that could be laid out on the different webpages of an online publication. In that setting, there is no need for the groups to have fixed names.

The reader will be able to notice that articles in a given cluster share something, such as being about sports, but the algorithm would be just grouping articles, not trying to name the clusters. The big plus of this approach is that you do not need a training set, so there is no costly process of going through labeling up the articles. The big negative is that the clusters might not be that intuitive. For example, if you cluster common words, one cluster often turns out to be the words "Monday", "Tuesday", "Wednesday", and "Thursday", with "Friday" off in another cluster. This is because Friday is the only weekday that frequently turns up following "Thank goodness it's ..."

5.3 Features and evidence

When we try to classify or cluster documents, the first step is to identify the properties that are most relevant to the decision we want to make. These properties are called features. In biology, a specimen could have features like scales or gills. If you observe these features, you can be fairly confident that your specimen is a fish. In the same way, when you are trying to decide whether a document is junk mail or not, you should pay attention to features of the document that are likely to help with the decision.

If you are trying to guess whether something is junk mail, these could include things like:

- Whether the document mentions a large sum of money.
- Whether the greeting used in the document is something weird like "Respected Madam" or not.
- Whether there are nonstandard honorifics like "DR. MRS." or not.
- Whether it has words written entirely in upper-case or not. (If the whole message is in upper case, then you might want to think that the writer was angry, or a little crazy, but that is a feature that is not very relevant to junk mail detection.)
- Whether the document uses the words "Viagra" and "sex" close to each other.

None of these features is a certain indicator of junk mail, but all are strong evidence that the document is more likely to be junk than if we had not seen the feature. To make a useful system, we need to tell the computer two things. First, we have to say exactly which features are used and exactly how to detect them. Secondly, we have to specify a way of weighting the evidence provided by the features. It often works well to use machine learning to weight the evidence, rather than doing it by hand, but it **feature** is much harder to automate the first stage of deciding what evidence is potentially **engineering** relevant. This first stage is often called **feature engineering**.

There are two common strategies for doing feature engineering. The first is to use lots of features, in the hope that some of them will be relevant and useful. We will **kitchen sink** call this the **kitchen sink strategy**, since we throw everything we have at the prob- **strategy** lem, including, perhaps, the kitchen sink. If you are building a junk mail detector, you could adopt a version of this strategy by using the words themselves as features: because there are lots of different words in the messages, there will also be lots of different word-based features. It is almost certain that some of these features (such as the presence or absence of the word *enlargement*) will be useful indicators. Of course, there will also be many irrelevant features, such as the presence or absence of the word "apple". If we adopt the kitchen sink strategy, we will need to choose a machine learning method that is good at focusing on the few but important relevant features, and also good at ignoring the many irrelevant features. We will return to this later in the chapter, when we discuss machine learning methods in detail.

Feature engineering actually has two parts. You need to decide which features you would like to collect, then write computer code to do the work of collecting them. One advantage of using words as features is that it is almost as easy to collect and count all the words in a document as it is to collect just a selected few.

The second common strategy for feature engineering is to use careful thought to try to identify, ahead of time, a small set of features that are likely to be relevant. **hand-crafted** We will call this the **hand-crafted** strategy, because it demands from the software developer the same kind of careful and sustained attention to the problem that a skilled woodworker might give to the creation of a beautiful piece of furniture. The software developer uses intuition and experience to select features that seem promising. An advantage of this approach is that there will be fewer irrelevant features, so the machine learning method does not have to be as good at ignoring them as was needed when we were using the kitchen sink features. A disadvantage is that the task of choosing relevant features ahead of time is very difficult. Human beings are not good at this task. Part of the reason is that it is hard to know whether the selected features are general enough. Testing for "DR. MRS." specifically is easy, but it is far harder to cover all the cases of similar features that might arise.

iterative In practice, most software developers use an **iterative method**. They pick an **method** initial set of features, train a classifier, measure how well it does, then try to work out which features are working well, and which less well. By analyzing the results, they come up with ideas for further features, add them in, and retry the machine learning. Depending on the problem, they might go around this cycle multiple times, until satisfactory performance is reached. The key to the success of this iterative approach, which is used on a much larger scale by firms such as Google, is to insist on systematically and thoroughly measuring success rates. With the luxury of very large numbers of users and correspondingly huge data centers, the big web firms can rapidly collect evidence about how well they are doing. This instant feedback makes it possible to try out all kinds of possible improvements, keeping only the ones that seem to work well.

Software developer time is a limited resource, so it may be better to collect a large number of easy but marginally relevant features quickly than to spend a lot of time trying to write code to extract the difficult features.

5.4   Application: Spam filtering

The Text Retrieval Conference (TREC) made available a sample collection of email consisting of about 57,000 junk emails and about 39,000 good emails. Computer scientists and engineers tend to call junk emails *spam*, for reasons that are slightly unclear, but that may involve the obsession that the Monty Python comedy team had with Hormel's processed pork product. They also tend to call nonjunk emails *ham*, presumably on the basis that real ham is to be preferred to any imitation. The authors feel that the spam/ham terminology is a bit geeky, and try to avoid overusing it, but sometimes we cannot help ourselves.

When writing this paragraph, we checked and found that one of us had received 20 instances of spam and 3 of ham in the last 12 hours. All of the spam was successfully filtered out. Many people (including us) trust the filters enough that we hardly **false** ever check for misclassified ham. We say that the **false positive rate** of the spam- **positive rate** detection task is very low (see more below on measurements).

Measuring success

If we are serious about spam detection, we need to be precise about how to measure success. It may seem obvious what we need to measure. We have a series of decisions to make, so we make them, and measure whether we got them right or not. If we classify all the spam as spam, and all the good mail as good, we have succeeded and all is well. Although this is definitely correct, we would be fooling ourselves if we believed that we can design a perfect system that gets every single decision correct. So we need measures that quantify our partial successes and failures and help us to build better systems.

Machine learning is a real-world science, like medicine, and we cannot always afford to wait for complete and reliable evidence to become available, so mistakes are almost inevitable. What we really want is a way of measuring performance that tells us what we need to know about ways in which an imperfect system could be improved.

To do this, we borrow some concepts and evaluation methods that were developed to meet the needs of medical science. These methods apply anywhere, but they turned up first in medicine because of the need to reason effectively with complex and uncertain data. When we run a classifier on a document to decide whether it is spam or not, it is much like running a diagnostic test to collect evidence about whether a patient has a disease or not. Here there are two two-way distinctions to be made:

1. The test can come out either positive or negative.
2. The patient may or may not really have the disease.

So there are four possible ways the situation could be after the test has been given, as shown in Table 5.1.

Table 5.1 A diagnostic test

	Has disease	No disease
Test positive	True positives	False positives
Test negative	False negatives	True negatives

true positive

true negative

false negative

false positive

Perhaps the patient has the disease, and the test correctly returns a positive result. We call this a **true positive**. When the patient does not have the disease, and the test correctly returns a negative result, it is called a **true negative**. In both of these cases, the test is doing its job. But there are two other possible outcomes. The test could return a negative even though the patient has the disease. This is called a **false negative** and is a bad thing, because a patient who needs treatment may not receive it. The fourth possibility is that the test returns a positive even though the patient does not have the disease. This is called a **false positive** and is again a bad thing, because the patient is then likely to receive unnecessary treatment.

probability

Epidemiology example You are an epidemiologist working on a disease (which means that you study health patterns across a population). You know from previous experience that about 10% of the population has the disease. You have a medical test for a disease. The solution is supposed to turn blue if the person has the disease; otherwise, it should stay clear. If the person has the disease, there is a 98% chance that the solution will turn blue and a 2% chance that it will stay clear. If the person does not have the disease, there is a 90% chance that the solution will stay clear and a 10% chance that it will turn blue.

Now suppose that you run the test and the solution does turn blue. You now know that you are dealing with either a true positive or a false positive, but you do not know which it is. Therefore, you cannot tell for sure whether the person has the disease. It surprises most people that in this situation the **probability** that the patient has the disease is only a little more than 50%, since many of us have an intuitive feeling that the answer should be around 90%. If you are not familiar with this kind of probability calculation, do not worry; we will give the details later in the chapter. If you are curious about where the intuitive sense that the answer should be 90% comes from, we will discuss that too. But first, we will introduce some concepts.

5.4.1 Base rates

The numbers in Table 5.1 are affected both by how well the test works, and by whether the disease we are testing for is rare or common. If the disease is rare, the vast majority of the patients tested will be in the second column of the table, and the first column will only have a few entries. If the disease is common, for example influenza, there will be more of a balance, with significant numbers of patients in the first column. In order to make the right decisions about how to interpret test results, medical scientists need to make a numerical estimate of how rare or common the disease is. Their best guess about how likely it is that a random person drawn from the population will have the disease is called the **base rate**. If we think that, at any given **base rate** time, about 1 in 80 of Ohio State students will have influenza, that makes the base rate 1.25%. Since there are about 50,000 Ohio State students, our guess is that around 50,000/80 = 625 students have the flu right now.

If 1 in 80 seems low to you, remember that this is your chance of having the flu right now. Since there are about 30 weeks in the Ohio State year, and the illness takes about a week, your chance of catching it at some point in the year would be something like 30/80 = 38%.

The probability of 1 in 80 is a guess, but what is important is that by making a guess we get some feel for what might be going on. By contrast, our estimate of the base rate of yellow fever among the same population is 1 in 250,000. This means that we think it is rather unlikely that even one student has yellow fever right now. This number is also a guess.

The airport security line   The analysis in Table 5.1 applies to many nonmedical situations, including the security line at airports. Suppose there is a scanner that is designed to detect guns in passenger baggage. Imagine that you are in charge of designing a sensible policy about how to use the scanner and interpret the results.

- You need to decide what should happen next if you get a positive result. Remember that the positive results will be made up of a mix of true and false positives.

  One option is to press the alarm immediately, call the airport police, and arrange for the arrest of anyone who gets a positive result. Another option is to arrange for further screening of the passengers with positive results.
- You need to decide what should happen next if you get a negative result. Remember that the negative results will be made up of a mix of true and false negatives.

  One option is simply to let all the passengers with negative results pass through unhindered. Another is randomly to select a small proportion of these passengers for further screening.
- In order to make rational decisions about the previous two questions, you need to have some idea about what proportion of passengers you think are trying to carry guns through security. This is where we estimate the base rate. You may wish to consider whether this base rate is going to be different in different countries

or in different regions of the same country, as some places have a strong gun culture and others do not.

Medicine uses two standard measures to assess the value of a test. An overview of these measures, and their relationship to false and true positives, is in Table 5.2.

Table 5.2 Measures of a diagnostic test

	Has disease	*No disease*	
Test positive	True positives	False positives	**Positive predictive value**
Test negative	False negatives	True negatives	**Negative predictive value**
	Sensitivity	**Specificity**	

Sensitivity

sensitivity The first is called **sensitivity**. This is the ratio

$$\text{Sensitivity} = \frac{\text{True positives}}{\text{True positives} + \text{False negatives}}$$

which focuses on what happens when the patient does really have the disease. Sensitivity is high when true positives massively outnumber false negatives; if you get a negative result in a high-sensitivity test, you can be pretty sure that you do *not* have the disease. In computational linguistics, we usually call sensitivity *recall*, as we discussed in Section 4.3.2. Precision corresponds to the positive predictive value, and the calculations are the same. If you know that your search engine typically has high recall, and your search for `fifty-year-old boy bands` produces no results, you can be pretty sure that there are no relevant documents out there. Sensitivity is important for ruling out the disease, and for making sure that people who do have the disease get treated, but it says nothing at all about what happens to patients who do *not* have the disease. So, the picture is incomplete.

Specificity

specificity A second measure, which focuses on what happens when the patient *does not* have the disease, is called **specificity**. This is the ratio

$$\text{Specificity} = \frac{\text{True negatives}}{\text{True negatives} + \text{False positives}}$$

Specificity will be high if true negatives massively outnumber false positives. The higher the specificity, the fewer the number of healthy people who will be subjected to follow-up tests.

Errors in medical tests Let us now revisit the question about medical diagnosis that was posed earlier. Suppose that you have a medical test for a disease. It has 90%

specificity and 98% sensitivity. The base rate of the disease among the population tested is 10%. You test 1,000 patients.

The questions we need to answer are:

- On average, how many of the 1,000 will have the disease and how many not?
- Starting from the number of people whom we expect to have the disease, what is the expected number of true positives and the expected number of false negatives? We need the **sensitivity** number to calculate this.
- Starting from the number of people we expect not to have the disease, what is the expected number of false positives and the expected number of true negatives? We will need to make use of the **specificity** figure for the test to do this.

On average, we expect that about 100 patients will have the disease and 900 will not. So we expect to see around $100 \times 0.98 = 98$ true positives, $100 \times (1-0.98) = 2$ false negatives, $900 \times 0.90 = 810$ true negatives and $900 \times (1-0.90) = 90$ false positives, as in Table 5.3.

Table 5.3 Expected numbers if you do 1,000 tests

	Has disease	No disease	Total
Test positive	98	90	188
Test negative	2	810	812
Total	100	900	1000

Notice the following:

- There are 908 correct decisions and 92 bad decisions. One summary of the situation is just to say that the test is 90.8% correct.
- There are 2 false negatives and 90 false positives.
- There are 98 true positives and 90 false positives. This means that nearly half of the people diagnosed are disease free.

Remember that there are four possible situations:

1. True positives: the patient has the disease and the test correctly detects it. We are expecting 1 in 10 patients to have the disease and also that the test will return a positive result for 98% of these patients. We can say that the probability of having the disease is 1 in 10 (that is, 0.1) and the probability of a positive test if you have the disease is 0.98. Multiplying the probabilities gives $0.1 \times 0.98 = 0.098$ as the probability of a true positive.
2. False positives: the patient does not have the disease, but the test incorrectly returns a positive result. Repeating the calculation, 9 in 10 patients will not have the disease, and in these circumstances 1 in 10 of them will get an

incorrect positive test. Multiplying the probabilities gives $0.9 \times 0.1 = 0.09$ as the probability of a false positive.

3. True negatives: the patient does not have the disease, and the test correctly detects this fact. 9 in 10 of the patients have no disease, and 9 out of 10 times the test successfully detects this, so the probability of a true negative is $0.9 \times 0.9 = 0.81$.

4. False negatives: the patient does have the disease, but the test incorrectly returns a negative result. 1 in 10 of the patients has the disease, but the test fails to detect this 2 times out of 100. Therefore, the probability of a false negative is $0.1 \times 0.02 = 0.002$.

To find out how likely it is that you really have the disease if you have a positive test, we need to consider the ratio between the probability of a true positive and the probability of any kind of positive. In the formula below, the numerator is the probability of getting a true positive and the denominator is the probability of getting either a true positive or a false positive. The result is the probability of having the disease, given that you got a positive test, which is what we want.

$$P(\text{disease} \mid \text{test positive}) = \frac{0.1 \times 0.98}{(0.1 \times 0.98) + (0.9 \times 0.1)} = 0.5213$$

The probabilities of false negatives and true negatives are not needed for this calculation, because we know that the test came out positive. They would be needed if you wanted to calculate the probability of having the disease after a *negative* test.

If this problem was new to you, and you used your intuition when we first asked the question, it would not be at all unusual to be surprised by the estimate of 52% as
cognitive bias the probability of having the disease given a positive test. This is because there is a
cognitive bias called **base rate neglect**, which tends to make human beings ignore
base rate neglect the effect of the base rate and focus far more on the connection between the symptoms and the disease. This leads us, almost without noticing it, to assume that about 50% of the people to whom the test is administered have the disease and the other 50% do not. If you do the calculation again, this time under the assumption that the base rates are equal, you will get:

$$P(\text{disease} \mid \text{test positive}) = \frac{0.5 \times 0.98}{(0.5 \times 0.98) + (0.5 \times 0.1)} = 0.9074$$

which will lead you to believe that nearly 91% of the people with a positive test are going to have the disease. In the same way, it is easy to fall into the trap of unintentionally assuming that the airport scanner sees about 50% terrorists and 50% nonterrorists. Unless you are particularly paranoid, next time you are in the line at an airport, you will be able to look at the people around you and decide that you really do not believe that 50% of them are terrorists. But, even knowing this, it is not easy to adjust your feelings about risk to match what you know to be true about the situation.

5.4.2   Payoffs

As you may have realized in thinking about the extended example on medical diagnosis, a third factor comes into the evaluation of a medical test. It is not enough to know how well the test works and how common the disease is, we also need to assess the costs and benefits of the various options available to us. To show how this works, we are going to use a simplified version of the calculations that a real doctor would need to do. To keep things gentle, we will say that the disease is always curable and that nobody ever dies of it. However, there are two different treatments: treatment A is cheap, costing the hospital $10, but treatment B is expensive, and would cost the hospital $1,000. For simplicity, and because we like the idea, we are going to say that the patient pays nothing, and the cost is all on the hospital. Treatment B will work any time, but treatment A works only in the early stages of the disease. The point of the test is to find people who should get treatment A now. The hospital's policy is to apply treatment A whenever the test comes back positive. It costs the hospital an unnecessary $10 whenever there is a false positive. We say that the **payoff**   payoff for a false positive is –$10. The payoff for a true positive is also –$10, because the hospital pays for the treatment in that situation too.

However, if the test misses a patient who does have the disease, that person will eventually come back in and require treatment B, which is much more expensive. So, the payoff for a false negative is –$1,000. The payoff for a true negative is $0, because no treatment is needed. In a real hospital situation, life would be more complicated, because there would be another choice to be made before this all happened: the doctors would have to consider the cost of the test itself. They might decide that some people are so unlikely to have the disease that it isn't even worth running the test.

Table 5.4   The payoffs for the four outcomes

	Has disease	No disease
Test positive	– $10	– $10
Test negative	– $1,000	$0

5.4.3   Back to documents

At this point, you are probably wondering whether this book has been taken over by medical researchers, biologists, or Homeland Security types. Not exactly, because the ideas we have used so far apply to document classification, too. In document classification, high specificity means that few of the irrelevant distractor documents will be classified into the target class. If the target class is *junk emails*, this means that few nonjunk emails will be placed in your junk mail folder. Similarly, high sensitivity means that few relevant documents will be missed.

Errors in junk mail filters   If you are using this book in a class, at some point the instructor is likely to ask you to spend five minutes discussing junk mail with your neighbor. Here are some questions to think about:

- Which do you find more annoying in the context of junk mail filtering: false positives or false negatives? In practice, what do you have to do to recover from a false positive? And what are the consequences of a false negative?
- Would you be prepared to accept a few extra false negatives for the sake of a reduction in false positives? (This is the same question that we had in the medical setting, but this time human suffering is kept to a low level.)
- Suppose that you win the lottery and become very rich. Now every scam artist in the universe starts sending you junk mail, but the number of real emails that you get is unchanged. Do you still want the same balance between false positives and false negatives? (This is a direct application of the ideas about base rates above.)

5.5   Some types of document classifiers

Most of the applications that we have looked at so far rely on some kind of technology for distinguishing between different kinds of documents. In this section of the chapter, we explain some of the tools that are used to do this.

5.5.1   The Naive Bayes classifier

In the earlier sections of this chapter, we talked about the need to collect and assess evidence about the appropriate classification for documents. The crucial technical decision is to choose an appropriate algorithm for weighting the evidence. One **Naive Bayes** simple and effective algorithm is known as the **Naive Bayes** classifier. We start by explaining the idea and then justify the math.

When we use the Naive Bayes classifier to classify documents, we run a competition between the hypothesis that the document is a piece of junk mail and the alternative hypothesis that it is not. This is expressed in math by doing a probability calculation for each of the two hypotheses. It is the evidence we collect that allows us to decide between these two hypotheses.

An example of the kind of data used in this calculation is given in Table 5.5. In order to make the example manageable, we are going to pretend that there are just a few words for which we have collected statistics. In reality, there would be many more. We have imagined an email user (we will call this user Sandy) whose usual mail conversations include recreational chat about horses, unicorns, and similar creatures, but who also gets some of the usual kind of spam. Sandy does not want genuine messages from friends (including particular friends Alice, Seth, and Emily) to be filtered out. Messages that mention rideable animals are usually good, but some of the ones mentioning stallions are suspect.

We are going to see some words that bias us to believe that the document is spam, and others that make us think it is not. The classifier needs a policy for how to reconcile the conflicting evidence.

The simplest policy is to pretend that we are dealing with a completely unstructured collection of words. We ignore the fact that the words were arranged into a particular order and that they go together to form sentences and paragraphs. All we worry about is which words occur in the document and how often they occur. This is done because it simplifies the math, not because it is realistic about how language is used. Computer scientists refer to this simplification as the **bag-of-words assumption** (see also Section 7.7 on word alignment). **bag-of-words assumption**

Imagine that we cut up a document and put the words in a bag. The document might be spam, or it might not. Now, we draw the words out of a bag one at a time. Each time we see a word, we ask whether that word is more likely to have come out of a document that is spam, or more likely to have come out of a document that is not spam. We can turn this idea into math using Table 5.5 and some simple reasoning.

Table 5.5 Some evidence from Sandy's email collection

	Spam	Ham
Cash	200	3
Alice	1	50
Seth	2	34
Emily	2	25
Viagra	20	0
Credit	12	2
unicorn	0	5
Cookie	1	5
hippogriff	0	18
Pony	9	50
stallion	3	8
TOTAL	250	200

For concreteness, imagine that the word that came out of the bag was "Emily". We are also going to pretend temporarily that the words in the table are the only ones that exist. We have seen this word in a spam document 2 times, out of a total of 250 spam words overall. This means that we can reasonably estimate that we are likely, on average, to see "Emily" 2 times in 250 (or 1 time in 125, or 0.8% of the time) if the document that we put in the bag was spam. We have seen the same word 25 times in Sandy's real messages, out of a total of 200 nonspam words overall. So, we can guess that we are likely to see the word 25 times in 200 (or 1 time in 8 or 12.5%) if the document is not spam. Since 12.5% is much bigger than 0.8%, we think, from seeing just one word, that the document in the bag is much more likely to be ham than spam. We can keep track of this by recording the **odds ratio** for ham to spam as 12.5/0.8, or nearly 16. This is **odds ratio** much greater than 1, which means that we think the document is ham.

Suppose that the next word is "credit." The counts for this are 12 in 250 for spam, 2 in 200 for ham. The odds ratio for this word is 2/200 against 12/250, or about 0.29. This is less than 1, so we think, on the basis of this word alone, that the document in the bag is probably junk.

To combine the evidence, we multiply the ratios, $16 \times 0.29 = 4.63$, and decide, because the combined ratio is greater than 1, that the two words together indicate a genuine document and not junk. We carry on in the same way, calculating a ratio for each new word as it comes out of the bag, and multiplying it into the combined ratio. Once we have put all this evidence in place, we can make an overall decision about the document. If the final value of the combined ratio is greater than 1, we claim that the document is genuine email; otherwise, we rate it as junk.

Under the Hood 9
Naive Bayes

Why does the Naive Bayes algorithm make sense, and why is it called Naive Bayes in the first place? The answer is that it is based on the ideas of an eighteenth-century British scientist called Thomas Bayes. Bayes was a Presbyterian minister, but also a member of the Royal Society, one of the first scientific organizations ever founded. His major contribution to science was a posthumous paper that laid out the key concepts of a probabilistic approach to reasoning about uncertain evidence. Here is the essence of his reasoning, as applied to junk mail filtering.

The leading mathematical idea of Bayes' approach is a decomposition of the reasoning process into two components. The first component is a so-called prior probability. This reflects what you assume about the situation before you have collected detailed evidence.

In spam filtering, you can safely assume that most documents in a typical mailbox are junk mail. So you can set the prior probability of junk mail to a high value, a probability close to 1. In spam filtering, the prior probability really reflects your beliefs or assumptions about the base rate of junk mail.

The idea of a prior probability works in more complicated situations, too. In spam filtering there are only two alternatives: either the document is spam or it is not. But there could be more alternatives: in the section on spelling correction (Section 2.3.2), we saw that the spelling error "nup" could be a result of a failed attempt to spell the words "nub", "nob", "nap", "nip", and "nut", among others. If we are using Bayesian reasoning, we start by asking ourselves which of these words the writer is *likely* to want to use. We might assume that a very sleepy person would tend to use "nap" a lot, or that a passionate vegan cook would often use the word "nut". These assumptions could be expressed by choosing different values for the prior probabilities of each word.

The second component of the reasoning process is called a likelihood. For junk mail, this component reflects your beliefs about the following questions:

- Suppose that the document we have *is* junk mail: are we surprised to see the particular words that are in the document, or not? We will translate this idea into math shortly.
- Suppose it *is not* junk mail: are we now surprised to see the words that are in the documents? Again, we will convert this into math and show how to run the competition between junk and nonjunk in a moment.

For spelling correction, we can do the same thing: we now ask, for each of the words "nub", "nob", "nap", "nip", "nut", and so on how likely it is that the writer would misspell them as "nup". We might decide that the likelihood for "nip" should be particularly high, because I is right next to U on the QWERTY keyboard. Bayes noticed that if you multiply together the prior probability and the likelihood, you get a probability that is useful for decision making. This is a generally useful principle of reasoning, not just for the specific situations we have discussed.

Here is the essence of Bayes' reasoning, as applied to spam filtering:

- We are interested in looking at a document D that may or may not be junk mail. We could make a decision if we knew the two probabilities $P(\text{spam}|D)$ and $P(\text{ham}|D)$. Read these formulas as "probability of spam given D" and "probability of ham given D". These are conditional probabilities, which were discussed in detail in Under the Hood 2.

  To understand the idea behind the word *given* here, think about the parallel with the medical tests we saw earlier. In that setting, the outcome of the test is a given, fixed fact. We know this because we have observed it directly. But we do not have direct knowledge of whether the patient has the disease, so we have to consider both possibilities and work out which is the more likely. In the same way, when we are doing spam filtering, the words of the document are given facts of which we are sure because we have observed them, but we do not have direct knowledge of whether or not the document was actually created by a spammer. Once again, we have to consider both possibilities and work out which is the more likely. If the spam probability is bigger than the ham probability, we will be right more often than not by guessing that the document is spam.
- With this assumption in mind, the mathematical formula for the likelihood of the document is actually $P(D|\text{spam})$ (the probability that the words in the document occur if it is spam) and not $P(\text{spam}|D)$ (the probability that the document is spam if we see those words). We want the second one, but

(Continued)

Under the Hood 9
Naive Bayes

(Cont'd.)

so far we only know how to calculate the first one. Fortunately, Bayes' theorem allows us to get the probability that we want by doing a little algebra. For spam documents it states that:

$$P(\text{spam} \mid D) = \frac{P(D \mid \text{spam})P(\text{spam})}{P(D)}$$

- We can also use Bayes' theorem on the nonspam documents, giving:

$$P(\text{ham} \mid D) = \frac{P(D \mid \text{ham})P(\text{ham})}{P(D)}$$

- If we take the ratio of these probabilities, $P(D)$ cancels out, giving:

$$\frac{P(\text{spam} \mid D)}{P(\text{ham} \mid D)} = \frac{P(\text{spam})P(D \mid \text{spam})}{P(\text{ham})P(D \mid \text{ham})}$$

- This last expression says that our competition between ham and spam can be run using the priors $P(\text{ham})$ and $P(\text{spam})$ along with the likelihoods $P(D|\text{ham})$ and $P(D|\text{spam})$. Nothing else is needed.

We can estimate a value for the ratio $P(\text{spam})/P(\text{ham})$ by remembering that spam is typically much more common than ham. If you feel that 95% of the mail you get is junk, you could estimate the ratio as $0.95/0.05 = 19$.

We still need to estimate the likelihood. In a spam filter, the likelihood model is built by paying attention to what the classifier has learned about the relationship between the labels that it wishes to assign and the features that predict them. In the spelling application (Chapter 2), the likelihood model is built by paying attention to what the classifier has learned about what happens when writers try (and sometimes fail) to write down the words that they intend accurately.

In the Naive Bayes classifier, to keep things simple, we imagine that the words in the document are being produced by a very simple random process, based on the "bag-of-words" assumption introduced earlier. We do not really believe this very simplistic assumption, but it is worth pretending that we do, because the calculations are simpler and the results of these calculations are useful. In spam filtering, we assign a value to the probability that a junk mail document will contain the word "enlargement", and another value, presumably lower, to the probability that a nonjunk document will contain the same word. We do this for every feature that we care about. Usually, we do this for most of the words in the document, but we ignore the very common stop words like "the" and "and", because we do not think that these words are going to be helpful (see a similar usage of stop words for searching in Section 4.3.4). We do not have to stick to words alone: we can also assign a probability to the hypothesis that a spam document will contain a high proportion of words that are written in bright colors and/or capital letters, and we can assign a corresponding probability that a non-junk document will have this feature.

The final step in the Naive Bayes process is to combine together all the feature probabilities. We assume that each feature is chosen independently, and that the relevant probabilities are $P(\text{feature}|\text{spam})$ and $P(\text{feature}|\text{ham})$. Under that assumption (which is the main reason Naive Bayes is called "Naive"), the probability of the document is the product of the probabilities of a series of independent events $f_1, f_2, ..., f_n$, one for each feature, and the ratio we need for our decision can be rewritten as:

$$\frac{P(\text{spam}|D)}{P(\text{ham}|D)} = \frac{P(\text{spam})\prod_f P(f|\text{spam})}{P(\text{ham})\prod_f P(f|\text{ham})}$$

Here, the symbol $\prod_f$ means "product over all features f." This tells you to multiply together the probabilities for each of the individual features, one time (in the numerator) for spam, one time (in the denominator) for ham. (If you recall your algebra classes you might remember the corresponding $\sum_i$ notation for sums. $\prod_i$ is just the same as this, but for products.)

The calculation for this ratio corresponds to the informal account given earlier in this chapter. In that account, we simplified by not bothering with the prior, and just started off with the features. You could redo the calculation by starting off with an odds ratio of 19:1 in favor of spam, then multiplying in the new evidence as each word arrives. Usually there will be plenty of evidence from the words, and the choice of prior will hardly affect the decision, but sometimes, especially for messages that have only a few words in them, the estimate of the prior will make a difference.

5.5.2   The perceptron

The Naive Bayes classifier depends on counting things that occur in the test set. A different approach to machine learning is the **perceptron**, which is based on the idea of **error-driven learning**. The perceptron maintains a collection of **weights**, where each weight links a feature with an **outcome**. The perceptron learns from

perceptron

error-driven
learning

weights

outcome

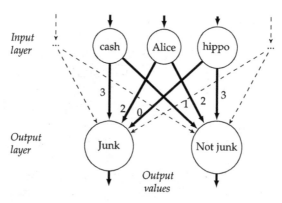

Figure 5.1   The perceptron

experience by trying to predict outcomes, then adjusting the weights when it makes
a wrong prediction. Initially, the weights are uninformative and the perceptron is
just guessing, but over time the perceptron builds up an ability to associate features
with outcomes in a useful way.

input layer   The perceptron (see Figure 5.1) is a network with two layers. The **input layer** has one
node for each possible input feature. In our running example of Sandy's email, there
would be one node for each of "cash", "Alice", "Seth", "hippogriff", and so on. This would
be unwieldy to draw in full, so we content ourself with three nodes in the diagram. The
output layer **output layer** contains one node for each possible outcome (in the case of Sandy's email,
one each for *junk* and *not junk*, exactly as in the diagram). The edges that link the input
and output layer are associated with weights. In order to do a prediction, the perceptron
reads a document and notes which words are present. We turn the nodes that correspond to these words on, and turn the others off. The role of the weights is to decide
how strongly to transmit the activity of the active nodes to the output layer. Suppose
that exactly three nodes ("cash", "Alice", "hippogriff") were active in Sandy's perceptron,
and the weights linking these words to *junk* and *not junk* are as in Table 5.6.

Table 5.6   Weights for a perceptron

Word	Junk	Not junk
cash	3	1
Alice	2	2
hippogriff	0	3

Under this supposition, the total activity of the *junk* output node would be
$3+2+0=5$ and that of *not junk* would be $1+2+3=6$, so *not junk* would win. If this
prediction is right, Sandy's perceptron can stay as it is, but if the message is actually
junk, then the weights need to change.

Let us suppose that this is what happens. The perceptron algorithm changes all the
relevant weights a little, in such a way as to move the result closer to a correct prediction.

So it would increase the weight of "cash" (and each of the other two words) as a predictor for *junk*, and downweight it as a predictor for *not junk*. A possible result (if "a little" is taken as 0.01 for the sake of demonstration) would be as in Table 5.7.

Table 5.7   Adapted weights for a perceptron

Word	Junk	Not junk
cash	3.01	0.99
Alice	2.01	1.99
hippogriff	0.01	2.99

This weight change is not enough to change the prediction, but it does move the result in the right direction (*not junk* still wins, but not by so much). To train the perceptron, we go through the training corpus, presenting each example to the current version of the perceptron, and adapting weights whenever we make a mistake. When we get to the end of the training corpus, we start again at the beginning. Each round of this process is called an **iteration**. After a sufficient number of iterations, the **iteration** weights will change enough that some of the predictions will flip. Gradually, the mistakes tend to go away (not completely, but to a reasonable extent). This is a result of the feedback mechanism under which features that contribute to wrong predictions get their weights changed. There is a mathematical proof that the perceptron will give perfect performance on the training set if that set has the mathematical property of being **linearly separable**. In two dimensions, the idea of linear separability is that a **linearly** dataset is linearly separable if it is possible to draw a straight line that has all the **separable** positive examples on one side of the line and all the negative examples on the other.

In three dimensions the line turns into a plane, and in four or more dimensions it turns into a mathematical object called a hyperplane. However, the idea is always that all the positive examples are on one side and all the negative examples are on the other. In Figure 5.2, positive examples are represented by hollow circles and negative examples by filled circles. The diagonal line is a nearly perfect linear separator, as only one positive example is on the wrong side of the boundary and the rest are correctly separated. For this dataset, this is the best that *any* linear separator can do.

In practice, as well as in the example shown in Figure 5.2, perfect performance is rare, because real world problems are usually not linearly separable, so some misclassifications remain, and training is stopped when the number of remaining mistakes has stayed stable for long enough. When this happens, we are probably doing as well as possible on the training set, but this does not give us certainty about how well we will do on an unseen test set. If the test set and the training set are similar enough, a perceptron that does well on the training set will also do well on the test set. Unfortunately, we are not completely sure how similar the test set will be, so there is an element of uncertainty in our guesses about how well we will do.

The perceptron is an algorithm for training a **linear model**. The technical details **linear model** of how linear models work would take us too far afield, but the discussion of linear

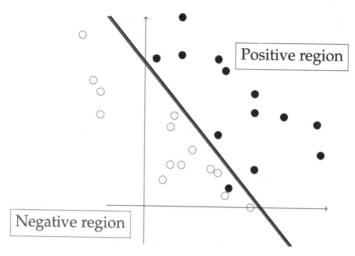

Figure 5.2   Linear separability

separability above is part of the story. The final weights can be understood as saying something about the importance of each piece of evidence in a combined solution to the classification problem. When there are a large number of potentially useful features in a classification problem, researchers have discovered that linear models often work well. The perceptron algorithm is not the only way of training linear models, or necessarily the best, but it is a good starting point for exploration.

5.5.3   Which classifier to use

The main reason for including a brief discussion of the perceptron is to show that there is more than one way to do machine learning. Intuitively, the idea of collecting statistics over a collection of examples is very different from maintaining a collection of weights that are updated in a mistake-driven way. But at a deeper level, both of these approaches are supervised learning, and it is likely that they will perform similarly a lot of the time. Usually, the most important part of a machine learning solution is the choice of features that provide information on the distinctions about which we want the classifiers to learn, and the choice of classifier plays an important but secondary role. Our advice is to try a few off-the-shelf classifiers and choose the one that seems to be working best for your problem. A toolkit containing state-of-the-art implementations of many classifiers is Weka (http://en.wikipedia.org/wiki/Weka_(machine_learning)), which is written in the programming language Java and is fairly easy to use.

    Weka also contains software for predicting numeric continuous values, such as the numbers of stars in a movie review (here we are imagining that the movie review site produces really detailed ratings, not just whole numbers of stars, and that the rating could be a decimal like 3.72). Predicting continuous values from features is called regression **regression**. By contrast, the perceptron and Naive Bayes produce predictions from a fixed set of discrete values, often just *yes* or *no*. Programs that predict discrete values are called **classifiers** in the machine-learning literature, and the term classification is used when it is important to make clear that they are predicting discrete rather than continuous values. **classifiers**

Another way of making our general point is that the choice of classifier should be based on thinking about the **context of use** of the technology. While programmers will certainly care about the details of how the algorithms work, users and managers will care more about what the system can do, what kind of errors it will make, and how this fits in with the real-world needs of the organizations or other clients who want to use the technology. One of the reasons for the substantial emphasis on evaluation in this chapter is that good evaluation focuses attention on the tradeoffs that are involved in using technology to the full. In the final section of this chapter, we provide a brief case study to illustrate how document classification technology is actually deployed. The important lesson is not that the authors think the technology is cool, although we do, but that we think it is useful for finding good solutions to real-world problems. **context of use**

5.6 From classification algorithms to context of use

In the early 2000s, companies such as Lexalytics, Attensity, and Scout Labs began to offer software and services for opinion mining. Starting at about the same time, there have been many academic papers on sentiment classification. These use several different techniques, some of them very sophisticated. Figure 5.3, for example, shows the result of an analysis by Lexalytics.

Julie Jones **superb**$^+$ performance in the **gubernatorial debate**$^+$ has all but **assured**$^+$ her of a **major victory**$^+$ in the **upcoming elections**$^+$. **Unfortunately**$^-$, the evening did not go as well for her opponent John Adams, his **nervous**$^-$ and **uncertain**$^-$ performance has all but **guaranteed**$^+$ a **loss**$^-$ and put his entire **political future**$^+$ into question.

Figure 5.3 **Positive**$^+$ and **negative**$^-$ phrases detected by Lexalytics

Lexalytics is well aware that sentiment classification is never going to be perfect. But neither are spelling correctors, internet searching, or spam filters. The advantages come when you are working with large volumes of data, or when you are doing other things that human beings find boring or complicated. One of the company's ideas is to concentrate on **monitoring** of sentiment, and on comparisons between the client's business offerings and those of its competitors. For example, it is easy to find public reviews of hotels in Las Vegas, but these reviews will mix up: **monitoring**

- comments that reflect the customer's experience with Las Vegas in general;
- comments that are really about the location of the hotel (which is going to be difficult to change); and
- comments that are specific to how the hotel is doing right now.

Table 5.8 Comparison of hotels by category

	Rooms	Price	Facilities	Location	Cleanliness	Service	Overall
Hotel X	34	39	25	35	38	37	35
Hotel Y	30	29	24	36	27	26	29

Only the third kind of comments is truly of interest to the hotel manager. This is a fact about what the hotel manager is looking for, not a fact that is evident from the reviews themselves. But Lexalytics understands what the hotel manager will be looking for, so rather than just counting positive and negative words in the whole article, the software can search the review site for sentences that say something specific about:

- the rooms
- the price
- the facilities
- the location
- the cleanliness of the hotel
- the service
- the overall rating

A point-by-point comparison could look like Table 5.8.

This might not mean that customers of Hotel Y were systematically less happy than those of Hotel X, but it could (and in this case did) mean that the unhappy customers of Hotel Y were much more inclined to write very negative reviews than those of Hotel X. Both hotels are in the same location on the Vegas strip, but in fact Hotel Y is very famous as a super-luxury hotel. The conclusion drawn by Lexalytics was that Y's unhappy customers, who are small in number but very vocal in their outrage, were expecting more, and felt even slightly negative experiences more keenly than did X's. Presumably Hotel Y can react to this by working especially hard on training staff to notice, acknowledge, and fix potentially negative experiences when they happen. By being nice to a few customers who are extremely irritated, the hotel can dramatically improve its public image.

Using insight and simple quantitative reasoning, sentiment analysts are able to provide information that is useful to businesses and others, even though the underlying document-classification techniques will make mistakes in detecting positive and negative words. Provided that the general trend is well enough represented, managers can use these kinds of techniques to gain insight and plan future service improvements. Comparisons can also be made week to week, to see whether satisfaction levels are changing. It remains important to keep a human in the loop, because blindly relying on the algorithms could be seriously misleading. Notice that the conclusion about Hotels X and Y depended on insight about how customers might be reacting, not just on the data or the mathematics. The theory of machine learning provides an understanding of the technology – which you need – but intelligent common sense is just as important. Add sensible experimentation and measurement, and you have a set of powerful tools for understanding the world.

Checklist

After reading the chapter, you should be able to:

- Discuss spam filtering and other document-classification tasks.
- Notice when other tasks, even those that are nothing to do with documents, turn out to be examples of classification.
- Understand the notions of precision, recall, specificity, and sensitivity.
- Explain base rates and the base rate fallacy.
- Define what a classifier that uses supervised learning does.
- Give reasons why sentiment analysis and opinion mining might be helpful.
- Understand how Naive Bayes classification works.
- Understand how the perceptron classifier works.

Exercises

1. **ALL**: Find aggregator websites for unlikely, amusing, or surprisingly useful topics. Do you think a specialist magazine exists for each of these topics? Why or why not?

2. **ALL**:
   (a) Table 5.4 gives a calculation of the payoffs associated with each outcome of the medical test in the extended example. Put this together with the population statistics in Table 5.3 to calculate the overall payoffs from: (i) always running the test, and (ii) never running the test. Which is the more cost-effective policy for the hospital ?
   (b) We carefully set up our example so that everyone was cured and the only effect of your decision is financial, but of course the mathematics also applies to decisions where much more is at stake. Now that you have learned about false positives, true positives, payoffs, and the rest, you have the conceptual tools to understand the tradeoffs that are involved in deciding whether a country should have a policy of offering mammography as a general screening tool for breast cancer. We recommend that you find information about this on the internet, read about it, and see what you think. Do not stop after the first article you read. It is a controversial issue, and you will find sensible articles advocating both for and against general screening.

3. **MATH**: You are the owner of a spam filtering service:
   (a) Currently, your server gets 2,000 spams per hour and only 500 good messages. The filter classifies 95% of the spams correctly, and misclassifies the other 5%. It classifies 99% of the good messages correctly, and

misclassifies the other 1%. Tabulate the results. How many false positives and how many false negatives do you expect to see each hour? Calculate the precision, sensitivity, and specificity of the spam filter.

(b) You receive word that a criminal gang is planning to double the amount of spam that it sends to your server. There will now be 4,000 spam messages per hour instead of 2,000. The number of good messages stays unchanged at 500. In your marketing literature, you have quoted the precision, recall, sensitivity, and specificity of your spam filter. You assume that the misclassification rates will stay the same (5% for spam, 1% for good messages). Should you put in a call to the technical writing department warning them that the literature will need to be revised? Why or why not? And if so, what will need to be revised?

4. **ALL:** You are the provider of an opinion mining service. You have been approached by a large airline that has been getting customer complaints about baggage handling. It wants to find out why and what to do about it. The airline will give you access to its database of complaints going back over the last two years. Each complaint is in the form of messages written by the customer, along with any letters written by the airline in response.

(a) What features will you look for as you examine these complaints? Do you think that any part of the process of analyzing the documents to find the features should be automated, and if so, which aspects?

(b) Can you think of any way of diagnosing how happy the complainants were with the company's approach to resolving the complaints? Can this be automated?

(c) Other than the complaints themselves, can you think of any other useful sources of information that could help you judge how your company is being perceived? (Hint: remember what was useful for hotels). If you have ideas, how would you go about collecting the extra information?

5. **MATH:** Continue the calculation in Section 5.5.1. Assume that the next word is "cookie". Using the frequency statistics from Table 5.5, carry out the next step of the calculation. What is the cumulative ratio for spam/nonspam?

Further reading

The statistical approach to junk mail filtering was popularized by Paul Graham's "A Plan for Spam" (http://www.paulgraham.com/spam.html). His article is an excellent starting point for learning about the technology and sociology of the junk mail phenomenon. Pang and Lee (2007) is a comprehensive introduction to opinion mining and sentiment analysis. The setting for the exercise about airline complaints comes from the infamous "United breaks guitars" incident (http://www.huffingtonpost.com/2009/07/24/united-breaks-guitars-did_n_244357.html). The discussion of base rate fallacy is based on Bar-Hillel (1980). Cognitive biases are discussed both in the psychology literature and in the relatively recent growth area of behavioral economics.

6

Dialog Systems

6.1 Computers that "converse"?

I'm sorry, Dave. I'm afraid I can't do that.
[Hal 9000, in Stanley Kubrick's 1968 film *2001: A Space Odyssey*]

In the film *2001*, Hal is a computer that can use and understand human language as well as we can. He knows how to say things that, while not strictly true, are effective in communicating with Dave the astronaut. The problem in the movie is that Hal becomes so intelligent that "he" starts disobeying Dave's commands.

In this case, Dave has just requested that Hal open the pod bay doors, and Hal says that he cannot. Both Hal and Dave know that Hal can really open the pod bay doors if he wants to, but they also both understand that he is choosing not to. Hal is being "polite" by using a phrase that disguises the conflict between what Dave wants and what Hal wants.

The reason this conversation works (even if opening the pod bay doors does not) is that Hal and Dave both understand a great deal about the hows and whys of dialog, as speakers and as listeners. From the speaker's perspective, the important organizing ideas are:

1. **Why to speak**. Dave is speaking because he wants Hal's cooperation in getting the pod bay doors open.
2. **What to say**. Dave chooses to express the request for cooperation indirectly, rather than using a direct command.

Language and Computers, First Edition. Markus Dickinson, Chris Brew and Detmar Meurers.
© 2013 Markus Dickinson, Chris Brew and Detmar Meurers. Published 2013 by Blackwell Publishing Ltd.

3.   **How to say it**. (To properly catch this, you need to hear the movie clip.) Dave sounds relaxed and professional, which ought to help keep the conversation on a friendly and nonconfrontational footing.

We shall see that practical dialog systems are based on these organizing principles.

From the other perspective, the listener's role is to make sense of what is being said by the speaker. The listener must:

1.   **Accurately notice what the speaker said**. This involves hearing what was said, then breaking up the speech signal into words and phrases. If this goes wrong, as it can, Hal will need to request that Dave repeat what he said.
2.   **Work out the literal meaning of what was said**. Hal has to understand that Dave is apparently asking a question about whether Hal is capable of opening the doors.
3.   **Work out the reason the speaker did what they did**. Hal needs to understand that Dave's question is really an indirect request.

In order to do this, the listener has to reason about the speaker's intent on the basis of the observed evidence. Competent listeners know about the conventions of dialog and use that knowledge to make inferences about what the other person must be thinking and intending. A first step toward building a computer that can do the same is to develop precise descriptions of how this process actually works in human–human dialog. In this chapter, we outline some of the concepts that dialog research-**speech act** ers use to describe dialogs and indicate how computers can use them. The key ideas **dialog move** are **speech acts**, **dialog moves**, and **conversational maxims**, all of which will be discussed. **conversational maxim** Neither the listener's perspective nor the speaker's is the whole story. Communicating is a collaborative event, so the speaker and hearer must interact in ways where each understands the other. Between them, the speaker and the listener must manage the following processes, in real time:

1.   Speaking and listening in an orderly way, without talking over each other more than is acceptable.
2.   Checking that the other person is understanding.
3.   Fixing confusions and misunderstandings before they cause the conversation to break down.

Human beings are skilled in this activity long before they enter preschool. We are so accustomed to this process that we hardly notice it. One of the first consequences of trying to involve a computer in dialog is that the difficulties become more evident. If you take nothing else from this chapter, try to remember to be impressed every time you see two or more people talking without getting confused or frustrated. This is a major accomplishment, and almost everyone does it ridiculously well.

In the film, Hal has clearly acquired the ability to participate fully in natural-seeming dialogs. Stanley Kubrick and Arthur C. Clarke, the writers of *2001*, seems to have imagined that Hal learned this in a human-like way, since toward the end of the film there is a scene in which Hal regresses to "childhood" as his memory banks are gradually shut down. It is not yet possible to design computer systems that have Hal's abilities (he turned out to have language skills beyond those of most humans), but it is possible to design systems that engage in reasonably natural dialog with their human users. Many modern dialog systems are trained by exposure to successful and unsuccessful dialogs, and do learn from experience, but the way in which they do this is quite different from the way a human child learns. (For a general introduction to what it might mean for a computer to learn, see Chapter 5 on classifying documents.) It is not practical to build systems that rely on learning for all their knowledge, so system designers always build in substantial knowledge of how dialog works. Most of this chapter is a description of this knowledge and how it is used in systems.

6.2   Why dialogs happen

One of the main reasons for using language is in order to collaborate with others on getting things done. If people, or other agents with some notion of intelligence, such as an **artificial intelligence** (AI) system, have everything they need, or can get it without asking for help, they have no pressing reason to speak. But, more often, people and computer systems need to work with others in order to achieve their goals. Dave the astronaut wants the pod bay doors opened and cannot immediately do this without Hal's help, so he **requests** Hal's collaboration. Hal turns out not to want to cooperate, but rather than saying this outright, he falls in with the standard **conventions** of human dialog and talks as if he basically wants to cooperate but is somehow prevented from doing so.

    Dialog is full of rules and conventions that have evolved over the years in order to make communication run smoothly. For example, a question is usually followed by an answer; a request is often made *indirectly* because outright demands feel rude; and a refusal is often heavily disguised so as to soften the impact of the unexpected and unwelcome response.

    Rules and conventions are easiest to notice when they break down. The American comedian Demetri Martin tells the following joke (near the end of the video at http://purl.org/lang-and-comp/identity):

> I went to a clothes store and the woman there got really annoyed because she asked what size I was and I said, "Actual! This ain't a trick, baby, what you see is what you get."
>   She took me to the changing room and said, "If you need anything, I'm Jill" and I thought to myself, "Whoa, I've never met a woman before … with a conditional identity. What if I don't need anything? Who are you?" "If you don't need anything, I'm Mike."

Good humor does not need explaining, but what has happened is that Martin has found a way of deliberately misinterpreting what the shop assistant said. Where is

(margin glosses: artificial intelligence · request · convention)

the misunderstanding? Everyone knows that the assistant must mean something like: "If you need anything, do call my name, which is Jill." We can fill in the details because we understand *why* the assistant is speaking, and we use that understanding to fill in the interpretation. What Demetri Martin noticed is that **literal meaning** fits better with the wildly incongruous situation in which Jill has "a conditional identity".

literal meaning

6.3 Automating dialog

If computers are supposed to participate in natural dialog with humans, they should be just as flexible as humans, or they should control the dialog so that this flexibility is not needed. One way to do this is to work in a **limited domain**, such as airline booking, where the system can keep tight control of the dialog, reducing the user to the bit-part role of providing strictly limited information as and when required. If a task can be reduced to simple form filling, and the user is prepared to play along, then this can be an efficient way of getting the job done. We do learn to work with these systems as they are, and to adjust to their abilities, but it is still very different from dealing with a real person.

limited domain

Figure 6.1 gives an example of what present-day dialog systems can do. The point of the system is to help callers with bus timetables. The system utterances are marked with S and the user responses with U. If you have access to a computer that can play sound, you should go to the URL mentioned in the caption and listen carefully to the dialog. It might be useful to listen a second time after reading the next few paragraphs.

6.3.1 Getting started

To begin the conversation, the system signals its willingness and ability to serve.

S: Thank you for calling the CMU Let's Go! Bus Information System. This conversation will be recorded for research purposes. If you do not want to be recorded, please hang up now. What can I do for you?

The first system utterance is simple canned text designed to ensure that the user has given informed consent to participation in a research study. In addition, it mentions the name and purpose of the system, so that people can hang up if that was not what they were expecting.

When the system says "What can I do for you?" part of the point of the polite question is to signal that the user now has the floor and should make a request for information. **Having the floor** is a useful idea that dialog analysts have borrowed from parliamentary procedure. When you have the floor, you have the opportunity, and sometimes the obligation, to contribute something to the dialog.

having the floor

S: Thank you for calling the CMU Let's Go! Bus Information System. This conversation will be recorded for research purposes. If you do not want to be recorded, please hang up now. What can I do for you?

U: I would like to go to the airport tomorrow morning.

S: To the airport. When do you want to arrive?

U: I'd like to arrive at 10:30.

S: Arriving at around 10:30 AM. Where do you want to leave from?

U: I'd like to leave from Carnegie Mellon.

S: From Carnegie Mellon. There is a 28X leaving Forbes Avenue at Morewood at 9:20 AM. It will arrive at Greater Pittsburgh Airport at Departure Stops at 10:15 AM.

U: When's the next bus?

S: There is a 28X leaving Forbes Avenue at Morewood at 9:40 AM. It will arrive at Greater Pittsburgh Airport at Departure Stops at 10:35 AM.

U: I'd like to go from the airport back to CMU on Friday.

S: From the airport to CMU. When would you like to leave?

U: At 6:15 PM.

S: Leaving at around 6:15 PM. There's a 28X leaving Greater Pittsburgh Airport at Departure Stops at 6:26 PM. It will arrive at Forbes Avenue at Morewood at 7:20 PM.

U: Thank you very much.

Figure 6.1   A sample dialog from the Let's Go system (http://www.speech.cs.cmu.edu/letsgo/example.html)

6.3.2   Establishing a goal

U: I would like to go to the airport tomorrow morning.

The user's first utterance announces the wish to go to the airport. Notice that this is *not* a direct request for bus information, but rather a statement about a desire that the caller has. Section 6.5 goes into detail on why conversations are often indirect. She does not need to say "I need some bus information.", because this is built in to the participants' understanding of the context in which the conversation is happening. In other words, this reflects the fact that the system and the user both understand the *why* of this conversation.

6.3.3   Accepting the user's goal

U: I would like to go to the airport tomorrow morning.

S: To the airport. When do you want to arrive?

The next system utterance includes two things. The first is a **confirmation** that the   **confirmation**
system has correctly understood the destination to be the airport. The second part

of the system response is a question about the caller's plan. Something quite subtle must be going on here, because nobody has mentioned a plan yet. Specifically, the system has assumed that the caller intends to make a bus journey to the airport, and it is therefore trying to help her out by finding a suitable bus. Notice that the caller has not said that she is *planning* to travel to the airport, only that she *wants* to do so. In context, it is a completely reasonable assumption that she does indeed have such a plan, and it is also an entirely reasonable thing for a cooperative dialog system to adopt the goal of providing the caller with the information she needs in order to execute that plan. Therefore, the system asks when the caller wants to arrive at the airport.

6.3.4   The caller plays her role

S: To the airport. When do you want to arrive?
U: I'd like to arrive at 10:30.
S: Arriving at around 10:30 AM. Where do you want to leave from?
U: I'd like to leave from Carnegie Mellon.

The caller provides the information. The system confirms its understanding of her intended arrival time, cleverly augmenting the caller's 10:30 to 10:30 a.m. This acts

implicit as an **implicit confirmation** of the system's assumption that it did correctly recognize
confirmation the word "morning" earlier on. Notice that it would be much less smooth for the system to ask explicitly: "Do you mean 10:30 a.m. or 10:30 p.m.?" Then the system prompts the user by asking for another necessary detail. The user provides Carnegie-Mellon as the departure point.

The system now has the information it needs to look up a bus, and it does so.
precondition It has collected all the **preconditions** for doing its database lookup, and can move ahead without further help from the user.

6.3.5   Giving the answer

U: I'd like to leave from Carnegie Mellon.
S: From Carnegie Mellon. There is a 28X leaving Forbes Avenue at Morewood at 9:20 AM. It will arrive at Greater Pittsburgh Airport at Departure Stops at 10:15 AM.

The next utterance confirms Carnegie-Mellon, then provides detail about a particular bus leaving at a particular time and arriving at Greater Pittsburgh Airport. The system gives the full name of the destination, which is perhaps more than a lay person would, but probably exactly what an experienced travel agent would do.

Avoiding misunderstanding

The reason the system gives more information than is strictly needed is in order to avoid misunderstanding. If the caller had really intended to travel to some other airport near Pittsburgh, now would be the time she would find out that the system was not understanding the phrase "the airport" in the same way as she was. In fact, when, earlier in the conversation, the caller used "the", she was relying on an assumption about what the system knows. In a city where there were multiple well-known airports, the system would have needed to **request clarification** with some utter- **request** ance like: "Hang on, which airport did you mean?" Clarification requests are among **clarification** the dialog moves covered in Section 6.5.

In fact, there actually are several different airports near Pittsburgh, but only one that has generally accessible flights open to the public, so the system would be justified in assuming that this is the one the caller means. Temporary ambiguity is OK, so long as the system and the caller finish up with a common understanding of what was meant. The system's strategy of explicitly confirming the full name of the destination is a good means to this end.

6.3.6 Negotiating the end of the conversation

S: From Carnegie Mellon. There is a 28X leaving Forbes Avenue at Morewood at 9:20 AM. It will arrive at Greater Pittsburgh Airport at Departure Stops at 10:15 AM.

U: When's the next bus?

S: ...

U: Thank you very much.

The system has finished its current task, but the conversation is not over. It would be over if the caller said "OK" now. But instead she asks: "When's the next bus?" The system does extremely well with this, correctly understanding that the caller is asking for a bus with the same departure and arrival points, but a later departure time. Even though her question could be seen as idle chit-chat, the system understands it as a request for a completely new plan. Notice that this bus does not exactly meet the caller's declared goal of arriving by 10:30. It looks as if the programmers built a certain amount of tolerance into the planning, because many callers are relaxed enough not to worry about five minutes one way or the other.

The rest of the conversation is a new plan for the return journey. Things work as before, then the whole interaction terminates with the caller's formulaic "Thank you very much", and the system can safely hang up.

6.4 Conventions and framing expectations

A running thread in the Let's Go dialog is that the system and the caller are making assumptions about beliefs, desires, and intentions, that these assumptions are silently tracked by the participants, and that this allows the conversation to be concise and efficient. Because the system and the caller both understand the goals of the dialog, there is no need for the conversation to mention these goals explicitly. The participants come to the conversation with a set of expectations that frame the dialog and allow it to proceed smoothly.

6.4.1   Some framing expectations for games and sports

There is much more to this idea of framing expectations than meets the eye. A useful analogy is to think of dialog as resembling a game of basketball. Games have rules, and when the players agree to participate, they also agree to be subject to the rules that control the game, rules that are designed to make the game enjoyable to play. The rules are designed to frame the game and set up expectations for how things will proceed; they are conventions rather than strict rules. A basketball game without any fouls would be a major surprise, and players who joined the game looking for an opportunity to exercise their physical skill and courage might actually be disappointed if this happened. In high-stakes settings, there is a referee, part of whose job is to apply appropriate sanctions for rule violations. In a neighborhood pick-up game, the rules will be enforced (or not) according to a tacit understanding between the players. In a mixed-ability or mixed-age group, there might be a general understanding that older and heavier players should be gentle with younger and lighter players (or not). In chess, which is a different kind of game from basketball, the rules are usually adhered to relatively strictly, but there are still gray areas: a player would never expect to be allowed to take back a move in a tournament, but might easily ask to do so in an after-dinner game with a friend. Chess is also different from basketball in that there is a strict rotation of moves: first white plays, while black waits, and then it is black's turn while white waits.

6.4.2   The framing expectations for dialogs

In the same way, dialog has conventions and rules. Discomfort can and does arise if the participants do not "play fair" in the game of dialog. For example, the caller would be quite right to be annoyed if she later found out that there is a perfectly good bus from Forbes Avenue to the airport, leaving at 9:55 and arriving at 10:20. Even though this is not the answer to "When's the next bus?", she is still entitled to expect that a well-informed and cooperative travel helper would offer it to her if it existed, because it is a better way of meeting her declared goal than the one that she was offered. So, she infers that no such bus exists. In so doing, she is relying on a deeper assumption, which is that the system understands and is playing by a generally accepted rule of dialog: one that can be stated as "Be cooperative." As in the other games, the ways the rules of dialog are applied depend on the situation. In law courts, the rules are tight, rather artificial, and managed by the judge, who plays the role, among others, of referee. Decision-making meetings often follow Robert's Rules of Order (http://www.robertsrules.com), which are again very formal. However, in everyday conversation, the rules and conventions are less obvious, partly because we are so used to them. Computers, of course, begin with no knowledge or under-standing of the conventions of dialog. If we want them to participate in conversation, and we are not satisfied by an inflexible form-filling approach, we are going have to study dialog, understand the implicit conventions, and draw these out into a form that can be used in computer programs. This is what we outline next.

6.5   Properties of dialog

We have just mentioned the idea of treating dialog as a game. Before this concept became established, the standard view was that language existed primarily in order to allow the speaker to generate and use accurate descriptions of the world. Many of the people who studied language were mathematicians, logicians, or philosophers of science, for whom the central preoccupation is how to establish whether or not something is true, so this is really not surprising.

In the 1950s and 1960s, an alternative view arose: language was instead seen as a tool for getting things done, especially getting things done in collaboration with others. This approach turns out to be extremely suitable for use in dialog systems. In this perspective, dialog is treated as a kind of cooperative game, and the things people say become moves in that game. This matches the needs of dialog systems, because dialog systems are usually goal driven.

We will investigate various properties of dialog, all of which help us see dialog as similar to a game. Researchers in this area talk about dialog moves, speech acts, and conversational maxims. These are useful concepts, and worth knowing about, whether you are interested in computer systems or not. We discuss each in turn.

6.5.1   Dialog moves

What kinds of things happen in a dialog? One way to answer this question is by view-ing dialog as a series of moves, like in a game. As in chess, what you can do at a given point in the dialog depends on what has gone before; a range of dialog moves are avail-able. Typically, the core of the matter is that the participants exchange information.

We can break down dialog moves into three basic kinds:

1. As an exchange has to start somewhere, we can group together a set of **initiating moves**. These include:
    -   Making an assertion (e.g., *You have a friendly face*).
    -   Issuing a command or making a request (e.g., *Let's go and have a bite to eat*).
    -   Asking a question (e.g., *Are you doing anything tonight?*).
2. Some moves are **responses** to the previous move. These include:
    -   Saying "Yes" or "No" to a question where the person was seeking information.
    -   Giving an answer to an information-seeking question that needs more than "Yes" or "No".

- Answering the question, but then providing more information than was strictly asked for (e.g., saying *Yes. I'm waiting for a bus, and I am really impatient* in answer to *Are you waiting for a bus?*).
- Agreeing to do something (e.g., saying *OK* to *Let's go and have a bite to eat*).
- Refusing to do something (e.g., saying *No* to *Let's go and have a bite to eat*).
- Maybe agreeing to do something (e.g., saying *Maybe* to *Let's go and have a bite to eat*).
- Partially agreeing to do something (e.g., saying *OK, if we're quick* to *Let's go and have a bite to eat*).
- Partially refusing to do something (e.g., saying *No, unless you pay* to *Let's go and have a bite to eat*).

3. Others are responses, more or less, but divert the conversation from its expected path. These can be called **dialog management moves**. These include:
    - Saying "Huh?" when you didn't hear.
    - Saying "I don't think I understand." in response to something you didn't understand.
    - Saying "I can't believe you said that." when you did hear what the other person said, find it offensive or unacceptable, and want them to retract it.
    - Saying "I take it back." when you want the other person to pretend that you haven't said what you just did. Note that this never entirely works: you can't actually unsay what you said.

These examples should be enough to give you an idea of the kind of give-and-take that can go on in conversation, and of the way in which previous moves can influence the choices that are reasonable as next moves. There is a lot of current research on dialog, and we are still short of a final consensus on what the repertoire of dialog moves should be, but the simplified version above is based on a comparative review of several frameworks, and is probably a good basis for extension and exploration. In general, this type of categorization is useful for determining a dialog system's next move.

6.5.2   Speech acts

A different kind of characterization of dialog is in terms of speech acts, which emphasize different aspects of utterances. To understand the history of speech acts, it helps to know that philosophers have often thought of sentences in terms of truth: the words in a sentence are combined in order to form a true or false statement. Part of the reason speech acts were developed was a philosophical concern with what is going on when people say things that are difficult to characterize in terms of truth, such as "I promise to pay you five hundred dollars." or "I pronounce you man and **performative** wife." The intuition is that these **performative utterances** are actions in their own **utterance** right, and it does not make sense to describe them as true or false. Speech act theorists note that a promise is an act that immediately incurs an obligation (typically, the obligation is simply to deliver on the promise). They also note that saying "I pronounce you man and wife." does not automatically result in a change in the legal status of the people addressed, but that it can have that effect when it is uttered by an officiant who has the appropriate legal and social status.

At a more mundane level, speech acts matter because they help us to understand what is really going on when people say, for example: "Could you pass the salt?" This utterance always has the syntactic form of a question, but in many contexts the speech act that it implements is obviously a polite request. There is a great deal of subtlety in what the speech act corresponding to an utterance can be, but what matters for practical dialog systems is the ability to recognize that utterances may not be exactly what they seem and to be aware of a few standard patterns, such as the use of questions to stand for commands, the use of objectively unnecessary, informative statements to stand for requests (e.g., using "You are blocking my view." rather than "Get out of my eyeline."), and so on. A customer service dialog system would probably do well to be able to recognize most of the patterns that people use to implement the speech act of *complaining*, for example.

Common speech acts include informing, reminding, inviting, complaining, refusing, accepting, requesting, and commanding. In artificial intelligence, we often describe actions in terms of their **preconditions** and their **effects**. For example, in order for bank robbers to pack their loot into a getaway van (an effect), they need to satisfy a range of preconditions, such as ensuring that the doors of the getaway van are open, the van has been backed up to the doors of the vault, both the loot and the loaders are available and in the right place, and so on. In order for the effect of the van doors being opened, the preconditions for that will in turn need to be satisfied: better not forget the key to the van doors! If they fail to satisfy a crucial precondition at any stage, or fail to sequence the operations properly, the whole operation will fail. It is useless to have the key to the van doors if the person carrying them is locked inside the van and cannot open the doors from the inside. And you have to worry about preconditions that may not have figured in your planning, such as the van turning out not to be empty or, worse, to be full of police. However, if you do it right, representing actions in terms of preconditions and effects can allow artificial intelligence software to work out solutions to problems that call for planning of sequences of actions. **precondition effect**

This kind of reasoning can work with speech acts as well as physical acts. You can represent the speech act of informing in terms of its preconditions and effects. A precondition of informing someone that a concert is on Friday is actually to know that the concert is on Friday, and the effect is that the other person also knows that. A second precondition, at least if we want a fully fledged act of informing, is that the other person did not previously know when the concert was. If they did, we would probably want to say that the speech act was in fact reminding rather than informing. Once you have a set of speech acts, along with a carefully worked-out understanding of their preconditions and effects, you can begin to piece together sequences of speech acts (and indeed other acts) that result in particular desirable effects in the world.

In stating "If you need anything, I'm Jill.", Demetri Martin's shop assistant was helping him out by offering a piece of information (her name) that is a precondition for an action that he might reasonably want to execute: namely, calling her if he wanted further advice. But Martin insists on reinterpreting Jill's remark as a free-floating act of information giving, forcing his audience to notice the weird alternative meaning that he had in mind.

In order to function in dialog, automated systems often use a level of explicit representation in which speech acts are represented in terms of preconditions and effects. Logically, this need not be the case. Indeed, most of you have been effortlessly navigating your way through dialogs without thinking much about preconditions and effects, so it might one day be possible to build systems that do things in the same way. For now, speech acts are useful because they give us a way of connecting choices about what to say with the real-world results that we would like our dialogs to achieve.

6.5.3   Conversational maxims

The philosopher H. Paul Grice had another take on dialog, similar to but not exactly the same as the speech act idea. He noticed that there are patterns in conversation **dialog** that can be explained if we think about **dialog conventions** and pay attention to **convention** what happens when these conventions are apparently violated. One of Grice's main interests was the phenomenon of nonliteral language, which he hoped to explain.

Typically, people who engage in conversation obey what Grice (1975) referred to **Gricean maxim** as the four **maxims** (or rules) of conversation. All of them are based on the **cooperative principle**: this is the assumption that speakers are trying to contribute to the **cooperative** **principle** purposes of the conversation. This is a safe working assumption, because if the speakers are not trying to do this, the conversation is more or less certain to go wrong. So, listeners can use the cooperative principle to infer what a speaker is really getting at, or to fill in details that were left out.

Quantity   The first Gricean maxim is called **Quantity**. Quantity asserts that speakers will be exactly as informative as required for the purposes of the current conversational exchange. You should not be less informative than the situation requires. Thus, when someone replies to "How many blackboard erasers do you have?" with the answer "Two.", the conversation partner knows that it means exactly two. If the person had three erasers, that is the more cooperative answer and should have been provided. If you have three, it is not a lie to say that you have two, but it is less informative than you could have been. As far as you know, your interlocutor might actually have a need for three erasers, in which case saying "two" is seriously uncooperative.

A second aspect of Quantity is that you should not be more informative than the situation requires. If you pass someone you know slightly on the way to class and they ask "How's it going?" the answer "It's complicated. Yesterday I was sick and stayed home all day, which was bad, but I did manage to do some scrapbooking ..."

is probably more than they were looking for. This is a violation of the maxim of Quantity, because the usual response would be conventional and largely content free. For midwestern Americans, who are taught to be positive, the expected reponse might be "Great, how about you?"; or for the British, whose culture encourages them to express stoicism in the face of life's irritations, it could be "Oh, you know, mustn't grumble." By providing a nonexpected response, one that violates the maxim of quantity, you would be inviting an escalation of the seriousness of the exchange. This is a perfectly reasonable social move, and might get you an invitation to go to coffee, but it is a disruption in the flow of the dialog. Grice's observation is that when the maxim of Quantity is violated, the hearer can and does interpret this as a signal that something unusual is happening.

The second maxim, similar to Quantity, is **Quality**. This states that people **Quality** typically make statements that they know to be true and that the hearer can accept that they have evidence for. When someone says "Everyone is counting on you to get the contract." and I reply "Yes, thanks, that really helps take the pressure off.", I am saying something that seems very unlikely to be true. This is a violation of Quality, since the knowledge that people are counting on me will, if anything, increase the pressure for success. The violation is supposed to lead the hearer to infer that I am not actually thanking them for being supportive, but instead chiding them for being insensitively pushy.

A third Gricean maxim is **Relevance**. Contributions are expected to be relevant to **Relevance** the conversation. If it looks as though they are not, maybe the hearer is supposed to be doing some inference. Thus, if you ask "Does Clara have a boyfriend?" and I reply "Well, I never see her around on Friday or Saturday nights any more.", I am not exactly saying "yes". However, by making a remark that initially appears to be irrelevant, I am inviting you to infer that she does have an ongoing relationship, since this is a probable cause – perhaps, in my mind, the only plausible cause – for Clara not being available to hang out with me.

The final Gricean maxim that we will cover is called **Manner**. It says that contri- **Manner** butions are expected to avoid obscurity, to avoid ambiguity, to be appropriately brief (that is, to avoid rambling on when they do not have to), and to be presented in a clear and orderly way. Violations of Manner trigger inference in much the same way as the other three maxims we have presented.

For example, if someone says "It is possible that the weather will be rainy.", this is a simple and direct statement, and most hearers take it to mean that there is a reasonably high probability that it will rain. If, however, someone instead says "It is not impossible that the weather will be rainy.", the hearer notes the (minor) violation of the maxim of Manner (the double negation is more complicated than the positive form) and infers that the speaker is warning against a rather more remote possibility of rain. In the same way, if someone is asked "Did you hear Doctor Brew's keynote address?" and the response is the verbose and obscure "Well, he came to the podium, moved his lips, exercised his larynx, and a series of words came out.", the questioner will infer from the violation of Manner (because the answer is much more obscure, verbose, and weird than the more obvious response of just saying "yes") that something nonstandard is intended, and will conclude that the speaker's true intent is to indicate, indirectly, a general dissatisfaction with the keynote.

Grice's maxims are all about inference. The examples given above are flashy ones in which the role of inference is made very obvious. Computer systems definitely need to use inference in order to keep track of what is going on in natural dialogs, and the need arises even in ordinary conversations. For practical purposes, speech acts and dialog moves cover most of what is needed, largely because real dialog systems currently get deployed in settings such as airline booking and traffic advice. In human–human dialogs, we typically notice the Gricean maxims when they are violated, and trigger the inference that a secondary meaning is intended. This happens because we know that the dialog partner is smart enough to avoid violations, so can assume that any violations are intentional.

We can see this even at an early age. One of the authors encountered a very early deployment of smart dialog tactics when a small child produced the following utterance: "I want something that is crunchy." The purpose of this vague request was not immediately evident until it was clarified to: "I want something that is crunchy and (points in direction of cookie jar) over there." We think that the child had noticed that direct requests for cookies were less successful than interactions in which the parent was the first to mention them, hence chose to start with an utterance that was intentionally obscure. This worked, once the parent had stopped laughing.

In human–computer dialogs, by contrast, since we cannot assume that the computer is clever enough to avoid unintentional violations, it is safer to assume that everything the computer says is intended to be taken at face value. If dialog systems ever get as good at managing dialog as Hal was in *2001*, we will need to revise this view, but for the moment it is correct. In the same way, until we have strong reason to believe otherwise, when we speak to a computer-based dialog system, it is probably safe to assume that it will be taking what we say at face value and not searching for hidden meanings.

6.6   Dialog systems and their tasks

Since real-world dialog systems are not as flexible as human speakers, and we still want them to perform well, it is useful to know the vocabulary that system designers use to describe the intended purpose of a particular system. This is helpful for establishing feasibility, setting realistic expectations for quality, and making plans for how much effort will be needed. When we try to make a precise description of the scenario under which the system is expected to perform well, we are carrying out **task analysis** an activity called **task analysis**. It is also an important part of task analysis to be clear about the scenarios under which the system is not required to perform well. This helps guard against over-engineering, which is what happens when a system is more elaborate than is really necessary. Looking back at Figure 6.1, Let's Go can be described as a mixed-initiative, task-oriented dialog system working in the limited domain of bus timetable advice. But what does this mean?

Dialog systems can be **system-initiative**, **user-initiative**, or **mixed-initiative** system-initiative systems. These categories are about the extent to which the system or the user takes charge and guides the conversation in a particular direction. As users, we would user-initiative prefer mixed-initiative systems, in which both conversational participants can take mixed-initiative the lead as needed, because that is what we are used to from people. As we will see in the next section, Eliza was an early dialog system that is a user-initiative system.

Let's Go is a mixed-initiative system because both participants (caller and system) take initiative. The caller takes control at the beginning of the interaction, then again by asking for a later bus, and finally when requesting the return journey. Otherwise, the system keeps control, and carefully prompts the user to provide particular pieces of information. Many telephone-based systems keep an even tighter rein on the conversation than Let's Go does; it would not have been surprising, for example, if the system had explicitly asked "Is that OK?" immediately after telling the user about each bus departure, thereby taking more of the initiative.

Dialog systems can be designed to work with the user in carrying out a task or can fulfill some other purpose such as selling a product, telling a story, or making the task oriented user laugh. Most research systems are explicitly **task oriented**. This is helpful, because it allows the system to make sane assumptions about what the user's goals are and then to focus the dialog on these assumed goals, as Let's Go did. Within the general frame of task-oriented systems, there is room for more and less ambitious tasks, requiring greater or lesser flexibility on the part of the system. Less ambitious would be a system designed to obtain a 10-digit phone number with area code; more ambitious a system that engages the user in conversation about a wide range of possible entertainment options, with the aim of recommending one that the user will like.

It is also helpful for the system designer to know ahead of time that the user is trying to carry out a particular task, such as getting travel information, because it can then make task-specific assumptions about what the user knows, wants, and believes. The set-up of Let's Go assumes that the user is trying to travel somewhere by bus and needs timetable information in order to do so. Dialog scientists call this a limited domain. Nobody really expects Let's Go to be any good at general conversation or to be able to give investment advice; that is not its role.

Limited-domain settings can be contrasted with general settings, in which less can safely be assumed about user goals. Hal the computer definitely has general-purpose dialog skills that operate across many possible domains, using general knowledge and extremely sophisticated reasoning. This is well beyond current technology.

6.7 Eliza

Let's Go is a good example of a modern dialog system very useful for modeling human conversation and fulfilling a task. But it is also too complicated to be explained fully in this textbook. We want you to have the full picture on what is involved in making a simple working system, so we are going to go back in time and look at a very early dialog system, called Eliza. You can find several versions of

Eliza by searching around online. The original Eliza was made in 1966 and was the first well-known program of its kind. Joseph Weizenbaum, Eliza's creator, only wanted to show that simple principles could produce a reasonably good dialog participant. But the idea caught the imagination of researchers in artificial intelligence, and Eliza became very famous.

chatbot Eliza is a simple limited-domain dialog system; such systems are often referred to as **chatbots** or chatterbots. It is based on a script that allows it to pretend to be a Rogerian nondirective psychotherapist. Weizenbaum chose the therapeutic setting because it is one of the few situations in which a conversational participant can get away without specific knowledge of what is being discussed. The primary role of the nondirective therapist is simply to keep the conversation going, allowing the patient to talk out his or her concerns. Eliza takes on this role, and turns out to be able to handle it well. Figure 6.2 shows part of a dialog that Eliza might have with a familiar mythological figure. The transcript of this dialog is in Figure 6.3.

It is tremendously important to the success of Eliza that it is emulating a "nondirective" psychotherapist. This is what allows the program to be so simple, because a nondirective therapist can usually get away with simply reflecting back things that the patient has said. A proper Freudian psychotherapist would need to have a more complex way of responding to King Oedipus and would need to provide a little more depth in the responses.

Basically, the Eliza program only reacts to what the user says (i.e., it is user-initiative). It watches for keywords such as "father" and "mother", and churns out items from a set of preplanned responses. Some of the things that it says, such as "Tell me more about your family.", are planned out in every detail and never changed. Others are a little more flexible: the system memorizes what the user says, changes it a little, and reflects some of the material back. Thus, it says "Why do you tell me that you were adopted by your stepfather now?" because the user has said "I was adopted by my stepfather." By reflecting back some of the material, it is increasing the chance that its contributions will conform to the Gricean maxim of providing *relevant* comments.

In this case, the words "I" and "my" have been converted into "you" and "your" (as well as "was" becoming "were"). While the placement of the word "now" is a little odd, this response works well. Later on, the system says "Perhaps I already know you were giving I your life history.", which is not quite right, because the routine that switches the personal pronouns made a small mistake. It would have been fine if the system had said "Perhaps I already know you were giving *me* your life history." In general, using the correct pronouns and understanding what the user is referring to with their pronouns (e.g., "I want help, and I want *it* now") is a challenge even today.

By carefully observing the behavior of the system, and making up new sentences that probe its capabilities, it is possible to find out much more about what the program must be doing. It clearly knows some words, has a store of templates for semirelevant responses, and remembers some of the things that the user says to it. The final response –"Does that have anything to do with the fact that your father is king of thebes?" – could easily be mistaken for psychological insight, but, as you will see if you read the Under the Hood section on Eliza, this is far from the case.

Eliza Test

This applet implements the classic "Eliza" program, a program that communicates in natural language. It pretends to be a Rogerian psychologist.

The original ELIZA was described by Joseph Weizenbaum in *Communications of the ACM* in January 1966. ELIZA was one of the first programs that attempted to communicate in natural language. The article was an attempt to demystify the behavior of the program, and included a detailed description of the program. ELIZA is based on a "script" consisting of patterns and corresponding responses. An appendix to the article contained the complete script for the Rogerial psychologist.

This rendition of ELIZA is a complete and faithful implementation of the program described by Weizenbaum. The script language has been reformatted for clarity, but is unchanged in its content.

>> I have just discovered that my father is king of Thebes.
Tell me more about your family.
>> I was left on a hillside to die, but rescued by a shepherd.
Were you really ?
>> Then I was adopted by my stepfather, Polybus of Corinth, and his queen, Merope.
Why do you tell me you were adopted by your stepfather now ?
>> I was giving you my life history.
Perhaps I already know you were giving I your life history

The Source

- Decomp.java - Decomposition rule.
- DecompList.java - List of decomposition rules.
- Key.java - A key is the first thing the program looks for in the input.
- KeyList.java - The list of all keys.
- KeyStack.java - The program arranges all keys found in the input into a rank-ordered stack.
- Mem.java - Used to store responses for later use.
- PrePost.java - Holds word parts for pre or post rewriting.
- PrePostList.java - List of all the pre or post rules.
- Reassemb.List.java - List of reassembly rules (goes with a decomp rule).
- EString.java - String matching and transformation helper functions.
- Synlist.java - List of EWordList synonym lists.
- WordList.java - List of words, used for synonyms.
- Eliza.java - The main applet program.
- ElizaApp.java The main application program. Use either this or Eliza.java, not both.
- ElizaMain.java - The main driver.

The Script

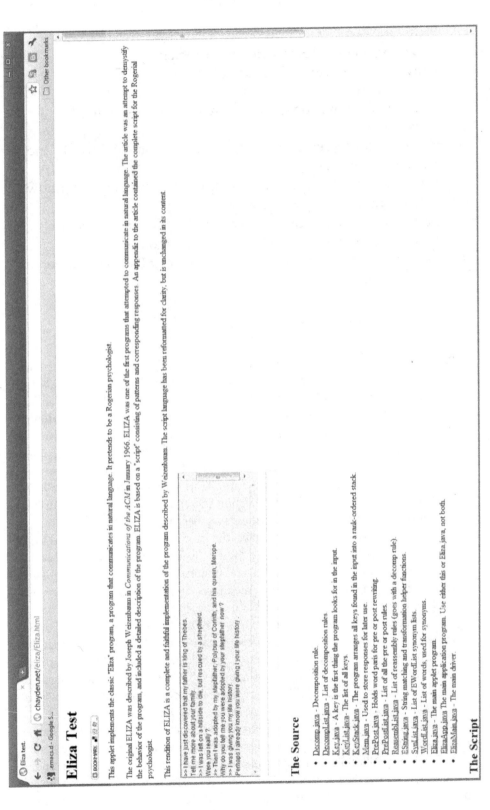

Figure 6.2 Screenshot of an ELIZA implementation (http://chayden.net/eliza/Eliza.html)

O: Hello.
E: How do you do. Please state your problem.
O: I have just discovered that my father is king of Thebes.
E: Tell me more about your family.
O: I was left on a hillside to die, but rescued by a shepherd.
E: Were you really?
O: Then I was adopted by my stepfather, Polybus of Corinth, and his queen, Merope.
E: Why do you tell me you were adopted by your stepfather now?
O: I was giving you my life history.
E: Perhaps I already know you were giving I your life history.
O: By the way, the oracle made a prophecy about me.
E: Does that have anything to do with the fact that your father is king of thebes?
O: ...

Figure 6.3 Transcript of Eliza's dialog with a figure from mythology

Part of the reason conversations with Eliza sometimes appear to succeed is that its conversational partners are very tolerant and adaptable. This is not surprising, because everyday dialog with a human partner also calls for flexibility and an ability to smooth over potential confusions. It is perfectly possible for human dialog partners to carry on a conversation in a noisy environment where almost every word is liable to be misheard, and the same kind of ability to keep going in the face of error operates at the level of meaning. When we talk with a human being, we are continually making sensible guesses and assumptions in order to fill in the details we need. This allows us to follow the conversation and chip in with our own contributions. It is natural to treat Eliza in the same way, generating the guesses and assumptions that are needed in order to make the conversation make sense. Eliza's conversation partner ends up actively working to maintain the illusion that this is a genuine conversation. Since Eliza has no real understanding, it will sooner or later say spectacularly unlikely and inappropriate things, and the illusion will shatter, but this can take a surprisingly long time if circumstances are favorable.

There is at least one well-attested account of a human being being misled by an Eliza-like program. Figure 6.4 is a story told to the *Stanford Humanities Review* by Daniel Bobrow, who is one of the pioneers of artificial intelligence. (Some historical pointers: *PDP-1* was an early type of computer; *LISP* is a programming language; *Weizenbaum* was the creator of Eliza; *teletype* was a typewriter used to type messages over a communication channel; and being *snotty*, we hope, is obvious.)

Eliza is important for two reasons. First, it works reasonably well using simple means, and this can be useful if your application calls for a straightforward but limited way of creating the illusion of an intelligent being at the other end of the wire. Secondly, it draws attention to the fact that human beings are tolerant dialog partners, who are prepared to cut their interlocutors a great deal of slack for the sake of keeping the

One Saturday morning about 9 a.m., a Vice President of Bolt, Beranek, and Newman in charge of selling our Telcomp commercial service arrived at our PDP-1 computer room hoping to be able to use the computer for a demonstration. He found a note on the PDP-1 teletype that read: "TYPE ALL MESSAGES INTO THIS TELETYPE AND END THEM WITH A PERIOD." This note was left there by one of the programming bums who had just succedeed in making run a LISP version of the DOCTOR program (based on ELIZA as developed by Weizenbaum). However, the VP thought that this note indicated that this teletype was linked with the one in my home, since I often use the computer all night. Therefore, he started typing to "me", but in fact was typing to this version of the DOCTOR program. The following conversation ensued:

VP: Do you think that I can use the computer this morning?
ELIZA: Why do you ask?
VP: I might be able to make some additional Telcom sales.
ELIZA: Why aren't you so sure?
VP: My perspective customers have never seen a demonstration of the system.
ELIZA: Does this mean very much to you?
VP: Of course it does.
ELIZA: You seem very positive about that.
VP: This is ridiculous.
ELIZA: What do you mean, this is ridiculous?
VP: Is there any reason why I can't use the computer now?
ELIZA: Tell me more about your perspective customers.
VP: Please dial me up on 491-1850 [*Note that after the last remark the VP did not obey instructions, and left out the period. Therefore, of course, the computer didn't answer him. This so infuriated the VP, who thought I was playing games with him, that he called me up, woke me from a deep sleep, and said:*]
VP: Why are you being so snotty to me?
BOBROW: What do you mean I am being snotty to you? [*The VP angrily read me the dialog that "we" had been having, and couldn't get any response but laughter from me. It took a while to convince him it really was a computer.*]

Figure 6.4   VP's dialog with Eliza, told by Daniel Bobrow

conversation going. Guesses and assumptions are just a built-in part of the process. This is obvious once you notice it, and really has nothing to do with computers, but it is something that everyone should remember. For example, eyewitness testimonies can be flawed because the witness cannot always tell the difference between the details they actually saw and the ones they used their common sense and world knowledge to fill in. In the same way, it is sometimes hard to tell the difference between what your conversation partner actually said and what you filled in using common sense, world knowledge, and awareness of dialog conventions. If you want to be more certain, record the conversation.

Under the Hood 10
How Eliza works

The software behind Eliza is conceptually simple. It carries out the following steps:

1. Read in a collection of templates. The templates are specified in a script (i.e., program) authored by the system designer and are the main means of controlling the dialog. These are outlined below.
2. Greet Eliza's patient. Possible greetings are again specified in the script.
3. Conduct a series of exchanges, where each exchange involves:
    - Reading a line of input and breaking it into words.
    - Matching the input against a template. This may involve storing some of the material from the user.
    - Creating a response. If necessary, material from the user input is incorporated into the response. Sometimes this requires postprocessing in order to, for example, convert the pronouns of "*I* hate *my* family." for use in "What makes you think that *you* hate *your* family?"
    - Printing out the response.
4. When the patient wants to quit, issue a farewell message. The choice of goodbyes again comes from the script.

As we can see, most of the processing involves working with a prespecified script containing very simple templates.

Templates

Here is an example template from the implementation shown in Figure 6.2. It is almost the same as the script used in Weizenbaum's original Eliza; the only differences are in the formatting of the text.

```
decomp: * i am *
    reasmb: Is it because you are (2) that you came
            to me ?
    reasmb: How long have you been (2) ?
    reasmb: Do you believe it is normal to be (2) ?
    reasmb: Do you enjoy being (2) ?
```

The first line, notated by decomp (for 'decompose the input'), says that this template is relevant when Eliza's patient says anything with the words i am in it. The stars before and after i am are special entities called wildcards, and they stand for any sequence of words (see also Section 4.2). If the patient says "At court I am nervous and sweaty.", the first star will match "At court", and the second will match "nervous and sweaty".

The second and subsequent lines, labeled with reasmb (for 'reassemble the output'), give Eliza options for how to reply. In these lines, variables like (1) and (2) are special markers, indicating places where material that matched the first and second stars should be inserted. For the example above, Eliza might respond: "Do you enjoy being nervous and sweaty?"

Here is another template, designed to deal with remarks like "Everyone hates me."

```
key: everyone 200
    decomp: * @everyone *
    reasmb: Realy, (2) ?
    reasmb: Surely not (2).
    reasmb: Can you think of anyone in particular ?
    reasmb: Who, for example?
    reasmb: Are you thinking of a very special
            person ?
    reasmb: Who, may I ask ?
    reasmb: Someone special perhaps ?
    reasmb: You have a particular person in mind,
            don't you ?
    reasmb: Who do you think you're talking about ?
```

This one has some extra features. The key is labeled with a priority of 200. This is so the program can know which template to choose if several different ones happen to match. A template with priority 500 would be preferred over anything with a lower priority. Also, the @ in @everyone is special, and indicates that Eliza should refer back to an earlier line of the script where synonyms (synon) were defined:

```
synon: everyone everybody nobody noone
```

The idea here is that the word can be either "everyone" or one of the alternatives, and the template should still fire. Also, the word that matched gets a number; in this case (2). So, if the patient says "Nobody loves me for who I really I am.", Eliza will reply "Realy, nobody?". Note the typo, which comes from the template: if that's what the script says, that's what Eliza does!

(Continued)

Under the Hood 10
How Eliza works

(Cont'd.)

Template matching

After reading in all the templates, the program begins to read lines from the patient, and responds as appropriate. Each line is broken down into words, mapped to lower case, and used to match against the templates.

A template is chosen. For the sake of variety, Eliza cycles through the options available with each template, choosing each of them in turn. The first time that the "i am" template is used, if the input was the one about being nervous and sweaty, Eliza will ask: "Is it because you are nervous and sweaty that you came to me?" And if the patient later says something that results in the template being used again, the result will be: "How long have you been nervous and sweaty?"

Postprocessing

In order to make responses sound more natural, the program has to post-process the patient's input, doing things like changing me into you. This too is specified as part of the script. It works reasonably well, but the line in Oedipus's dialog about

E: Perhaps I already know you were giving I your life history.

shows that it doesn't always work perfectly. In exercise 5 we invite you to write patterns to predict where "me" occurs and where "I" occurs. For more robust dialog systems, this would involve more complicated natural language generation, where part of speech (POS) and syntactic properties would indicate which pronoun is appropriate.

6.8   Spoken dialogs

Eliza produces its output in written form, on the screen. This is not what we usually do as humans, although we can. For us it is more natural to produce the dialog in spoken form. Programs for text-to-speech synthesis are available for most modern computers (see Section 1.4.5) and can, for example, play back the text of a document. It would be quite easy to make Eliza speak by hooking into this software.

Unfortunately, this may not be enough because, in dialog, the speakers must do more than speak the right words; they must also speak them in the right way, with appropriate emphasis and intonation. We know this already: the scripts of plays often have stage directions, and even when they do not, actors are expected to perform the words in a way that is expressive of the underlying intentions of the characters. The only way they can do this is to understand those intentions, and to imagine how a person with those intentions would speak the words.

In practice, what this means is that the core dialog system needs to produce more than just the words themselves, and pass them along to the speech synthesizer. There are standard markup languages called SSML and voice XML, both of which aim to do for speech what HTML does for well-laid-out text on the web (see Under the Hood 6 in Chapter 4). The idea is that instead of saying where you want paragraphs, line breaks, bold fonts, and so on, as you would with HTML, you instead provide tags that specify emphasis, timing, and pitch at a more or less detailed level. This field is in its infancy; more work is needed on finding good ways to describe the ebb and flow of expressive spoken language, and then yet further research will be needed to make the connections between the top-level plans and the ways in which they ought to be expressed in dialog.

For now, dialog systems are probably going to sound flatter and more robotic than their human counterparts. This may in fact be helpful in managing expectations, because a very natural sound might draw users into unreasonable expectations about what the system is really able to do.

6.9   How to evaluate a dialog system

If we want to make dialog systems better, we have to devise methods for making sure that we can measure their performance and work out which features of the systems contribute to success.

In principle, we know exactly how to evaluate the performance of a dialog system. Suppose that its job is to help customers make airline bookings. All that we have to do is to monitor the conversations it has, measuring how often it succeeds in booking a flight for the customer, how often the customer hangs up in frustration, and perhaps even the number of times it lures a gullible customer into paying extra money for a first-class seat. This is exactly what well-organized businesses do with human customer service representatives. (In call centers, the somewhat questionable activity of guiding customers to high-profit additional items is called **upselling**, and it is exceptionally important in determining your commission.) Unfortunately, this style of evaluation will not work until the system is good enough to be worth deploying in the first place, so it is not useful for the initial development. Until the system is good enough, users will simply be unable to interact with it in any useful way. In particular, until the system is minimally capable of holding up its own end of the conversation, users will be unable to have a dialog with it at all, and no progress will be made in improving it.

In response to this conundrum, researchers have developed two approaches. Both approaches temporarily give up on the idea of human–computer dialog, but try to

upselling

collect information that will be useful in shaping the design of the final system. The first of these approaches replaces human–computer dialog with a carefully disguised human–human dialog. As far as the user is concerned, the system seems like a computer, but actually, behind the scenes, it is being driven by a human being who takes **Wizard of** on the role of the computer. This approach is called the **Wizard of Oz simulation**, **Oz simulation** because, like the Wizard of Oz in the movie, it relies on using a trick to maintain the illusion of magic.

The second approach replaces the human–computer dialog with a computer–computer dialog. Here there are two computer systems. The main system is a straightforward dialog system, one that tries to be flexible and efficient in the ways we have discussed earlier in the chapter. In addition, there is a second computer system that is designed to take on the role of the user. This is similar to an idea that has been used by chess computers in which the system learns by playing a large number of simulated games against itself. In just the same way, two linked dialog systems can rapidly simulate a large number of dialogs and work out which strategies will work best in achieving the goals of the system. Of course, this only works if the simulated dialogs are sufficiently similar to what the system will encounter with real, live users.

A third approach to evaluation is to give up on the idea of doing fully general dialog systems, and to focus instead on dialogs that take place in well-understood and highly structured domains. One such domain is teaching. Teaching, especially individual or small-group teaching, can definitely be seen as a dialog, but **role** it is one where the **roles** are very well defined and formal. The teacher is trying to get the student to think in particular ways and may also be trying to evaluate the student's level of knowledge. Typically, the teacher asks carefully targeted questions, then pays attention to the student's answers, looking for evidence that the student is thinking in the expected ways, or that particular expected **tutorial dialog** misconceptions have arisen. This kind of **tutorial dialog** is highly structured and has attracted a lot of research, both from people who want to automate it and from those who want to help human teachers develop effective ways of getting ideas across.

6.10   Why is dialog important?

Dialog crosses the boundary between language and action. In order to play well with others in dialog, computers need not only to use language well, but also to understand the mental and social worlds of their interlocutors. Current dialog systems work well when the designers manage to arrange for a situation in which the system can get away with limited linguistic and social skills, and poorly when the situation calls for real flexibility. Realistically, the near future is likely to bring continued clever exploitations of the niches in which limited dialog skills are enough, along with improvements in surface features such as vocabulary choice and the naturalness of spoken responses. Major improvements in flexibility and responsiveness will only come, however, if researchers are able to crack some of the very hard problems of giving computers common sense and the ability to reason effectively with everyday knowledge.

Your working assumption should probably be that any impressive-seeming dialog system is probably more limited than it seems. Our guess is that a careful and systematic effort to probe such a system will reveal the limitations, just as it did with Eliza. Alan Turing, a British mathematician and early computer scientist, turned this idea around. Imagine that you find yourself in a (written medium) chat conversation, with a partner who, unknown to you, is actually a computer, and that the conversation is so natural that you really cannot be sure whether or not you are dealing with a machine. If a machine can do that, says Turing, perhaps we ought to agree that it has met all the important criteria for intelligence. This idea struck a chord among philosophers and many others, and contributed much to the development of the academic field of artificial intelligence. Turing's successors called his imaginary experiment the **Turing Test**.   **Turing Test**

The Loebner Prize is a competition for chatbots, where the set-up is essentially Turing's, and the designer of a successful program could win a large monetary prize. It has been suggested that any winning program ought to be allowed to keep the money, and make its own decisions about how to spend it, since it would, by definition, be intelligent enough to do so. This is a joke, because a special-purpose system designed to carry on a good dialog would not necessarily have any claim to general intelligence. However, for practical dialog needs, there is nothing wrong with a well-judged special-purpose system. It is certainly realistic to hope that there will be limited-domain dialog systems that are appropriately responsive, sound good, work well in their niche, and offer an improvement in terms of consistency and cost-effectiveness over what could be done before they existed.

Checklist

After reading the chapter, you should be able to:

- Explain why explicit modeling of the dialog partner's beliefs, desires, and intentions is sometimes necessary.
- Distinguish between system-initiative and mixed-initiative systems.
- Distinguish between dialog moves and speech acts.
- Explain the basic idea of Gricean maxims and the cooperative principle.
- Classify tasks according to the complexity of the dialog that is needed.
- Identify different types of errors that can arise in a dialog system.
- Explain why chatbots like Eliza can seem reasonably natural under good circumstances and disastrously unnatural when the interlocutor is less cooperative.
- Remember what a Wizard of Oz experiment is and why such experiments are necessary.

Exercises

1. **ALL**: A well-meaning friend with an MBA suggests replacing the Let's Go bus information system with a tape recording of someone reading out the whole of the bus timetable. Is this a good idea? Why or why not? If you think it is a bad idea, can you suggest any way of rescuing it?

2. **ALL**: Make a recording of yourself taking part in a conversation, preferably one in which you are trying to make a plan or get something done. (Make sure that you get permission from the person or people you are talking to.) Listen back to the conversation, and try to write down:
    (a) The words that were said.
    (b) Any hesitations or corrections that you notice.
    (c) Which of the utterances are statements, which are requests or commands, and which questions. Also, which are requests that sound like questions, requests that sound like statements, and so on.
    (d) Anything that you notice about assumptions that the speakers are making about each others' beliefs, desires, and intentions.

3. **ALL**: We claimed that dialog can be seen as a game, and drew an analogy to basketball. How far does this analogy go? In this exercise, we want you to push the analogy as far as you can. You might want to consider some of the following concepts, most of which seem to us to have interesting equivalents:
    *   Playing as a team (and its converse, playing selfishly).
    *   Committing so many fouls that you get ejected.
    *   Doing sneaky fouls behind the referee's back.
    *   Man-to-man coverage and zone defense.
    *   Misdirection and disguise.
    *   Tactics and strategy.
    *   Alley-oops and slam dunks.
    *   Free throws.
    *   Working the referee.
    *   Running out the clock.
        Write up your ideas about how some of these concepts map onto dialog (or think up new ones of your own and map them). You should give specific examples of how a dialog could match each situation. We do not promise that all our items make sense, since we intentionally put in a few strange ones to challenge your imaginations.

4. **CS**: Much of Eliza's success depends on clever design of the templates. If you have the skills to run a Java program on your website, you can have a lot of fun by making your own version of Eliza run with a script of your own design. We have seen versions of Eliza that do nontherapeutic things, such as showering the user with robot-flavored verbal abuse. The author of that version had some very funny ideas for things that a robot made of metal and

silicon could say to the frail, wet, and disgusting organic life-forms with which it was being forced to interact. Try your hand at authoring an Eliza that does something impressive or funny. If you succeed, you will have made something impressive or funny. If you fail, you will learn something about the limits of the Eliza approach.

5. Look at the scripts for the Eliza described in the text, and:
   (a) **ALL**: Redesign the templates to do a better job of transforming personal pronouns in the input into the correct ones in the output.
   (b) **CS**: Test these templates and make a quantitative evaluation of how well they do.

6. By considering the ideas in this chapter, or otherwise, think of a potential application of current dialog system technology that is new to you, but that you think would be useful and might work.
   (a) **ALL**: Research this application to see whether it has been attempted and write a short report on the results. If you still like the idea, and think it would work, consider starting a company to develop it. Let us know how you do!
   (b) **CS**: Implement an Eliza-type system that provides a crude approximation of the need you have identified.

7. **ALL**: Do a study to find out what strict "push to talk" feels like, and how easy it is to use it in task-oriented dialogs. One way to do this is get hold of a pair of cheap walkie-talkies, then find a friend with whom you want to have a reasonably complicated conversation (something like planning a trip or hosting a social event might be good). Instead of doing this face to face, try it using the walkie-talkies. Maybe take notes of your impressions and/or make a recording. The next time you and the friend have the same kind of conversation, do it face to face, and pay attention to the differences between the two ways of having the dialog. Another way, which works at the time of writing but might be "improved" out of existence at any time, is to chat with friends using the Google Hangout service. You get a "push-to-talk" button if you are watching a YouTube video, but not if you are just chatting. Can you work out a way of turning this fact into a design for an experiment?

Further reading

H.L. Austin's book *How to do things with words* (Austin, 1975) is an excellent introduction to the idea that dialog can be thought of in terms of speech acts. This book sparked a series of major contributions to the philosophy of language, including H. Paul Grice's *Studies in the Way of Words* (Grice, 1989), which includes detailed discussion of the conversational maxims discussed in this chapter.

In the world of technology and computer-supported cooperative work. Terry Winograd and Fernando Flores develop the idea of "tools for conversation" in their book *Understanding*

Computers and Cognition: A New Foundation for Design (Winograd and Flores, 1987). This is a remarkable and thought-provoking book that does not fit into any known academic discipline, but is full of interesting and potentially very useful ideas. Their framework for thinking about conversation has found its way, in simplified form, into widely used software for email and calendaring.

Turing (1950) introduces the idea of the Turing Test and, despite being over 60 years old, is still fresh and challenging today, as well as beautifully written and full of sly humor.

Jurafsky and Martin (2009) is a good review of modern dialog systems. In Jurafsky and Martin (2000), the corresponding chapter is 19, but the one from the second edition is a complete rewrite and has a great deal of extra material. The quote from *2001* at the head of this chapter is also used by Jurafsky and Martin, as a general illustration of what computers might be able to do with speech and language. Weizenbaum, the creator of Eliza (Weizenbaum, 1983), was sufficiently shocked by the sensation caused by Eliza to write *Computer Power and Human Reason: From Judgment to Calculation* (Weizenbaum, 1976). A set of dialogs between Eliza and other human and computer entities, including the interaction with the anonymous VP of BBN, can be found at http://www.stanford.edu/group/SHR/4-2/text/dialogues.html.

The dialog moves discussed are simplified versions of those discussed in a review paper by Staffan Larsson (Larsson, 1998).

7

Machine Translation Systems

7.1   Computers that "translate"?

This chapter is about technology for automatic translation from one human language
to another. This is an area where the gap between (science) fiction and (science)
reality is especially large. In *Star Trek*, the crew uses a Universal Translator that
provides instantaneous speech-to-speech translation for almost all alien languages.
Sometimes there is a short pause while the Universal Translator adapts to a
particularly challenging language, and very occasionally the system proves
ineffective, but most of the time everything simply works. In *The Hitchhiker's Guide
to the Galaxy*, Douglas Adams' affectionate parody of the conventions of science
fiction, the same effect is achieved when Arthur Dent puts a Babel Fish in his ear. In
Matt Groening's *Futurama* (another parody), one of the characters invents a
Universal Translator that translates everything into French (in *Futurama*, nobody
speaks French any more, and almost everyone knows standard English anyway, so
this device, while impressive, has no practical value whatsoever). In the real world
however, instantaneous general-purpose speech-to-speech translation is still a far-
off research goal, so this chapter will focus on simpler uses of translation.

Before discussing uses of translation, it is useful to define the concept and introduce some terms. **Translation** is the process of moving text or speech from one
human language to another, while preserving the intended message. We will be
returning to the question of what exactly is meant by **preserving the intended message** throughout the chapter. For the moment, please accept the idea at its intuitive
face value. We call the language that the translation starts from the **source language**
and the language that it ends up in the **target language**. We say that two words, one

— translation

*— preserving the
intended
message*

— source language

— target language

Language and Computers, First Edition. Markus Dickinson, Chris Brew and Detmar Meurers.
© 2013 Markus Dickinson, Chris Brew and Detmar Meurers. Published 2013 by Blackwell Publishing Ltd.

In a Swiss mountain inn: Special today – no ice cream
In a doctor's office: Specialist in women and other diseases
In a Norwegian cocktail lounge: Ladies are requested not to
have children in the bar
In a Paris hotel: Please leave your values at the front desk.
On a Chinese menu: Stir fried Wikipedia
On the same Chinese menu: Steam eggs with Wikipedia
On sign above a Chinese dining hall: Translate server error

Figure 7.1 Some overconfident translations into English

translation
equivalents
from the source language, one from the target language, are **translation equivalents** if they convey the same meaning in context. The same idea applies to pairs of phrases and sentences.

Figure 7.1 contains some examples of difficulties that can arise if you are not careful to check whether a translation is saying the right thing. If you are ever asked to put up a sign in a language that you do not fully understand, remember these examples, and get the content checked.

It is unclear what happened with the first one. Perhaps the source text was about some kind of special ice-cream, and the adjective that described the ice-cream was mistranslated. Or perhaps the word "fat" was omitted, and the translation should have been "no-fat ice cream". The second one is presumably trying to describe a doctor who specializes in women's and other diseases, but the possessive marker is omitted, making the sentence into an unnecessary suggestion that women are a kind of disease. The third one happens because the sense of "have children" as "give birth" was not salient in the mind of the person who created the sign. The fourth one is just a poor word choice: "valuables" is the word that the translator was searching for, and "values" is unintentionally funny. The French word "valeurs" means "values" and the French phrase "valeurs familiales" is used in much the same way as "family values" is in English. Of course, this kind of ambiguity can also happen when English native speakers write notices in a hurry and do not check them carefully.

The last three are a little different, because they are failures of the *process* of translation. Presumably Wikipedia was used to find an article about some foodstuff, but the amateur translator mistook the name of the website for the name of the foodstuff. We have a great deal of sympathy for the translator here, because "Wikipedia" does feel like a good name for a foodstuff, possibly some kind of seafood with legs. For the dining hall, the graphic artist must have thought that the string "Translate server error" actually was the translation.

We chose the examples in Figure 7.1 because we hope that they are funny. But in other settings, translation errors can have serious consequences. This happened when a young male patient was brought into a Florida hospital's emergency room in a coma. His mother and girlfriend, speaking in Spanish, talked to the non-Spanish-speaking emergency room staff. They used the word "intoxicado", which can mean several things, including "nauseous". Because the emergency room staff were not professional interpreters, they thought that "intoxicado" must mean the same as the English "intoxicated" and treated him on the assumption that he was under the influence of drugs or alcohol. The patient was eventually diagnosed with a brain aneurysm and became quadriplegic. This case is famous, because it led to a lawsuit and drew attention to the principle that hospitals, courts, and other institutions that work with the public should plan for the needs of a multilingual population and provide the necessary translation and interpretation services. This is an issue of basic fairness, public safety, and perhaps also civil rights.

7.2   Applications of translation

7.2.1   Translation needs

In web search and information retrieval, the user can be thought of as having an information need (Section 4.3.1). In the same way, a potential user of translation technology can be thought of as having a **translation need**. If you have taken com- **translation need** parative literature classes at high school or college, you will have encountered translations into English of foreign-language poetry and novels. A publisher who wants to make a new English version of a novel by José Saramago has a translation need. This need is far beyond the capabilities of any present-day automatic system, because for this purpose, a good translation needs to be a literary work in its own right. As well as getting across the content, it must capture the "feel" of the original writing. The only way to do this is to employ a human translator who has excellent literary skills in both English and Portuguese. Because there are so many English-speaking readers in the world, and the author is a Nobel prize winner, the publisher can expect a good return on investment in expert help. Nobody would expect a machine-generated translation to be good enough for this purpose, although it would be cheap.

Another quite demanding translation need is that of a scholar needing to understand an academic paper written in a foreign language. Here, the scholar does not care much about the "feel" of the article, but will want to be sure about the arguments that are being made, the conclusions that are being drawn, and the evidence that is being used to support these conclusions. To do this well, even if the paper is in your native language, you need to have some training in the relevant academic field or fields. Academic papers are designed to be read by informed experts, so if the paper is on linguistics, what you are looking for is a translator who is expert enough in linguistics to be able to understand and accurately translate the arguments in the text. A translator who is a specialist in translating business documents will almost certainly struggle to make a useful translation of a linguistics paper. We should not expect a machine translation system to be any better at meeting this specialized need.

7.2.2   What is machine translation really for?

In Chapters 2 and 4, we described technology that supports the everyday scholarly activities of information gathering and writing. Each one of you already knows much about these activities. The role of the computer is to help out with the aspects of the process that it does well, and to keep out of the way when the human writer knows better. Translation is a little different, because it is usually done by trained experts rather than the general public. Professional translators sometimes worry that machines are going to take over their role, or that free web-based services will lead to big changes in the market for their skills. These worries are reasonable, since all knowledge workers will need to adapt as technology changes, but the reality is that professional translators are still going to be required in future. Unless you have had an internship with a translation company, you probably do not know as much about the market for translation as you do about the activities of writing and information gathering. In this chapter, as well as explaining some of the technology, we will go into detail about the business needs for translation and the changes that are resulting from the easy availability of free online translation.

From this perspective, literary translations are interesting to think about when we are trying to understand the process of translation, but are not the first place to look for practically important uses of translation technology. For that, we need to focus on more everyday translation needs. For example, if you are considering buying a new mobile phone, but the model you want is not yet available in your country, you may want to read customer reviews from another market, perhaps ones written in a language you do not know well.

This is a translation need, but literary quality is no longer a relevant criterion. You want to know about battery life, quality of the input devices, usability of the built-in software, and so on. (See Chapter 5 on classifying documents for other ways in which computers can assist in this.) If there are points in the review that you can understand, errors may not matter. The German text says that the phone is a little slimmer (*schmaler*) than the iPhone, and the English version is "The Magic is smaller, and therefore slightly better in the hand". A human translator might write this as "The Magic is slimmer and therefore more pleasant to handle", but the rather literal automatic translation serves the purpose perfectly well, even though, strictly speaking, it is inaccurate. Free web-based translation (specifically, Google Translate, in July 2009) is quite adequate for this translation need.

A third type of translation need turns up in large multinational organizations such as electronics companies. For them, there is often a legal requirement that the instruction manuals and other documentation be available in the native language of the user. Here, accuracy obviously matters, but fine points of literary style are not important. Indeed, if there is a choice between elegant literary phrasing and an uglier version using simple and direct language, the latter is preferable. For this translation need, there is an especially good choice of translation technology, called **example-based translation**. This relies on the fact that most of the sentences in an instruction manual are either the same as or very similar to sentences found somewhere in a collection of previously translated manuals. Electronics companies keep copies of all the manuals that they produce, as

example-based translation

well as the translations. The software that does this is called a **translation memory**.
The first step is for the human translator to use the search capability of the translation
memory to find relevant sentences that have already been translated. These previously
translated sentences can be used as a basis for the translation of the new sentence. For
example, suppose that the sentence to be translated into German is:

(33)   The FX380B has a color LCD screen and an automatic rangefinder.

and we have the following example sentences already translated:

(34)   a. The ZX65 has a color LCD screen.
           = <u>Die ZX65 hat einen LCD-Farbbildschirm</u>.
       b. The FX809 has a 4 cm screen <u>and</u> a flashgun.
           = Die FX809 hat einen 4 cm-Bildschirm <u>und</u> ein Blitzgerät.
       c. The larger model has <u>an automatic rangefinder</u>.
           = Das größere Modell verfügt über <u>einen automatischen</u>
           <u>Entfernungsmesser</u>.

Then it should not be too hard to piece together the underlined fragments to get:

(35)   The FX380B has a color LCD screen and an automatic rangefinder.
       = Die FX380B hat einen LCD-Farbbildschirm und einen automatischen
       Entfernungsmesser.

The simplest way of doing this is to write a program that uses search technology to
find the best matching sentences, leaving to a human the task of working out how to
put the fragments together. Alternatively, a fairly simple program could get most of
the way. There would need to be a special routine to make sure that the name of the
product "FX380B" was transferred appropriately, but the rest is pretty straightforward. The output should be checked by a human being, to make sure that the legal
requirement for adequate documentation has been met. Once again, the standards
that apply depend on the nature of the documentation need. The documentation for
a medical x-ray machine that is going to be used by a multilingual staff, and that
could hurt people if it is used incorrectly, needs to be excellent in all the relevant
languages. The translations of the documentation for a mobile phone are not so
safety-critical, so it may be acceptable to be a little less careful.
       The important lesson of this section is that the translation technology that is used
should depend on the details of the translation need, not just on some abstract
notion of what counts as a good translation.

7.3   Translating Shakespeare

For fun, let us return to the idea of translating Shakespeare. Figures 7.2, 7.3, 7.4,
and 7.5 contain a range of versions of Shakespeare's Sonnet 29. One is the original
Shakespeare, one a brilliant translation into German by the twentieth-century poet

When, in disgrace with fortune and men's eyes,
I all alone beweep my outcast state
And trouble deaf heaven with my bootless cries
And look upon myself and curse my fate,
Wishing me like to one more rich in hope,
Featured like him, like him with friends possess'd,
Desiring this man's art and that man's scope,
With what I most enjoy contented least;
Yet in these thoughts myself almost despising,
Haply I think on thee, and then my state,
Like to the lark at break of day arising
From sullen earth, sings hymns at heaven's gate;
For thy sweet love remember'd such wealth brings
That then I scorn to change my state with kings.

Figure 7.2   Shakespeare's Sonnet 29 in the original

Wenn ich verbannt von glück und menschenblick
Bewein allein mein ausgestossnen-los ·
Mich selber sehend fluche dem geschick ·
Zum tauben himmel schreie aussichtlos:

Möcht ich wie einer sein mit freunden viel ·
Wie er geformt · wie er von hoffnung voll
Und wünsche eines kunst · des andren ziel –
Dess mindest froh was meist mich freuen soll.

In solchem sinnen fast mich selbst verachtend
Fällst du mir plötzlich ein: ich steig empor
Und · wie die lerche mit dem frührot trachtend
Aus trüber erd · lobsing am himmelstor.

Dein · süsse liebe · denken bringt solch glück ..
Nun weis ich tausch mit königen zurück.

Figure 7.3   Shakespeare's Sonnet 29 as translated by Stefan George

Als in Ungnade Glück und die Augen der Männer,
Ich ganz allein meine <u>beweep</u> Ausgestoßenen Zustand
Und tauben Himmel <u>weint mein begehret</u>
Und ich betrachte mein Schicksal und Fluch,

Figure 7.4   Google's translation of Sonnet 29

If I exiled from happiness and human-looking
    (from: *Wenn ich verbannt von glück und menschenblick*)
Lament but my outcast, los ·
    (from: *Bewein allein mein ausgestossnen-los ·*)
Curse myself seeing the cleverest ·
    (from: *Mich selber sehend fluche dem geschick ·*)
For the deaf sky hopeless cry:
    (from: *Zum tauben himmel schreie aussichtlos:*)

Figure 7.5   Google's translation of Stefan George's version

Stefan George. Then there are two machine translations from English to German, and a back-translation by Google Translate of George's German into English.

When translating poetry, it is important to do more than just get the meaning across: you have to also aim for a similar overall impression. Stefan George's translation is almost line for line, and uses the same rhyme scheme as Shakespeare. "Deaf heaven" in Shakespeare's third line finishes up as "tauben himmel" in George's fourth, and the "rich in hope" in Shakespeare's fifth becomes "von hoffnung voll" in George's sixth. The crunchy contrast of "with what I most enjoy contented least" turns into the alliterative "Dess mindest froh was meist mich freuen soll".

German and English are quite closely related – words like "king" and "König" or "earth" and "Erde" come from the same original source and mean the same. Linguists call these corresponding words **cognates**. Cognates sometimes make it possible to   **cognate** work out which lines go with which even if you don't speak German well enough to read the text in detail.

Figures 7.4 and 7.5 show what happens with automatic translation. In Google's German, the word "beweep" has defeated the system, and simply been transferred over unchanged. Also, the fourth line translates the English word "curse" as a noun "Fluch" when it should be a verb. Because the verb is missing from the German, the translation engine has a hard time finding an acceptable way of fitting in the material that should have been attached to it, and the result is very messy.

In Google's English (which is a back-translation of George's good German), there are lots of good word-for-word translations. But "los" (= "fate") has been "translated" in the same way that "beweep" was: the system has given up. The term "human-looking" is not quite right for "Menschenblick": Shakespeare had "men's eyes", and "human view" is probably what a modern writer would produce. Also, the "For" in "For the deaf sky hopeless cry" should be "To", thus rendering the final line as "To the deaf sky hopelessly cry".

Overall, the conclusion regarding poetical translation has to be a qualified negative. Current systems are designed for quite a different translation need. Certainly, the output is not good poetry, or indeed particularly convincing English, but there might be circumstances in which knowing what the poem is about has some usefulness. For example, it comes through clearly that Shakespeare's sensitive protagonist is not having an especially good time. And, more seriously, a human translator might be able to use the machine-translated output as a starting point for revisions.

7.4 The translation triangle

Figure 7.6 shows a diagram that explains one of the main tradeoffs in designing translation systems. At the bottom corners of the triangle in Figure 7.6 are the source and target languages. The captions in the body of the triangle indicate possible relationships between source and target language. If we are lucky, the words and concepts in the target language will match those in the source language, and direct word-for-word translation will just about work. In that case, there is no need to design a complex system, or to use linguistically sophisticated representations.

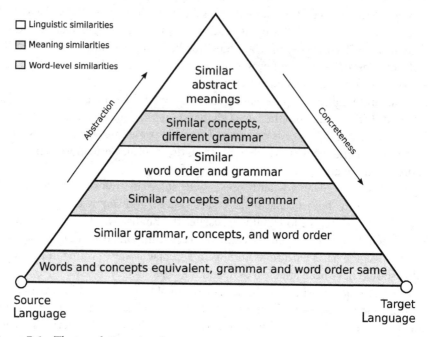

Figure 7.6 The translation triangle

The example-based translation that we discussed in Section 7.2.2 is a method that works directly with the words of the sentence, not analyzing them in any deep way. The translation triangle illustrates the fact that if you work at the level of words, source and target languages are quite far apart. For some uses, such as example-based methods for highly stereotyped and repetitive texts, such **direct approaches to translation** work well enough, but broadly speaking they are insufficient for more general tasks.

direct approaches to translation

The labels on the body of the triangle represent various different kinds of similarities and differences that might turn up in translation. There can be differences in the linguistic rules used by the two languages and also differences in the way in which the languages map concepts onto words. If you are prepared to do work to produce abstract representations that reconcile these differences, you can make translation easier. The captions are placed according to our judgment of how easy it would be for an MT system to create them, with the ones that would take more work nearer the top.

The arrow labeled *Abstraction* points in the direction of increasing abstraction, as well as increasing distance from the specifics of the source and target languages. The higher you go, the fewer the differences between source and target languages, and the easier the task of converting the source language representation into the target language representation. This is represented by the fact that the sides of the triangle get closer as we go up. The corresponding arrow, labeled *Concreteness*, points in the direction of increasing concreteness (therefore, also, in the direction of decreasing abstraction).

However, although translation itself gets easier as the representation becomes more abstract, the task of moving from the words of the source language to a more abstract representation gets harder as the representation becomes more abstract, as does the task of moving from the abstract representation of the target language back down to the words of the target language. This is represented by the fact that the distance between the representations and the bottom of the triangle grows larger as we go up. Unless the consumers of your translations are highly sophisticated linguists, it will not do to give them abstract representations: they need words.

At the apex of the translation triangle we would have a so-called **interlingua**. At this point there would be no difference between the source and target language representations. If you could do full linguistic analysis and get all the way to a common *language-neutral* meaning, there would be no translation work to do.

interlingua

Thus, an interlingua is a representation that can be reached by analyzing the source language, and that can then be used, unchanged, to generate the equivalent sentence in the target language. If this could be achieved, it would have the tremendous advantage that in order to add a new language (e.g., Hungarian) to our translation system we would only need to build a Hungarian-to-interlingua module and an interlingua-to-Hungarian module. Once that was done, we could translate to or from Hungarian into or out of any of the other languages in the system.

The fundamental problem with this approach is that the interlingua is an ideal rather than a reality. Despite great efforts, nobody has ever managed to design or build a suitable interlingua. Worse, it has turned out to be very difficult to build fully

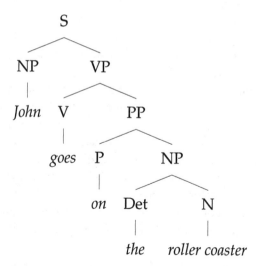

Figure 7.7 English phrase structure rules for *John goes on the roller coaster*

adequate solutions for the step that analyzes the source words and produces the interlingua. A useful partial solution for this task, which is known as parsing, is described in detail in Section 2.4.1. Finally, the remaining step, the one that generates the target language words from the interlingua, is also a difficult research topic on which much effort and ink has been spent. In summary, the interlingua idea is useful because it clarifies what would need to be done in order to build an excellent MT system based on solid linguistic principles. This is helpful as a focus for research, but it does not offer a ready-made solution.

So, while an interlingua-based system would be good in theory, we probably cannot have one any time soon. For practical purposes, it is often best to be somewhat less idealistic, and build systems that do simple things well. Sometimes a direct approach will work well, because the given languages express things in similar ways.

Figures 7.7 and 7.8 give an example of two sentences for which everything is parallel, so the direct approach would work well. If you know German, you will realize that the only really tricky aspect of this pair of sentences is getting the right feminine dative ending on the article "der" that translates "the". For the record, the German is actually a little less ambiguous than the English: the German unambiguously says that John is riding on the roller coaster, not going *onto* the roller coaster, but the English allows either situation. In translating, you often have to make an educated guess about what was meant in order to translate correctly. An automatic system has to do the same, by whatever means it can.

In practice, many systems fall in the middle ground between the direct method and interlinguas, doing some linguistic analysis in order to move a little way up the translation triangle. The result of this is a language-specific transfer representation for the source language sentence. Then the system designer writes transfer rules to move the language-specific source language representation into a language-specific target language representation. Finally, a third module moves from the language-specific target

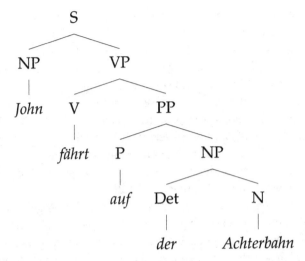

Figure 7.8 German phrase structure rules for *John fährt auf der Achterbahn*

language representation to an actual target language sentence. Systems that use this design are called **transfer systems**. The advantage of this approach is that the transfer representations can be designed in such a way that the transfer rules are reasonably easy to write and test; certainly easier than the kind of rules you have to write in order to switch around the word order in a direct approach to the translation between English and German. The disadvantage is that if you have N languages you have to write $N(N-1)$ sets of rules, one for each pair of languages and direction of translation.

transfer systems

7.5 Translation and meaning

The main requirement that we can realistically expect from machine translation is that the translation process **preserves meaning**. That is, we want a person who speaks only the target language to be able to read the translation with an accurate understanding of what the source language original was saying. Before we can tell whether a translation is good, we will need to have a clear way of talking precisely about the meanings we are aiming to preserve. Therefore, before studying the details of translation, we will need to introduce some ideas from the linguistic subfield of **semantics**, which is the study of the part of human language grammar that is used to construct meanings (see also Section 3.3 for a discussion of semantic relations in the context of language tutoring systems).

preservation of meaning

semantics

Notice that we are no longer asking for the translated text to preserve aspects of the message other than meaning. The style of the translation could be very different from the style of the original. So long as the meaning is preserved, we will call the result a success.

In our discussion of grammar checking (Section 2.4.1), we saw that it is helpful to break up English sentences into smaller components, and give these components names like *noun phrase* and *verb phrase*. These components may in turn be broken down into subcomponents, with the whole process bottoming out either in words or in a unit slightly smaller than the word that is called the **morpheme**. The same kind of process happens in semantics and we thus need to study two aspects. The first is **lexical semantics**, which is the study of the meanings of words and the relationships between these meanings. Lexical semantics includes the study of synonym (words that mean the same thing), **antonyms** (words that are opposites), and **word senses** (the subdivisions of meaning that a particular word can have). This matters for translation, because lexical semantics gives you the tools to understand some of the ways in which elements can change as you move from one language to another.

morpheme

lexical semantics

antonym

word sense

The other part of semantics explains how a sentence like "Roger outplayed Andy" means something quite different from "Andy outplayed Roger". The words are the same, but the way they are arranged differs, and this affects the meaning. But "Roger outplayed Andy" means much the same as "Andy was outplayed by Roger". Here the words differ, but the meaning somehow comes out almost identical. The part of semantics that studies this is called **compositional semantics.**

compositional semantics

The reason that this term (*compositional*) is used is that the meaning of a whole expression is *composed* of the meanings of its component parts. Thus, the meaning of the phrase "triangular hat box" is constructed (one way or another) from the meanings of the individual words "triangular", "hat", and "box". It could mean a triangular box for hats, a box (shape unspecified) for triangular hats, or even a triangular box made out of hats, but each one of these meanings can be built out of the meanings of the smaller parts. Researchers in compositional semantics begin with the assumption that there is some kind of kind of mechanism for assembling the word meanings into a sentence meaning and spend their research efforts on experiments and theories designed to shed light on the way this mechanism works. Different languages typically assemble meanings in similar ways, but the fine details of the process differ from language to language, so an automatic translator has to smooth over the differences somehow.

For example, in German, when you want to say that you like skiing, you use an adverb (*gern*) to express the idea of liking:

(36) Ich fahre gern Ski
I drive (gladly) on-skis
'I like skiing'.

There are two aspects to notice about this translation:

1. The word "skiing" translates into two words of German, one of which (*fahren*) means something like the English verb "to drive", and the other (*Ski*) is rather like "on skis".
2. "Gern" doesn't really mean the same as "gladly", but this is the best available English word if you want a literal translation.

The meaning comes across, and in each language it is easy to see how the meaning of the whole is related to the meaning of the parts, but the details differ.

Some phrases are not like this at all. Both German and English have idiomatic phrases for dying, but the usual English one is "kick the bucket" and the German one is "ins Gras beissen", which is literally "to bite into the grass". The German idiom is rather like the English "bites the dust", and a tolerant reader can probably accept that the meaning is somehow related to the meaning of the component parts, but the English idiomatic meaning has no obvious connection with buckets or kicking, so **non-** linguists label this kind of phrase **non-compositional**. To understand "kick the **compositional** bucket" you just have to learn the special idiomatic meaning for the phrase. As a bonus, once you have done that, the slang-term "bucket list" becomes more comprehensible as a way of talking about the list of things you want to do before you die. Later in the chapter, we will see a technology called phrase-based machine translation. This technology learns from data and would probably be able to get the translation right for many idiomatic phrases.

7.6   Words and meanings

7.6.1   Words and other languages

George W. Bush is reputed to have said: "The trouble with the French is that they don't have a word for entrepreneur". This is an example of a common type of claim made by journalists and others. But, of course, "entrepreneur" *is* a French word, listed in the dictionary, and means just about the same as it does in English. Claims like this are not really about the meanings of the words, but rather about cultural attitudes. If President Bush did actually say what was reported, people would have understood him as meaning something like: "The French people do not value the Anglo-Saxon concept of risk-taking and the charismatic business leader as much as they should". When people say "<languageX> doesn't have a word for <conceptY>", they want their readers to assume that if the people who speak <languageX> really cared about <conceptY>, there would be a word for it. So if you want to assert that a culture does not care about a concept, you can say that there is no word for it. It is not important whether there really is a word or not: your intent will be understood. This is a good rhetorical trick, and a mark of someone who is a sensitive and effective language user, but it should not be mistaken for a scientific claim.

Vocabularies do differ from language to language, and even from dialect to dialect. One of the authors (who speaks British English) grew up using the word "pavements" to describe what the other two (speakers of standard American English) call "sidewalks", and also prefers the terms "chips" and "crisps" to describe what the other two call "fries" and "chips", respectively. These are actually easy cases because the words really are one-for-one substitutes. Trickier are words that could mean the same but carry extra senses, such as "fag", which is an offensive term for a gay male in the USA, but (usually) a common slang term for a cigarette in Britain. In elite British private schools, "fagging" is also a highly specialized term for a kind of institutionalized but (hopefully) nonsexual hazing in which younger boys are required to, for example, shine the shoes of older boys. This one can be a source of real misunderstanding for Americans who are unaware of the specialized British meaning.

7.6.2   Synonyms and translation equivalents

In school, you may have been exposed to the concepts of synonyms and antonyms. Words like "tall" and "short", "deep" and "shallow", "good" and "bad", "big" and "small" are called antonyms because they have opposite meanings. Words that have the same meaning are called synonyms. Examples of very similar words include pairs like "eat" and "devour" or "eat" and "consume", "drink" and "beverage", "hoover" and "vacuum". As linguists, we actually doubt that there are *any* true synonyms, because there is no good reason for a language to have two words that mean exactly the same thing, so even words that are very similar in meaning will not be exactly equivalent. Nevertheless, the idea of synonyms is still useful.

Cross-linguistically, it also makes sense to talk about synonyms, but when you look carefully at the details it turns out that word meanings are subtle. The French word "chien" really does mean the same as the English word "dog", but there is no single French word corresponding to all occurrences of the English word "know". You should use "connaître" if you mean "to know someone" and "savoir" if you mean "to know something". Translators have to choose, and so does a machine translation system. Sometimes, as below, you have to choose two different translations in the same sentence.

(37)   Do you **know** that Freud and Conan-Doyle **knew** each other?
(38)   **Savez**-vous que Freud et Conan-Doyle se **connaissent**?

The right way to think about the relationships between words in different languages is to note when they are translation equivalents. That is, we try to notice that a particular French word corresponds, in context, to a particular English word.

7.7   Word alignment

This idea of translation equivalence is helpful, because it leads to a simple automatic method that a computer can use to learn something about translation. Called the **bag-of-words method**, this is based on the use of **parallel corpora**. As an example, we use the English and German versions of a Shakespeare sonnet that we discussed in Section 7.3. This text is not typical of real translation tasks, but makes a good example for showing off the technology.

The main idea is to make connections between the pairs of sentences that translate each other, then use these connections to establish connections between the

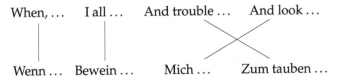

Figure 7.9   Correspondence between the two versions

words that translate each other. Figure 7.9 is a diagram of the **alignment** between
the first four sentences of Shakespeare's original and the first four lines of the German
translation. Because this is a sonnet, and is organized into lines, it is natural to align
the individual lines. In ordinary prose texts you would instead break the text up into
sentences and align the sentences, producing a so-called **sentence alignment**.

alignment

**sentence
alignment**

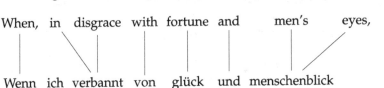

Figure 7.10   Word alignment for the first line

Once you have the sentence alignment, you can begin to build word alignments.
Look carefully at Figure 7.10. Notice that the word "menschenblick" is associated
with two words, and that the word "ich" is not associated with any word, because the
line we are matching does not have the word "I" anywhere in it. It is useful to make
sure that every word is connected to something, which we can do by introducing a
special **null word** that has no other purpose than to provide a hook for the words
that would otherwise not be connected. This is shown in Figure 7.11.

null word

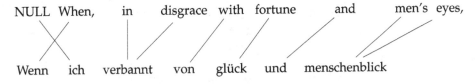

Figure 7.11   Revised word alignment for the first line

Once we have the word alignment, we have collected some evidence about the
way in which individual German words can go with corresponding English words.
We are saying that "wenn" is a possible translation of "When", that "in disgrace"
could be translated by "verbannt", that "men's eyes" could go with "menschenblick",
and so on. Notice that these are not supposed to be the only answers. In another
poem "menschenblick" could easily turn out out to be translated by "human view",
"verbannt" could go with "banned", and "wenn" could turn out to correspond to "if".
But in Sonnet 29, the correspondences are as shown in the diagram.

In order to automate the idea of word alignment, we rely on the fact that it is fairly
easy to identify corresponding sentences in a parallel corpus. Then, to get started,
we just count the number of times each word pair occurs in corresponding sen-

tences. If we try this for a little fragment of Hansard (the official record of Canadian parliamentary debates), which is conveniently published in French and English, we can find out that the French word "gouvernement" lines up with the frequent English words in the second column in Table 7.1.

Table 7.1 Word alignment of gouvernement in Hansard

French	English	Count
Gouvernement	the	335
Gouvernement	to	160
Gouvernement	government	128
Gouvernement	of	123
Gouvernement	and	81
Gouvernement	that	77
Gouvernement	in	73
Gouvernement	is	60
Gouvernement	a	50
Gouvernement	it	46

Likewise, the English word "government" lines up with the frequent French words in the first column of Table 7.2.

Table 7.2 Word alignment of government in Hansard

French	English	Count
De	government	195
Le	government	189
Gouvernement	government	128
Que	government	91
?	government	86
La	government	80
Les	government	79
Et	government	74
Des	government	69
En	government	46

We have left out the infrequently paired words in both lists, because we are expecting many accidental matches. But we are also expecting that word pairs that truly are translations will occur together more often than we would expect by chance. Unfortunately, as you see, most of the frequent pairs are also unsurprising, as the word for government is lining up with a common word of the other language, such as "the". However, one pair is high up in both lists:

Gouvernement   government   128

Table 7.3 Selected word-pair statistics in a small aligned corpus

φ^2	French	English	fe	f	e
0.823	D'accord	Agreed	14	17	14
0.500	Bravo	Hear	6	12	6
0.111	Interpellation-Suite	Inquiry-Debate	4	8	18
0.094	Législation	Legislation	6	16	24
0.083	appelle:	Order:	7	21	28
0.083	L'ordre	Order:	7	21	28
0.067	Étude	Study	6	18	30
0.067	spéciale	Study	6	18	30
0.044	Deuxième	Reading	4	20	18

This gives us a clue that these words probably do translate as each other. You can do the same with phrases. You can use the word-pair statistics about: "Président", "Speaker", and "Mr" to work out, just by counting, that "Monsieur le Président" and "Mr Speaker" are probably translation equivalents. Here is the data that you need to decide this:

	...	
Président	Mr	135
Président	Speaker	132
	...	
Monsieur	Mr	129
	...	
Monsieur	Speaker	127
	...	

Because these numbers are all roughly the same, you can tell that this set of words are tightly linked to each other.

The tables we are showing are based on 1,923 sentences, but in a full system we would process many thousands, hundreds of thousands, or millions of sentences, so the tables would be correspondingly bigger. To make further progress on this, we need to automate a little more, because it is hard work poring over lists of word pairs looking for the interesting patterns.

The way to deal with this is to do statistics on the word pairs. Table 7.3 contains some of the higher-scoring pairs from a single file of the Canadian Hansard. Now, instead of calculating the number of times the word pair occurs together, we also collect other counts. The first column of the table is a statistical score called φ^2 (**phi-squared**) which is a measure of how closely related the words seem to be. The second column is the French word, the third the English word, and the fourth through seventh are, respectively:

phi-squared (φ^2)

- The number of times the two words occurred in corresponding sentences (fe).
- The number of occurrences of the French word (f).
- The number of occurrences of the English word (e).

In reality, the table would be much bigger and based on more words, but you can already see that good word pairings are beginning to appear. The point of this table is to motivate you to believe that statistical calculations about word pairings have some value.

7.8   IBM Model 1

Many of the tools of statistical machine translation were first developed at IBM Research in the 1980s. This work completely changed the nature of academic research in machine translation, made it much more practical to develop web services such as Google Translate, and will probably be recognized as the most important work in machine translation for several decades. IBM made five models

IBM Model 1 of the translation process. The first and simplest one, called **IBM Model 1**, is explained here.

Taking the task of translating from English to French, Model 1 is based on the idea that in each aligned sentence each English word chooses a French word to align to. Initially, the model has no basis for choosing a particular French word, so it aligns all pairs equally.

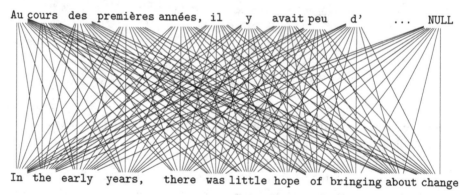

Figure 7.12   Part of an initial alignment

Figure 7.12 shows part of the initial alignment between two sentences. The point of making such alignments is as a step along the road toward making a so-called translation model; we are not doing translation yet, just working with the aligned sentences in order to produce a mathematical model, which will later be used by the translation software to translate new sentences. Notice that we add a special *NULL* word, to cover the possibility that an English word has no French equivalent. We make an alignment like this for each of the sentences in the corpus, and count the number of times that each word pair occurs. After that, words that occur together frequently will have larger counts than words that occur infrequently. This is what we saw in the previous section. Now we use those counts to form a new alignment that drops some of the weaker edges from the original figure.

An idealized version of what might happen in this process is shown in Figure 7.13. The connections between the first part and the second part of the sentence have been broken, reflecting the fact that there are two distinct phrases.

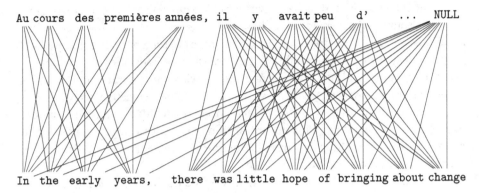

Figure 7.13   Part of a second-stage alignment

The details of what really happens depend on the statistics that are collected over the whole corpus. The hope is that "années" will occur more in sentences aligned with ones having the word "years" than it does with ones aligned with "change", thereby providing more weight for the "années"–"years" link.

Once we have created a new alignment for each sentence in the parallel corpus, dropping some edges that do not correspond to likely translation pairs, we have a new and more focused set of counts that can be used to form a third series of alignments, as shown in Figure 7.14.

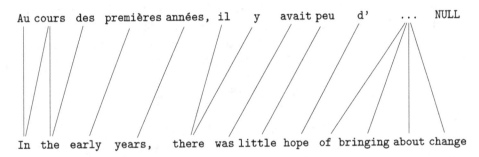

Figure 7.14   Part of a third-stage alignment

The principle here is to use the statistics over a whole corpus to thin out the alignments such that the right words finish up aligned. We are going to create a model that represents the probabilities of many of the ways in which words can combine to form a translation. To do this, we use the information contained in the bilingual corpus of aligned sentences.

Since the model is just a representation of what has been learned by processing a set of aligned sentences, you may wonder why we bother with the whole elaborate apparatus of alignments, model building, and probabilities. Could we not simply memorize all the sentence pairs? That would allow us to achieve a perfect translation of the sentences in the bilingual corpus, but it is not really good enough, because we want a solution that generalizes to new sentences that we have never seen before. To do this, we need a way of assigning probabilities to sentence pairs that we have not previously seen. This is exactly what the translation model provides.

When we come to translate new sentences, we will choose a translation by using the probabilities provided by the translation model to piece together a good collection of words as equivalents for the French. Model 1 provides a translation model. We will soon see how to combine this translation model with a language model. This is order to make sure that the translation output not only matches the French, but also works as a fluent sentence in English.

IBM Model 1 is clearly too simple (else why would the IBMers have made Models 2, 3, 4, and 5?) Specifically, Model 1 has the following problems:

- It ignores the order in which the words occur. We know that words at the beginning of the French sentence are more likely to go with words that are at the beginning of the English sentence, but this model has no way of coping with this.
- It does not model the number of words that each French word chooses to be aligned with. We know that words mostly translate 1-1 (i.e., one English word to one French word), and that 2-1, 1-2, and 2-3 are reasonably common, but that 1-17 and 17-1 are unlikely. Again, Model 1 has no way of using this fact.
- It has some other technical deficiencies that are less easy to explain in a general-audience textbook. For more detail, see the *Further reading*, for example Koehn (2008).

Models 2, 3, 4, and 5 introduce different ways of building alignments, ones that are carefully tuned to avoid the deficiencies of Model 1. For a long time, systems based around variants of Models 3, 4, and 5 were state of the art, but lately a new and related idea of phrase-based translation has gained ground. This will be discussed later.

Under the Hood 11
The noisy channel model

To understand how much of machine translation works, we need to step back and look at something called the noisy channel model. The science of information theory was developed in the 1930s and 1940s in response to a need for mathematical tools for reasoning about telegraphy, and also about codes and ciphers. A key concept of information theory is the noisy channel. Standard telephones have a very limited frequency range (from 300 Hz to 3500 Hz), but human hearing goes from roughly 20 Hz to as much as 20,000 Hz, and typical

Figure 7.15 The noisy channel model

human voices have significant energy in the range from 80 Hz to 5000 Hz (see more in Section 1.4). Male voices have a fundamental frequency that is well below the frequency range transmitted by the telephone. Yet, even over the telephone, we still perceive the low fundamental, and male voices still sound male. This is because hearing is an active process: our perceptual system *reconstructs* the missing fundamental by extrapolating from the higher harmonics that are transmitted through the telephone. In the same way, over the telephone it is very difficult to hear any difference between /f/ and /s/, because the acoustic differences between these sounds are in frequency bands that are too high to be transmitted. We say that the telephone is a *noisy channel*, because it fails to transmit the whole of the input signal. This is shown in Figure 7.15.

The task of the listener at the far end of the noisy channel provided by the telephone is to guess successfully what the speaker actually said. Fortunately, after a little experience, we become accustomed to the effects of the noisy channel, and get better at interpreting telephone speech. We call this knowledge about the channel the channel model: it describes the way in which the channel degrades the input speech. Unfortunately, on its own, the degraded signal passed by the noisy channel may not be enough to recover the original message reliably. Fortunately, however, we have additional information, because we know something about the kinds of messages that we expect to hear. For telephone speech, we know, for example, that the strongest harmonics of the signal will be simple multiples of the missing fundamental frequency, which is why we are able to reconstruct the fundamental frequency even though it is not really transmitted. This knowledge about which messages are likely can be referred to as the message model. Taken together, the channel model and the message model can be used in a process that consumes the degraded form of the input message and produces a well-informed best guess about the original clean message.

The noisy channel idea is widely applicable. We can think of spelling correction as a channel-encoding problem. Consider the nonword errors discussed in Section 2.2.1. Suppose that you get an email inviting you to a party at "Dsvid's house". Think of the original clean signal as being what the user meant to type and the degraded signal as what the user's fingers actually did type. It is easy to tell that the clean signal must have been "David's house", and that the error is a

(*Continued*)

Under the Hood 11
The noisy channel model
(Cont'd.)

key-for-key substitution of *s* for *a*. Here, the channel model says that substitutions of adjacent keys are common, and the message model says that "David" is a more plausible name for the mutual friend than "Dsvid". (Can you see what must have happened if the degraded signal was instead "Dsbif'd houfr"?)

We can turn the noisy channel model into math by writing

$$\hat{y} = \arg\max_{y} P(y)P(x\,|\,y)$$

where *x* is the observed output of the channel (that is, the degraded message) and *y* is the hypothesized clean message. The notation $\arg\max_{y} P(y)P(x|y)$ is a mathematician's way of saying "search for the *y* that gives the highest value for the probability expression $P(y)P(x|y)$". $\hat{y}$ is therefore the system's best guess at what the original message must have been. The message model is expressed as $P(y)$, which is the probability that the writer will have intended a particular word *y*. This is what tells us "Dsvid" is unlikely and "Dscis" very unlikely. $P(x|y)$ is the channel model, and tells us that the *s* for *a* substitution is likely. Obviously, all bets are off if you *do* have friends called "Dsvid" and "Dscis", or if the writer was using a nonstandard keyboard.

At the end of the chapter, in the exercises, there are a couple of rather more exotic examples of the noisy channel model: part-of-speech tagging and cryptography. If you want to stretch your mind, do those exercises! After that, there is a risk that you will start seeing the noisy channel model everywhere.

You may already be able to see why this discussion belongs in a chapter about translation. In 1949, Warren Weaver put it this way:

> It is very tempting to say that a book written in Chinese is simply a book written in English which was coded into the "Chinese code". If we have useful methods for solving almost any cryptographic problem, may it not be that with proper interpretation we already have useful methods for translation?

Modern machine translation technology builds on this appealing idea. Indeed, the noisy channel idea works perfectly. If we have a message in Chinese *c* that we would prefer to read in English *e*, we can factor the task into three parts:

1. Estimating a translation model $P(c|e)$
2. Estimating a language model $P(e)$

3. Maximizing the product $P(e)P(c|e)$ and returning the resulting English. This process is usually called decoding by analogy with the cryptography example above.

This decomposition gives rise to a pleasing division of labor. Imagine that we are trying to translate the Latin phrase "summa cum laude" into English, and that the system is considering three possible candidates. (This example is adapted from a lecture slide by Jason Eisner.)

(39)   topmost with praise
(40)   cheese and crackers
(41)   with highest distinction

1. The language model is responsible for making sure that what is proposed as a translation actually looks like a reasonable piece of English. On this metric (40) and (41) should get fairly high probabilities, but (39) should get a low score, because nobody ever says anything like "topmost with praise".

2. The translation model is responsible for making sure that the intended content gets across. (39) scores especially well on this, because "summa" goes well with "topmost", "cum" with "with", and "laude" with "praise". (41) does pretty well too, because "summa" goes well with "highest", "cum" and "with" still go well with each other, and "distinction" and "laude" are not horrible. The word matches with (40) are pretty awful, except perhaps for "cum" with "and", so its score is low.

3. The decoder multiplies together the two components and (we hope) finishes up giving the highest overall score to "with highest distinction". One of the two bad alternatives is vetoed because the language model hates it (as an unlikely phrase in English), the other because the translation model hates it (as an improbable equivalence between foodstuffs and academic honors).

It is not easy to build a good decoder, language model, or translation model. Each of these tasks has resulted in decades of research, but the basic idea of factoring the problem into these three parts has stood the test of time. The point of this section is to persuade the reader that the noisy channel model is a useful abstraction and can be used effectively in many situations, including the design of machine translation systems. In the translation setting, one major advantage is that the language model needs only monolingual text, and can be built separately using huge volumes of text from newspapers or from the web. The translation model still needs parallel text (as discussed in Section 7.7), which is much more difficult to find, but because the models can be built separately it is possible to make progress even if you do not have that much parallel text.

Under the Hood 12
Phrase-based statistical translation

We have been discussing translation models based on translating a single word into a single other word. But notice the word-pair statistics in Table 7.4.

Table 7.4   Word pairs in French and English

φ^2	French	English	*fe*	*f*	*e*
0.0100883766096	orthodoxe	Orthodox	9	99	81
0.0100883766096	orthodoxe	Church	9	99	81
0.0100883766096	l'Église	Orthodox	9	99	81
0.0100883766096	l'Église	Church	9	99	81

Modern statistical machine translation systems are phrase-based. What this means is that instead of aligning individual words, the system aligns longer phrases as well. What is really going on here is that the phrase "l'Église orthodoxe" is lining up with the English phrase "The Orthodox Church". Intuitively, translation is based on phrases rather than individual words. All we mean by phrase here is "sequence of words that might be longer than just one"; these phrases often turn out to have nothing to do with the verb phrases and noun phrases that we talked about in Chapter 2. The idea of phrase-based statistical translation is to build statistical models that reflect the intuition that phrases should be involved. We make the units of translation phrases instead of words, and build a table, called the phrase table, that takes over the role that was played by the word-pair tables earlier on. Everything that could have been part of the word-pair table can still be a part of the phrase table, but we can now also have pairings between collections of words.

We hope that in a system trained on the corpus we have been working with, the phrase table will contain the pair:

"l'Église orthodoxe" = "The Orthodox Church"

with a moderately high score. The phrase table will also contain numerous pairs that are matched 1-1, and these pairs correspond to entries that were in the word-pair tables earlier. What is important is that when the data has enough evidence to be confident about a translation relationship that is many-to-one or many-to-many, the phrase table can include the relevant entry. This approach works well; current research focuses on methods for finding good ways of choosing which phrases should be placed in the phrase table and how the scores should be assigned (see *Further reading*).

Returning to the discussion of idioms earlier in the chapter, you can probably see why a phrase-based system might be able to successfully translate the French idiomatic expression for dying, which is "casser sa pipe", with the English "kick the bucket". The system does not really have to understand what is going on with these phrases, it just has to notice that they occur together, put them in the phrase table, and use them in the translation. If the aligned sentences happened to make heavier use of some *other* common English idiomatic expression for dying, then "casser sa pipe" could equally well be translated as "meet one's maker".

It is not obvious exactly where phrase-based translation belongs in relation to the translation triangle. There is certainly no interlingua in sight, and there is little explicit linguistic analysis going on, so it is tempting to call it a direct approach. However, the kinds of reasoning and generalization that it is doing about the properties of chunks are very similar to the kinds of reasoning and generalization that traditional transfer systems do about verb phrases, noun phrases, and sentences, so one can definitely make the case that these systems have something in common with transfer systems. The big difference is that the statistical systems learn directly from data, whereas more typical transfer systems rely on linguists and language technologists to create the necessary transfer rules. The statistical systems often work well, but because they represent their knowledge in the form of complex mathematical models, it can be very difficult for human beings to understand them or to correct the mistakes they make. Carefully built transfer systems are easier to understand and test, but require constant care and maintenance by experts.

7.9 Commercial automatic translation

In this section, we discuss the practicalities of using (or not using) automatic translation in a real-world commercial setting. This discussion is not concerned with difficult literary translations, or with the complexities of the technology, but with what the technology lets you do.

7.9.1 Translating weather reports

A system built for Environment Canada was used from 1981 to 2001 to translate government weather reports into French, as Canadian law requires. A typical report is shown in Figure 7.16.

This is a very structured text, as shown in Figure 7.17, but it is not really written in conventional English at all. The main part of each "sentence" is a weather condition such as "CLOUDY WITH A FEW SHOWERS", "CLEARING", "SNOW", or "WINDS". These do not correspond to any standard linguistic categories: the main part can be an adjective, a verb in the *-ing* form, a noun, and probably other things.

To translate into French, the METEO system relies on a detailed understanding of the conventions about what weather reports say and how they say them, and on a

```
FORECASTS FOR YUKON AND NORTHWESTERN BC
ISSUED BY ENVIRONMENT CANADA AT 5:30 AM PDT
FRIDAY JULY 11 1980 FOR TODAY AND SATURDAY
KLONDIKE
BEAVER CREEK
STEWART RIVER
RAIN OCCASIONALLY MIXED WITH SLEET TODAY CHANGING TO
SNOW THIS EVENING. HIGHS 2 TO 4. WINDS INCREASING TO
STRONG NORTHWESTERLY THIS AFTERNOON. CLOUDY WITH A FEW
SHOWERS SATURDAY. HIGHS NEAR 6.
```

Figure 7.16   A typical Canadian weather report

`FORECASTS FOR YUKON AND NORTHWESTERN BC`
`ISSUED BY ENVIRONMENT CANADA AT 5:30 AM PDT`
`FRIDAY JULY 11 1980 FOR TODAY AND SATURDAY`
	dateline

`KLONDIKE`
`BEAVER CREEK`
`STEWART RIVER`
	locations

`RAIN OCCASIONALLY MIXED WITH SLEET TODAY`
 	
`CHANGING TO SNOW THIS EVENING.`
 	
`HIGHS 2 TO 4.`
 	
`WINDS INCREASING TO STRONG NORTHWESTERLY`
`THIS AFTERNOON.`
 	
`CLOUDY WITH A FEW SHOWERS SATURDAY.`
 	
`HIGHS NEAR 6.`
	body

Figure 7.17   The parts of Canadian weather report

special grammar, largely separate from traditional grammars of English, which explains which words are used to mean what and in what combinations. This is
sublanguage called a **sublanguage**. The translation of the dateline is completely straightforward, since it simply consists of the date plugged into a standard template. Similarly, place names are easy to translate: they are the same in the English and French version. The

body text does change, but the sentences are highly telegraphic, and mostly very similar from day to day.

Finally, METEO benefits from two facts about the way it is used. First, it is replacing a task that is so crushingly boring for junior translators that they were not able, even with the best will in the world, to do it consistently well. Secondly, by law, METEO's output had to be checked by a human before it was sent out, so occasional mistakes were acceptable provided that they were obvious to the human checker. METEO was used until 2001, when a controversial government contracting process caused it to be replaced by a competitor's system. By that time, it had translated over a million words of weather reports.

7.9.2 Translation in the European Union

The European Union (EU) is a group of European countries that cooperate on trade policy and many other aspects of government. It was founded by 6 countries in 1957, has expanded to include 25 countries, and now has 23 official languages. There is a rule that official documents may be sent to the EU in any of the 23 languages and that the reply will come back in the same language. Regulations need to be translated into all the official languages. In practice, European institutions tend to use English, French, and German for internal communications, but anything that comes in front of the public has to be fully multilingual.

One way of meeting this need is to hire $23 \times 22 = 506$ teams of good translators, one for each pair of source language and target language. You might think that 253 would suffice, because someone who speaks two languages well can translate in either direction. This idea has been tested and found to be wrong, however, because a translator who is good at translating English into French will usually be a native speaker of French, and should not be used to translate from French into English. It is harder to write well in a foreign language than to understand it. Translators are expensive, and government documents long and boring, so the cost of maintaining the language infrastructure of the EU is conservatively estimated at hundreds of millions of euros. In practice, it makes little sense to employ highly trained teams to cover every one of the possibilities. While there will often be a need to translate from English into German, it is unusual to have a specific need to translate a document originally drafted in Maltese into Lithuanian. Nevertheless, the EU needs a plan to cover this case as well. In practice, the solution it adopts is to use English, French, and German as **bridge languages**, and to translate between uncommon language pairs by first translating into and then out of one of the bridge languages. With careful quality control by the senior translators, this achieves adequate results.

Because of the extent of its translation needs, the EU has been a major sponsor of research and development in translation technology. This includes **fully automatic machine translation**, but also covers **machine-aided human translation**. The idea is that it may be more efficient to provide technology that allows a human translator to do a better and faster job than to strive for systems that can do the job

bridge languages

fully automatic machine translation

machine-aided human translation

without human help. Despite substantial progress in machine translation, nobody is ready to hand over the job of translating crucial legislative documents to a machine, so, at least for the EU, there will probably always be a human in the loop. Since the EU was early in the game, it makes heavy use of highly-tuned transfer systems, with transfer rules written and tested against real legislative documents. Over time, it may begin to make more use of statistical translation systems, especially if future research is able to find good methods for tuning these systems to do well on the very particular workloads of the EU. For the moment, the EU, with its cadre of good translators, is likely to stick with transfer methods. By contrast, Google, with statisticians aplenty, computational power to burn, and access to virtually limitless training data, seems likely to continue pushing the frontiers of statistical methods. For the casual consumer of machine translation, this diversity of approaches can only be good.

7.9.3   Prospects for translators

Translators entering the professional market will need to become experts on how to use translation memories, electronic dictionaries, and other computer-based tools. They may rely on automatic translation to provide first drafts of their work but will probably need to create the final drafts themselves thus the need for expert human judgment will certainly not disappear. In part, this is because users of commercial translation need documents on which they can rely, so they want a responsible human being to vouch for the accuracy and appropriateness of the final result. Specialist commercial translators will certainly continue to be in demand for the foreseeable future; there is no need to worry about the risk of being replaced by a computer. As in most other workplaces, you have to be comfortable *using* technology, and you should expect to have to keep learning new things as the technology changes and offers you new ways of doing your job more efficiently.

The range of languages for which free web-based translation is available will continue to grow, in large part because the statistical techniques that are used are very general and do not require programmers to have detailed knowledge of the languages with which they are working. In principle, given a parallel corpus, a reasonable system can be created very rapidly. A possible example of this was seen in June 2009, when Google responded to a political crisis in Iran by rolling out a data-driven translation system for Persian. It appears that this system was created in response to an immediate need due to the fact that the quality of the English translations from Persian did not match up to the results from Google's system for Arabic, a system which used essentially the same technology but had been tuned and tested over a much longer period.

Improvements in the quality of web-based translation are also likely. We think this will happen for three reasons: first, the amount of training data available will continue to increase as the web grows; secondly, the translation providers will devote effort to tuning and tweaking the systems to exploit opportunities offered by the different languages (notice that for this aspect of the work, having programmers with detailed knowledge of the source and target languages really would be useful after all); and thirdly, it seems likely that advances in statistical translation technology will feed from the research world into commercial systems. There will be a continuing need for linguists and engineers who understand how to incorporate linguistic insights into efficient statistical models.

Literary and historical translators could be unaffected by all of this, although some of them will probably benefit from tools for digital scholarship such as those offered by the Perseus Project. These allow scholars to compare different versions of a text, follow cross-references, seek out previous works that might have inspired the current work, and so on. For example, a scholar working on a Roman cookbook might want to check up on all uses of the word "callosiores" in cooking-related Latin, to see how often it seems to mean "harder" and how often it means "al dente."

Many potential users want to use automatic translation as a tool for gathering a broader range of information than they otherwise could. Marketers who already do the kind of opinion mining mentioned in Chapter 5 will also want to collect opinions from their non-English-speaking customers. This is much the same as what we did to decode the German cellphone review.

Checklist

After reading the chapter, you should be able to:

- Explain the idea of a translation need and give examples. You should be able to provide examples that are demanding, such as literature and poetry, and those that are not, such as help with multilingual shopping. You should also be able to explain some of the reasons why the hard ones are hard and the easy ones are easy.
- Draw and explain the translation triangle. You should be able to use the idea of more abstract and less abstract representations, and explain why the distance between the source language and the target language narrows as we move up the triangle toward more abstract representations.
- Explain the idea of word alignment. You should be able to take a pair of sentences and draw lines to indicate which words in the source language are aligned with which words in the target language.
- Discuss IBM Model 1 and its pros and cons.
- Explain the noisy channel model and how it can be applied to different types of tasks, including machine translation.
- Explain the basics of phrase-based machine translation and why it has a chance of working.
- Produce an orderly and informed discussion of what web-based machine translation services are likely to be able to do well, and why.

Exercises

1. **MATH**: The three procedural languages of the EU are English, French, and German. There are 20 other official languages, making a total of 23. You want to make sure that it is possible to translate from any of these languages to any other. As we discussed, having a separate translation team for each language results in a need for 506 teams. How many expert translation teams do you need if you adopt a policy that all documents will be first be translated from the source language into English, French, or German, then translated back out into the target language? How many would you need if you managed to agree that there should be just one procedural language (for example German) and that all translations would either begin, end, or pass through German?

2. **ALL**: Find a native speaker of a language other than yours (and other than English) and sit down with them with a short passage of text in their native language. Discuss what problems there are in translating from their language into English (or into your own native language). Which kinds of sentences/constructions are fairly easy to translate? Which ones border on impossible?

3. **ALL**: Go to http://translate.google.com/. This online automatic translation system provides free translations between languages such as French, English, Spanish, Arabic, Chinese, and Russian, among others.
    (a) Try translating three sentences from English into another language and then *back to English*. To do this, first translate from English to one of the other languages. Then, copy and paste the response and translate back to English. Try using different languages for each example. Write down your sentences, the languages you translate to/from, and what the back-translations are.
    (b) Rate the intelligibility of the translations. Is the word order correct? Does the system choose words that make sense? How close is the back-translation to the original input sentence? Can you figure out the meaning or is it gibberish?
    (c) Do some languages offer better back-translations than others? For example, does an English–Spanish–English translation produce better results than English–Russian–English? Why or why not?

4. **ALL**: Take the following German and English sentence pairs and do the following (you might find a German–English dictionary helpful, although it is not strictly necessary):
    (42) a. Das Kind ist mir ans Herz gewachsen.
             I have grown fond of the child.
         b. Sie ist bloß ein Kind.
             She is but a child.
         c. Sie nahm das Kind mit.
             She took the baby with her.

(a) Describe how the bag-of-words method will derive a translation/alignment for "Kind" and for "but". Address why we have to use several iterations when calculating alignments between words.

(b) How will phrase-based translation improve on the translation models here?

5. **MATH**: The math for the noisy channel can also function as a way of working out the parts of speech mentioned in Sections 2.4.1 and 3.4.2. We have to imagine that speakers were once really cooperative, and that instead of speaking normally and saying things like:

(43) He checked out a book from the library.

they actually used to say:

(44) He/pronoun checked/verb out/adverb a/article book/noun
      from/preposition the/article library/noun ./punctuation

helpfully spelling out all the parts of speech for us. Unfortunately for us, people no longer speak like this, so, if we want the parts of speech, we must guess them. We can think of example (44) as *y* (the clean message) and example (43) as *x* (the degraded form of the message). In other words, we are imagining that people still really speak in a form that spells out the parts of speech, but that everything they say is filtered through a horrible channel that deletes the parts of speech and retains only the words. Of course, this is not actually what is going on, but we can still go through the steps of searching for the part-of-speech sequence that is most likely to go with the words we saw.

Finish this story by designing a part-of-speech tagging model that:

(a) Uses probabilities of the form $p(tag_2|tag_1)$ to model the chance that, for example, a noun will follow a verb.

(b) Builds up the probabilities of longer series of tags by chaining together the individual probabilities $p(tag_2|tag_1)$.

(c) Uses probabilities of the form $p(word|tag)$ to model the chance that, for example, a randomly chosen noun will turn out to be the word "dog" (or *zebra* or *axolotl*).

Test whether you fully understand your model by seeing whether you can explain to yourself how it would give different probabilities to two different interpretations of the sentence "He saw her duck."

If you can spell out the details of this model on your own, without further clues, you will have reproduced one of the better achievements of computational linguistics. If you need further hints, go to the *Further reading*, especially Jurafsky and Martin (2009), which covers this approach to part-of-speech tagging.

6. **ALL**: You can apply the noisy channel model to cryptography. Imagine that you receive a coded message mentioning an impending invasion of Britain by "MXOLXV FDHVDU". As an expert in cryptography, you know to shift the letter three letters back in the alphabet and identify the culprit: "JULIUS CAESAR". Here *y* is the original Latin name, *x* is the encoded message, the

channel model says "shift three letters forward", and the message model is about "who is a likely invasion threat". The channel is specifically designed so that those who are in the know can undo its corrupting effect.

You now receive a message using the *rail fence cipher*, which involves laying out the message in the form of a rail fence, then reading it off row by row. Here is an example of how the message TRANSPOSITION CIPHERS ARE FUN would be laid out in a four-rail cipher:

```
T.....O.....N.....R.....U.
.R...P.S...O.C...E.S...F.N
..A.S...I.I...I.H...A.E...
...N.....T.....P.....R....
```

In cryptography we leave out the spaces between the words, and group the encoded message into fives, so this message would be encoded as TONRU RPSOC ESFNA SIIIH AENTP R. In order to read the message, the recipient has to know that when the message was sent, the writer used four rails. Knowing that, it is possible to recreate the layout and read off the message, once again in the conventional cryptographic groups of five, as TRANS POSIT IONCI PHERS AREFU N. All that remains is to regroup the letters into words, and the reader has decoded the message. If the reader uses three rails instead of four, this happens:

```
T...O...N...R...U...R...P.
.S.O.C.E.S.F.N.A.S.I.I.I.H
..A...E...N...T...P...R...
```

and the "decoded" message is TSAOO CEENS NFRNT AUSPI RIRIP H. The fact that this is unrecognizable gibberish proves that a mistake has been made somewhere.

The process for encoding is:
- Lay out a grid with the right number of rows. If you use four rows and your friend uses three, this is not going to work.
- Start at the top of the grid, and fill in cells diagonally downwards, until you reach the bottom row.
- Turn around and write diagonally upwards until you get to the top.
- Keep writing diagonally up and down until you run out of message text.
- Read off the text by rows.

Consider the rail fence message TAEIS HRIFN ESAYE LCE.
- What does the decoded version of the message say? You might have to try a few different numbers of rows.
- How many rows are there in the rail fence that worked?
- In the noisy channel formulation of the rail fence, we know that the channel model is "it was corrupted by the railfence cipher." Describe the message model that you used, and how it helped you to decide whether you had solved the problem. How would this message model need to change if there was a possibility that the sender was from a foreign country?

7. **ALL**: When translating from English into the Native American language
    Mam (in Guatemala), a translator reported the following terms used among
    siblings (in phonetic transcription here):
    - [ntzʔica] = "older sibling"
    - [witzin] = "younger sibling"

    Both words are used for males and females.

    (a) In terms of hyponymy/hypernymy, describe the relationship between the
         English word "sibling" and these words.
    (b) Draw a Venn diagram showing how the English words "brother" and "sister"
         overlap with the Mam words "ntzʔica" and "witzin".
    (c) You come across the text "Maxwell is the brother of Santiago", but it gives
         no indication who is older. If you had to translate this into Mam and were
         being forced to preserve this age ambiguity, how would you do it?

Further reading

There is a large and growing literature on translation and machine translation. We provide a
few pointers into this literature.

Chapter 25 of Jurafsky and Martin's textbook (Jurafsky and Martin, 2009) covers modern
machine translation in depth. Phillipp Koehn (Koehn, 2008) has written a comprehensive
technical introduction to statistical machine translation.

An older but more general introduction to machine translation is provided by John
Hutchins and Harry Somers (Hutchins and Somers, 1992). *Language Files* (Mihaliček and
Wilson, 2011) has a full chapter on machine translation.

Doug Arnold and his colleagues have made a good introductory textbook available for free
on the internet: http://purl.org/lang-and-comp/mtbook.

The cautionary tale about "intoxicado" is from Harsham (1984).

There have been a few attempts to make machine translation systems more capable of
translating poetry. In Genzel, Uszkoreit, and Och (2010), the authors describe a system that
aims to produce translations with appropriate meter and rhyme. This is an impressive technical achievement, but does not address the bigger problem of how to produce translations that
have the beauty and precision of good human-created poetic translations.

The Perseus project (Crane, 2009) presents beautiful web versions of literary texts,
including 13 million words of Latin and 10 million words of Ancient Greek. These include
commentary, translations, and all kinds of support for multilingual scholarship.

8

Epilogue
Impact of Language Technology

In this book, we have explored real-life applications involving language and what is needed to make them work, from investigating writers' aids to addressing how computers can be relevant in learning a foreign language, from tools supporting effective search in structured and unstructured data to several applications that involve sorting of documents into different classes, on to applications supporting human–computer dialogue and machine translation. While we have now given you a good hold on how computers deal with language and the concepts we need to understand what is going on, in this epilogue we want to wrap things up by asking what happens when such language technology (LT) is actually used. In other words, we want to raise some questions about the **impact of computers and language technology on society** and our self-perception. impact of LT on society

    Let us start by considering an example of how language technology can change jobs. For example, when you call an airline to book a flight and you find yourself talking to the speech recognizer front-end of a dialog system, what do you think happened to the people who used to answer the phone? There essentially are two options. On the one hand, some of the people in the call center will no longer have been needed in the company after the automated flight-booking system was introduced and have therefore lost their jobs. On the other, some of the employees may have received or sought out additional training to learn how to deal with the difficult cases that the automated system cannot handle – and to deal with those customers who learned to press the right button to reach a human, because they cannot or do not want to deal with an automated system.

    The first of these options is an instance of **deskiling** of the workforce. Deskilling deskiling is a broad term characterizing the process of dividing up tasks so that each worker

Language and Computers, First Edition. Markus Dickinson, Chris Brew and Detmar Meurers.
© 2013 Markus Dickinson, Chris Brew and Detmar Meurers. Published 2013 by Blackwell Publishing Ltd.

will need fewer skills in order to complete their part. Workers needing fewer skills can then be paid less, and some subtasks can be automated so that those workers are no longer needed.

upskilling   The alternative is known as **upskilling**. The idea, as you probably can guess, is that mechanization, the introduction of a machine or automated process, takes over some of the menial work, but requires workers to acquire new skills to be able to use that machine. With the menial work out of the way, workers then are free to spend more of their time on complex and conceptual tasks beyond the scope of the technology. A good example of upskilling in the context of language technology is mentioned in Doug Arnold and colleagues' Machine Translation book (http://purl. org/lang-and-comp/mtbook). The example involves one of the early success stories in machine translation, which you may remember from Section 7.9.1, the METEO system. It was designed to translate Canadian weather reports from English into French and vice versa. After METEO was introduced in the early 1980s, it was no longer necessary to translate all weather bulletins by hand. Instead, the job of the translators became checking translations and trying to find ways to improve the system output. This significantly increased the job satisfaction of human translators in the Canadian Meteorological Center, as was evident from the greatly reduced turnover in translation staff at the Center.

nature and   While deskilling and upskilling here are characterized in terms of their impact on
quality of   the workers, another relevant perspective to consider is how the **nature and quality**
automated tasks   **of the task** change when it is automated. When a dialog system replaces a human answering the phone, the dialog system may be able to carry out the core functions of routing calls, but it naturally lacks the human ability to react to unexpected requests, calm down frustrated customers, explain why a given person is not reachable and when they will be back, or simply serve as an interlocutor for a lonely caller.

The overall performance on a task often depends on a combination of automated and human interventions, the division of labor between which may lead to unintended results. Consider the introduction of spell checkers, discussed in Chapter 2. Such writers' aids in principle free the writer from worrying about the form of what they write, so that they can spend more time on the conceptual side of what they want to express – an instance of upskilling. At the same time, a study at the University of Pittsburgh showed that students using spell checkers make more errors than those writing and correcting by hand. So the nature and quality of a task may change significantly when it is being automated by language technology – which also brings us back to the dialog system example from the beginning of this section, providing a partial explanation for why people may at times try to opt out of such automated systems.

impact of LT   A related issue to consider is how we react to computers that can speak and listen
on self-   to language. For this we need to take a step back and think more broadly about what
perception   is involved in using language and how it reflects our identity. Using language is more
                 than merely conveying information and voicing requests. We have many options for
language and   expressing a given message, from the particular words and expressions we choose, to
identity   the way we pronounce them, on to how directly or indirectly we convey a message.

This was particularly apparent in our discussion of dialogue and conversational maxims in Section 6.5.3. Importantly, by making these choices, we can convey that we belong to a particular group and many other aspects of our identity. The question of how the specific use of language relates to questions of **individual and social identity** is studied in **sociolinguistics**, a subfield of linguistics that is closely related to anthropology and sociology. While we can only scratch the surface of those issues here, they clearly play an important role in how we react to computers that are equipped with language technology so that they can produce and react to language. **individual and social identity**

sociolinguistics

For example, we may ask in which situations it is easier to talk to a computer than to a human. Given that humans generally do a much better job of recognizing and interpreting spoken language than current automatic speech-recognition technology, you may think that the answer is obvious. But think about other aspects of using language than the quality of the speech recognition. When you are trying to find out whether your account is overdrawn, would you prefer to ask the teller in your local bank branch or a machine? A similar situation arises in language teaching, the application context we discussed in Chapter 3. Language teachers often report that some students practice extensively when they are given the opportunity to receive immediate, computer-based feedback on pronunciation and other computer-based exercises; yet those same students shy away from practicing with the teacher to avoid loss of face by making a mistake.

Taking the relation between language use and our social and individual identity one step further, the ability to use language is often mentioned as an important characteristic that sets humans apart from animals. Of course, animals do make use of communication systems, even rather complex ones. But human languages differ from **animal communication systems** in several **characteristic** ways. First, the relationship between the form of words (how they are pronounced and written) and what these words mean in general is arbitrary. By **arbitrariness** of the form–meaning relationship, we mean that there is nothing inherent in, for example, the three letter sequence *c*, *a*, and *r* that predestines the English word "car" to be used to refer to automobiles – as also supported by the existence of words like "automobile" and "vehicle", which are different forms with the same or similar meaning. What a word means must be learned, just like other aspects of a language. Human languages are learned by **cultural transmission**: every child acquires the language anew from the environment around them. Different from animal calls and communication systems such as the bee dance communicating the direction and distance where food was found, human languages are not inherited genetically. But many researchers believe that humans have a genetic predisposition for learning human languages, an **innate language faculty** that ultimately is the reason human languages cannot be learned by other animals. All human languages also make use of **discrete** units, such as words and phrases, which can be combined to create complex units, such as sentences. This **productivity** of a language makes it possible to produce an unlimited number of new sentences. Crucially, it is possible to understand the meaning of those new sentences by understanding the meaning of the discrete parts and how they are combined – the so-called **compositionality** of the meaning. Complementing the **animal communication systems**

characteristics of human language

arbitrariness

cultural transmission

innate language faculty

discreteness

productivity

compositionality

ability to compose new sentences to express new meanings when the need arises,
displacement human languages support **displacement**. This means that it is possible to use language to talk about ideas and aspects that are not in the immediate environment, which may have happened a long time ago, are assumed to happen in the future, or are not likely to happen at all. And finally, it is possible to talk about language using **metalinguistics** language, which is referred to as **metalinguistics**. While some of these properties can be found in some animal communication systems, the full set of properties seems to be realized by human languages alone.

self-perception Considering that language is so tightly connected to what it means to be human, what does it mean for the way we see ourselves, our **self-perception**, when computers now can use language to interact with us? There indeed seems to be some evidence that assumptions we make about every speaker of a language are transferred onto computers that use a language-based interface. This is particularly apparent in reactions to dialog systems such as the chatbot Eliza we discussed in Section 6.7. Eliza's creator Joseph Weizenbaum was astonished by the reactions of some of the staff at the MIT AI lab when he released the tool. Secretaries and administrators spent hours using Eliza and were essentially treating it like a human therapist, revealing their personal problems. Weizenbaum was particularly alarmed by the fact that Eliza's users showed signs of believing that the simple chatbot really understood their problems. The language-based interaction was apparently natural enough for people to attribute a human nature to the machine and to take it seriously as an interlocutor. Based on this experience, Weizenbaum started to question the implications of such dialog systems and artificial intelligence in general, which in 1976 resulted in *Computer Power and Human Reason*, an early influential book questioning the role of computers and their impact on human self-perception.

Weizenbaum's critical perspective on computer technology and its impact also points to another relevant distinction, which is nicely captured in one of our favorite quotes from *Jurassic Park*: "your scientists were so preoccupied with whether they could that they didn't stop to think if they should" (http://purl.org/lang-and-comp/jurassic). Language technology opens up a range of opportunities for new applica-
ethical tions and new uses for existing ones – and it is far from trivial to evaluate the **ethical**
impact of LT **impact** of these opportunities. Document classification as discussed in Chapter 5, for example, can be used for anything from spam to opinion mining, and more generally opens up the opportunity to classify and monitor huge sets of documents based on their contents. Governments and companies can monitor opinions expressed in emails, discussion boards, blogs, the web, phone conversations, and videos – we clearly live in an age where an unbelievable amount of information is available in the form of written or spoken language.

On this basis, governments can detect extremist opinions and possibly identify terrorist threats – yet they can also use language technology to automatically censor the documents available to their people or to monitor and crack down on opposition movements. Using opinion mining, companies can determine which aspects of their new products are discussed positively or negatively in discussion boards on the web, and improve the products accordingly. Or they can send targeted ads to customers based on automatic analysis of their profiles and blogs – which can be useful but is also scarily like Big Brother in George Orwell's book *1984*. Should a company be required to respect the level of **privacy** that its individual users are comfortable with **privacy** by giving them a choice to keep their data truly private?

The new opportunities opened up by language technology – providing an unprecedented ability to classify and search effectively in vast repositories of documents and speech – thereby raise important ethical questions.

Checklist

After reading the chapter you should be able to:

- Explain the notions of deskilling and upskilling and how they relate to the use of language technology.
- Give an example of how the nature and quality of a task are changed when it is automated through language technology.
- Point to aspects of language that go beyond the functional use of conveying information and voicing requests.
- Provide an example of a situation in which interaction with language technology may be preferred over interaction with a human, and one where this would not be the case.
- Mention characteristic properties of human language, which set it apart from animal communication systems.
- Give an example of the attribution of human-like properties to machines that use language.
- Discuss in which way privacy concerns and the ethical use of information are issues that arise in the context of language technology.

Further reading

A good starting point for going deeper into some the topics discussed in this chapter is *Language Files* (Mihaliček and Wilson, 2011, http://purl.org/lang-and-comp/languagefiles). In the 11th edition, Chapter 10 talks about language variation related to regional, social, and individual identity, and Chapter 14 discusses animal communication systems and how human languages differ from those.

If you want to learn more about the criteria distinguishing human language from animal communication systems, the classic article by Charles Hockett in *Scientific American* (Hockett, 1960) works them out in detail. For a vivid picture of how this issue has been explored, there are several interesting experiments that tried to teach great apes communication systems that satisfy the properties of human languages discussed in this chapter. Two well-known case studies involve Koko the gorilla and Nim Chimpsky the chimpanzee, both of whom were raised in human families and taught American Sign Language (ASL). The results are difficult to interpret, but are generally taken to support the view that animals cannot fully acquire a human language such as ASL. There is a wealth of material on those studies, including "A conversation with Koko" available from PBS online (http://purl.org/lang-and-comp/koko) and a 2011 documentary about Nim Chimpsky entitled "Project Nim" (http://purl.org/lang-and-comp/nim). Two of the original articles in *Science* (Terrace *et al.*, 1979; Patterson, 1981) are useful for anyone interested in a deeper understanding of the issues involved.

For a deeper look at issues of identity in the context of technology, Sherry Turkle's book *Life on the Screen: Identity in the Age of the Internet* (Turkle, 1995) is a classic book discussing the impact of the internet and online games on human identity and self-perception. A discussion of the broader context of the deskilling/upskilling debate can be found in Heisig (2009).

Finally, the University of Pittsburgh study on the (non)effectiveness of spell checking technology mentioned in the context of how the nature and quality of tasks are changed by automation can be found in Galletta *et al.* (2005).

References

Alias-i (2009) LingPipe 3.7.0 Tutorial, http://alias-i.com/lingpipe/demos/tutorial/query SpellChecker/read-me.html, accessed on April 7, 2012 (cited on p. 66).

Amaral, L. and Meurers, D. (2008) From recording linguistic competence to supporting inferences about language acquisition in context: Extending the conceptualization of student models for intelligent computer-assisted language learning. *Computer-Assisted Language Learning* 21(4), 323–338, http://purl.org/dm/papers/amaral-meurers-call08.html, accessed April 7, 2012 (cited on p. 89).

Amaral, L. and Meurers, D. (2011) On using intelligent computer-assisted language learning in real-life foreign language teaching and learning, *ReCALL* 23(1), 4–24, http://purl.org/dm/papers/amaral-meurers-10.html, accessed April 7, 2012 (cited on p. 89).

Austin, J.L. (1975) *How to Do Things with Words*, Cambridge, MA: Harvard University Press (cited on p. 179).

Bar-Hillel, M. (1980) The base-rate fallacy in probability judgments, *Acta Psychologica* 44(3), 211–233 (cited on p. 152).

Baroni, M. and Bernardini, S. (2004) BootCaT: Bootstrapping corpora and terms from the web, in *Proceedings of LREC 2004*, http://sslmit.unibo.it/~baroni/publications/lrec2004/bootcat_lrec_2004.pdf, accessed April 7, 2012 (cited on p. 125).

Baroni, M. and Kilgarriff, A. (2006) Large linguistically-processed Web corpora for multiple languages, in *Proceedings of EACL-06, Demonstration Session*, Trento, Italy, http://aclweb.org/anthology/E06-2001.pdf, accessed April 7, 2012 (cited on p. 125).

Crane, G.R. (2009) Perseus Digital Library, the Perseus Project, http://www.perseus.tufts.edu, accessed April 7, 2012 (cited on p. 213).

Crystal, D. (2011) *The Cambridge Encyclopedia of Language*, Cambridge Cambridge University Press, 3rd edn (cited on p. 31).

Cucerzan, S. and Brill, E. (2004) Spelling correction as an iterative process that exploits the collective knowledge of web users, in *Proceedings of 2004 Conference on Empirical Methods in Natural Language Processing (EMNLP)*, 293–300 (cited on pp. 62, 64).

Language and Computers, First Edition. Markus Dickinson, Chris Brew and Detmar Meurers.
© 2013 Markus Dickinson, Chris Brew and Detmar Meurers. Published 2013 by Blackwell Publishing Ltd.

Damerau, F. (1964) A technique for computer detection and correction of spelling errors, *Communications of the ACM* 7(3), 171–176 (cited on p. 66).

Daniels, P. and Bright, W. (eds.) (1996) *The World's Writing Systems*, Oxford: Oxford University Press (cited on pp. 3, 31).

Díaz Negrillo, A., Meurers, D., Valera, S., and Wunsch, H. (2010) Towards interlanguage POS annotation for effective learner corpora in SLA and FLT, *Language Forum* 36(1–2), Special Issue on Corpus Linguistics for Teaching and Learning, in Honour of John Sinclair, 139–154, http://purl.org/dm/papers/diaz-negrillo-et-al-09.html, accessed April 7, 2012 (cited on p. 80).

Fellbaum, C. (ed.) (1998) *WordNet: An Electronic Lexical Database*, Cambridge, MA: MIT Press (cited on p. 67).

Galletta, D., Durcikova, A., Everard, A., and Jones, B. (2005) Does spell-checking software need a warning label? *Communications of the ACM* 48(7), pp. 82–85 (cited on p. 220).

Genzel, D., Uszkoreit, J., and Och, F.J. (2010) "Poetic" statistical machine translation: Rhyme and meter, in *Proceedings of the 2010 Conference on Empirical Methods in Natural Language (EMNLP)*, 158–166 (cited on p. 213).

Golding, A.R. and Roth, D. (1999) A winnow-based approach to context-sensitive spelling correction. *Machine Learning* 34(1–3), 107–130 (cited on pp. 61, 67).

Gordon, R.G. (ed.) (2005) *Ethnologue: Languages of the World*, Dallas, TX: SIL International, 15th edn, http://www.ethnologue.com/ (cited on p. 31).

Grice, H.P. (1989) *Studies in the Way of Words*, Cambridge, MA: Harvard University Press (cited on p. 179).

Harsham, P. (1984) A misinterpreted word worth $71 million, *Medical Economics* 61(5), 289–292 (cited on p. 213).

Heift, T. (2010) Developing an intelligent language tutor, *CALICO Journal* 27(3), 443–459, http://purl.org/calico/Heift-10.html, accessed April 7, 2012 (cited on p. 89).

Heift, T. and Schulze, M. (2007) *Errors and Intelligence in Computer-Assisted Language Learning: Parsers and Pedagogues*, London: Routledge (cited on p. 88).

Heisig, U. (2009) The deskilling and upskilling debate, in Heisig, U., Maclean, R., and Wilson, D. (eds.). *International Handbook of Education for the Changing World of Work*, 1639–1651 (cited on p. 220).

Hirst, G. and Budanitsky, A. (2005) Correcting real-word spelling errors by restoring lexical cohesion, *Natural Language Engineering* 11(1), 87–111 (cited on pp. 61, 67).

Hockett, C.F. (1960) The origin of speech, *Scientific American* 203, 88–96, http://www.isrl. illinois.edu/~amag/langev/paper/charles60theOrigin.html, accessed April 7, 2012 (cited on p. 219).

Holland, V.M., Kaplan, J.D., and Sams, M.R. (eds.) (1995) *Intelligent Language Tutors: Theory Shaping Technology*, Hillsdale, NJ: Lawrence. Erlbaum (cited on p. 89).

Hopcroft, J.E., Motwani, R. and Ullman, J.D., (2007) *Introduction to Automata Theory, Languages, and Computation*, Reading, MA: Addison-Wesley, 3rd edn (cited on p. 67).

Hutchins, W.J. and Somers, H.L. (1992) *An Introduction to Machine Translation*, San Diego, CA: Academic Press (cited on p. 213).

Johnson, K. (2003) *Acoustic and Auditory Phonetics*, Oxford: Blackwell, 2nd edn (cited on p. 31).

Jones, M.P. and Martin, J.H. (1997) Contextual spelling correction using latent semantic analysis, in *Proceedings of the Fifth Conference on Applied Natural Language Processing (ANLP)*, Washington, DC, 166–173 (cited on p. 67).

Jurafsky, D. and Martin, J.H. (2000) *Speech and Language Processing: An Introduction to Natural Language Processing, Computational Linguistics, and Speech Recognition*, Upper Saddle River, NJ: Prentice Hall (cited on p. 180).

Jurafsky, D. and Martin, J.H. (2009) *Speech and Language Processing: An Introduction to Natural Language Processing, Computational Linguistics, and Speech Recognition*, Upper Saddle River, NJ: Prentice Hall, 2nd edn, http://www.cs.colorado.edu/~martin/slp.html, accessed April 7, 2012 (cited on pp. 31, 67, 180, 211, 213).

Kernighan, M.D., Church, K.W., and Gale, W.A. (1990) Spelling correction program based on a noisy channel model, in *Proceedings of the 13th International Conference on Computational Linguistics (COLING)*, Helsinki, Finland, 205–210 (cited on p. 66).

Kilgarriff, A. (2007) Googleology is bad science, *Computational Linguistics* 33(1), 147–151 (cited on p. 125).

Koehn, P. (2008) *Statistical Machine Translation*, Cambridge: Cambridge University Press (cited on pp. 200, 213).

Kukich, K. (1992) Techniques for automatically correcting words in text, *ACM Computing Surveys* 24(4), 377–439 (cited o n pp. 36, 66).

Ladefoged, P. (2005) *A Course in Phonetics*, Stamford, CT: Thomson Learning, 5th edn (cited on p. 18, 31).

Larsson, S. (1998) Questions under discussion and dialogue moves, in: *Proceedings of 13th Twente Workshop on Language Technology and the 2nd workshop on Formal Semantics and Pragmatics of Dialogue (TWLT 13/Twendial 98)* (cited on p. 180).

Leacock, C., Chodorow, M., Gamon, M., and Tetreault, J. (2010) *Automated Grammatical Error Detection for Language Learners*, Synthesis Lectures on Human Language Technologies, Redwood City, CA: Morgan & Claypool (cited on p. 67).

Lu, X. (2007) A hybrid model for Chinese word segmentation, *LDV-Forum* 22(1), 71–88 (cited on p. 77).

Madnani, N. (2009) Querying and serving n-gram language models with Python, *The Python Papers* 4(2), http://www.desilinguist.org/pdf/langmodel.pdf, accessed April 7, 2012 (cited on p. 31).

Mangu, L. and Brill, E. (1997) Automatic rule acquisition for spelling correction, In *Proceedings of the International Conference on Machine Learning*. (cited on pp. 66, 67).

Manning, C.D., Raghavan, P., and Schütze, H. (2008) *Introduction to Information Retrieval*, Cambridge: Cambridge University Press (cited on pp. 101, 124).

Mays, E., Damerau, F. J., and Mercer, R.L. (1991) Context based spelling correction, *Information Processing and Management* 23(5), 517–522 (cited on p. 67).

McCarthy, D. (2009) Word sense disambiguation: An overview, *Language and Linguistics Compass* 3(2), 537–558 (cited on p. 67).

McEnery, T., Xiao, R., and Tono, Y. (2006) *Corpus-Based Language Studies*, New York: Routledge (cited on p. 125).

Meurers, D. (2012) Natural language processing and language learning, in C.A. Chapelle (ed.), *Encyclopedia of Applied Linguistics*, Oxford: Blackwell, http://purl.org/dm/papers/meurers-11.html, accessed April 7, 2012 (cited on p. 88).

Mihaliček, V. and Wilson, C. (eds.) (2011) *Language Files: Materials for an Introduction to Language and Linguistics*, Columbus, OH: Ohio State University Press, 11th edn (cited on pp. 31, 50, 67, 213, 219).

Mitton, R. (1996) *English Spelling and the Computer*, London: Longman (cited on pp. 44, 66).

Naber, D. (2003) *A rule-based style and grammar checker, Master's thesis*, Technische Fakultät, Universität Bielefeld, http://www.danielnaber.de/languagetool/download/style_and_grammar_checker.pdf, accessed April 7, 2012 (cited on p. 67).

Odell, M.K. and Russell, R.C. (1918) *U.S. Patent Numbers 1,261,167 (1918) and 1,435,663 (1922)*, Technical report, Patent Office, Washington, (cited on p. 67).

Page, L., Brin, S., Motwani, R., and Winograd, T. (1999) *The PageRank Citation Ranking: Bringing Order to the Web*, Technical report, Stanford InfoLab, Stanford, CA, http://ilpubs.stanford.edu:8090/422/, accessed April 7, 2012 (cited on p. 125).

Pang, B. and Lee, L. (2007) Opinion mining and sentiment analysis, *Foundations and Trends in Information Retrieval* 2(1–2), 1–135 (cited on p. 152).

Partee, B.H., ter Meulen, A., and Wall, R. (1990) *Mathematical Methods in Linguistics*, Dordrecht: Kluwer (cited on p. 125).

Patterson, F.G. (1981) Ape language. *Science* 211(4477), 86–87, http://www.sciencemag.org/content/211/4477/86.1.short, accessed April 7, 2012 (cited on p. 220).

Sharoff, S. (2006) Creating general-purpose corpora using automated search engine queries, in M. Baroni & S. Bernardini (eds.), *WaCky! Working Papers on the Web as Corpus*, Bologna: Gedit, http://wackybook.sslmit.unibo.it/pdfs/sharoff.pdf, accessed April 7, 2012 (cited on p. 125).

Sproat, R. (2000) *A Computational Theory of Writing Systems*, Cambridge: Cambridge University Press (cited on p. 31).

Sproat, R. (2011) *Language, Technology, and Society*, Oxford: Oxford University Press (cited on p. 31).

Stolcke, A. (2002) SRILM – An extensible language modeling toolkit, in *Proceedings of the International Conference on Spoken Language Processing*, Denver, CO (cited on p. 31).

Swartz, M.L. and Yazdani, M. (eds.) (1992) *Intelligent Tutoring Systems for Foreign Language Learning: The Bridge to International Communication*, Berlin: Springer (cited on p. 89).

Terrace, H.S., Petitto, L.A., Sanders, R.J., and Bever, T.G. (1979) Can an ape create a sentence? *Science* 206(4421), 891–902, http://www.sciencemag.org/content/206/4421/891.abstract, accessed April 7, 2012 (cited on p. 220).

Turing, A.M. (1950) Computing machinery and intelligence, *Mind* 49, 433–460 (cited on p. 180).

Turkle, S. (1995) *Life on the Screen: Identity in the Age of the Internet*, New York: Simon and Schuster (cited on p. 220).

Verberne, S. (2002) Context-sensitive spell checking based on trigram probabilities, Master's thesis, University of Nijmegen (cited on p. 67).

Weizenbaum, J. (1976) *Computer Power and Human Reason*, San Francisco, CA: W.H. Freeman (cited on p. 180).

Weizenbaum, J. (1983) ELIZA – a computer program for the study of natural language communication between man and machine, *Communication of the ACM* 26, 23–28, http://doi.acm.org/10.1145/357980.357991, accessed April 7, 2012 (cited on p. 180).

Wilcox-O'Hearn, L.A., Hirst, G., and Budanitsky, A. (2006) Real-word spelling correction with trigrams: A reconsideration of the Mays, Damerau, and Mercer model, http://www.cs.toronto.edu/compling/Publications/Abstracts/Papers/WilcoxOHearn-etal-2006-abs.html, accessed April 7, 2012 (cited on pp. 60, 67).

Williams, J. and Kane, D. (2008) *Exploring the National Student Survey. Assessment and feedback issues*, Heslington: Center for Research into Quality (CRQ)/The Higher Education

Academy, http://www.heacademy.ac.uk/assets/York/documents/ourwork/nss/NSS_assessment_and_feedback_issues.pdf, accessed April 7, 2012 (cited on p. 71).

Wing, A.M. and Baddeley, A.D. (1980) Spelling errors in handwriting: A corpus and distributional analysis, in U. Frith (ed.), *Cognitive Processes in Spelling*, London: Academic Press, 251–285 (cited on p. 67).

Winograd, T., and Flores, F. (1987) *Understanding Computers and Cognition: A New Foundation for Design*, New York: Addison-Wesley (cited on p. 180).

Concept Index

n-gram, 26, 59
   character *n*-gram, 40

abjad, 4
abugida, 6
acoustic phonetics, 18
acoustic signal processing, 25
aggregator sites, 127
agreement, 80
alignment, 195
alphabet, 3
alphabetic system, 3
alphasyllabary, 6
ambiguity, 5
   covering ambiguity, 77
   lexical ambiguity, 98
   overlapping ambiguity, 77
   structural ambiguity, 54
amplitude, 19
animal communication system, 217
annotation, 116
antonym, 192, 194
arbitrariness, 217
article, 70
articulatory phonetics, 18
artificial intelligence, 155
ASCII, 14

aspiration, 23
asterisk (*), 38
automatic speech recognition (ASR), 24
automatic spelling corrector, 38

babbling, 70
back off, 28
backtrack, 55
bag-of-words assumption, 141
bag-of-words method, 194
base rate, 135
base rate neglect, 138
Bayes' theorem, 144
Big Endian, 13
bigram, 28
binary, 13
bit, 13
Boolean expression, 94
bottom-up, 55
branching CALL system, 73
bridge languages, 207
byte, 13

canned text response, 72
capitalization, 98
center-embedded structure, 56
channel model, 201
character n-gram, 40

Language and Computers, First Edition. Markus Dickinson, Chris Brew and Detmar Meurers.
© 2013 Markus Dickinson, Chris Brew and Detmar Meurers. Published 2013 by Blackwell Publishing Ltd.

CPSIA information can be obtained
at www.ICGtesting.com
Printed in the USA
FSHW02n0930140618
49285FS

9 781405 183055